.Net Knowledge]

C000110429

Web Development with Asp.Net MVC and Entity Framework

Volume 1

First Edition

Patrick Desjardins

Copyright © 2014 Patrick Desjardins

Author: Patrick Desjardins

Self-Publishing

Email: mrdesjardins@gmail.com

WebSite: http://patrickdesjardins.com

Printed in the United States of America

Mention de dépôt legal:

Dépôt legal - Bibliothèque et Archives national du Québec, 2014

Dépôt legal - Bibliothèque et Archives national du Canada, 2014

All rights reserved.

ISBN: 978-2-9813110-1-6

DEDICATION

I dedicate this book to my wife, Mélodie Savaria, who has been patient during the time I took to write these blog articles and hereafter this book. I also dedicate this work to my parents, who opened the path to all my realizations present and future.

CONTENTS

ACKNOWLEDGMENTS

I wish to thank, first and foremost, everybody who has been patient with me during this process. I wrote twice a week on my blog and the results are in this book. I owe my deepest gratitude to those who challenged me at my work, during conferences and by comments directly on my website. You have helped me to improve every day.

1. ASP.NET MVC

This chapter groups every post written during 2011 and 2012 about Asp.Net MVC. Most of them are still coherent and effective two years later. If some information is outdated, I still believe it can provide some positive insight to you by relating the evolution of the Microsoft MVC framework. Like all chapters in this book, every article is a snapshot of a real scenario that has a high probability of happening if you are using these technologies. You will notice that every article that has been chosen to be included in this book contains the release date to identify when it was written. A permanent link is also provided that allows you to go in and read updates and comments. Feel free to go on the website to add your own comment if you wish.

Asp.Net MVC Template EditorFor priorities

Release Date: 21-Sep-12
Url: http://patrickdesjardins.com/blog/?post_type=post&p=1435

When using **EditorFor,** the system searches for the right HTML input to produce. This is done in a cascade fashion.

If the user had used the **EditorFor** with the signature that contains the template name, this one will be used in first priority.

```
v class="editor-field">
 @Html.EditorFor(model => model.Avatar.Name,|)
  @Html.Validatio  (this HtmlHelper<Customer> html, Expression<Func<Customer,LocalizedString>> expression):MvcHtmlString
iv>
                   (this HtmlHelper<Customer> html, Expression<Func<Customer,LocalizedString>> expression, object additionalViewData):
v class="editor-   MvcHtmlString
  @Html.LabelFor(  (this HtmlHelper<Customer> html, Expression<Func<Customer,LocalizedString>> expression, string templateName):
iv>                MvcHtmlString
v class="editor-   Returns an HTML input element for each property in the object that is represented by the Expression expression, using
  @Html.EditorFor  the specified template.
  @Html.Validatio  templateName: The name of the template to use to render the object.
```

At first, this HTML helper may look useless because it relies on a **parameter** and doesn't directly use the correct helper.

For example, instead of doing:

```
@Html.EditorFor(x=>x.Name, "Textbox")
```

you might use:

```
@Html.TextBoxFor(x => x.Name)
```

In fact, if you do so, you might see the textbox in the rendered HTML, but it isn't showing the textbox because you wrote it, but simply because it has not found the template in the **EditorTemplates** folder. If you want to use the named template EditorFor you need to ensure that it is inside the **EditorTemplates**. Otherwise, the Asp.Net MVC Framework will pass on to its next template priority.

The second priority for the choice of the correct template is **ModelMetadata.TemplateHint**. This attribute is set at the top of the property. The attribute is inside the namespace *System.ComponentModel.DataAnnotations*. This takes one parameter that is the name of the template located in EditorTemplates or DisplayTemplates, depending on whether EditorFor or DisplayFor is used.

```
[UIHint("MyTemplate")]
public string FirstName
{
    get;
    set;
}
```

This is quite simple to use but, from my perspective, it is a "code smell"[1]. Why would you want to set up a UI element inside the model? It breaks the separation of concern (SOC). The model should not care about how it will be represented. It would be better to specify the type of the data instead, which is the third priority. However, keep in mind that it is a good practice to use **UIHint** in the scenario when you are using **ViewModel** and not directly the Model.

The third priority is another attribute called **DataType**.

---

[1] Code Smell: (From Wikipedia) In computer programming, code smell is any symptom in the source code of a program that possibly indicates a deeper problem. Code smells are usually not bugs—they are not technically incorrect and do not currently prevent the program from functioning. Instead, they indicate weaknesses in design that may be slowing down development or increasing the risk of bugs or failures in the future.

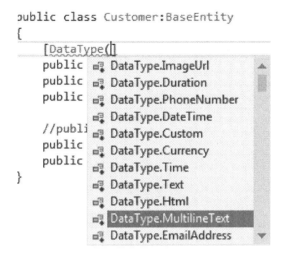

```
public class Customer:BaseEntity
{
    [DataType(]
    public
    public
    public

    //publi
    public
    public
}
```

It comes with a list of predefined values (enum). This is of interest for basic data type and you can define a template for each of those types inside the **EditorTemplates** and **DisplayTemplates** folders. The separation of concern is respected because the model only specifies the type of its property and not how it will be represented.

The fourth priority is the Model type. If you have defined a Template for one of your class, this will be used automatically. This works pretty much in the same way as the DataType except that you do not have to specify the type; .Net Framework will figure it out from the property type by reflection.

In a previous post (see page 78), we had created a LocalizedString class that displayed, depending on the user culture, differently. It requires its own template. This is done by adding inside EditorTemplates and DisplayTemplates a template that defines the type.

```
@model EFCodeFirst.General.LocalizedString

@Html.LabelFor(s => s.Current)
```

This is also how UI library works to override a basic template. For example, the Telerik or DevExpress suite add their own templates for String, Date, Int, Double to override the default input with their enhanced ones. This is the last, and fourth, template mechanism priority based on the type.

How to kill current session in Asp.Net

Release Date: 10-Jul-12
Url: http://patrickdesjardins.com/blog/?post_type=post&p=1173

If you need to kill your current session, which is the case if a user logs out, you need to kill cookies and sessions.

To kill cookies, you have to set the expiry to something already passed. For example, you can set the cookies' expiration time to yesterday. For the session, you can use the method **Abandon**.

The Abandon method destroys all the objects stored in a Session object and releases their resources. The resources are not deleted right away, which means that you still have access to the data of the session until the page is generated.

```
HttpContext.Current.Session.Abandon();
```

Session are stored in a cookie with the name *ASP.NET_SessionId*. You need to kill this cookie like you would do with any cookie.

```
var sessionCookie = new HttpCookie("ASP.NET_SessionId", string.Empty);
sessionCookie.Expires = DateTime.Now.AddDays(-1);
sessionCookie.Domain =
UrlInformation.GetHostDomain(HttpContext.Current.Request.Url.Host);
HttpContext.Current.Response.Cookies.Add(sessionCookie);
```

With those two snippets of code, the session should be killed for good. If you are wondering about the UrlInformation.GetHostDomain, here it is:

```
public static string GetHostDomain(string hostUrl) {
    string domain = string.Empty;

    if (hostUrl.Count(x => x == '.') == 2) {
        var dotIndex = hostUrl.IndexOf(".");
        domain = hostUrl.Substring(dotIndex + 1, hostUrl.Length - dotIndex - 1);
    }
    else {
```

```
        domain = hostUrl;
    }

    return domain;
}
```

Unable to launch the IIS Express Web server

Release Date: 01-Oct-12
Url: http://patrickdesjardins.com/blog/?post_type=post&p=1454

This morning, I started a new project where the team uses *IIS Express* instead of *Visual Studio Web Server* or *IIS*. For me, this is new. Even though I have developed for several years with Visual Studio, I always used Visual Studio Web Server (Cassini) or the full IIS.

The installation of IIS Express is quite simple with **Microsoft Web Platform Installer** and can be easily configured by Visual Studio (in the property window of the project) and from the configuration file inside the IISExpress folder of your My Documents.

Unable to launch the IIS Express Web server

This happened when the project was launched. After checking if the port is blocked, check if all projects are correctly compiled. I decided to remove IIS Express completely. I have to say that IIS 7.5 was installed and once the problem occured I tried to install 8.0 over it. So, everything got uninstalled and I installed from scratch. I also did not use my teammate's configuration file (which was edited to link to the correct path). I also installed directly IIS Express 8.0 and decided to let Visual Studio on the first launch create the Virtual Directory with a new configuration file. From there, everything worked.

I suggest you start by uninstalling everything, removing the configuration file from your My Documents folder, then re-install and let Visual Studio on the first launch create everything.

Getting 404 error after publishing with .Net4.5 from Visual Studio 2012

Release Date: 06-Sep-12
Url: http://patrickdesjardins.com/blog/?post_type=post&p=1361

After the migration to the new .Net Framework 4.5 you could have a scenario where it works on your computer but not when publishing. Even publishing to the local IIS on your computer may work but not on a remote one.

The 404 page is shown without any more information. To solve this issue, I created an MVC3 web application and published. It worked! I did the same with an MVC4 and it was also working.

The difference between the two projects was that the web.config file has a different assemblies version in the config file.

```xml
<?xml version="1.0" encoding="utf-8" ?>
<compilation debug="true" targetFramework="4.0">
  <assemblies>
    <add assembly="System.Web.Abstractions, Version=4.0.0.0, Culture=neutral,
PublicKeyToken=31BF3856AD364E35" />
    <add assembly="System.Web.Helpers, Version=1.0.0.0, Culture=neutral,
PublicKeyToken=31BF3856AD364E35" />
    <add assembly="System.Web.Routing, Version=4.0.0.0, Culture=neutral,
PublicKeyToken=31BF3856AD364E35" />
    <add assembly="System.Web.Mvc, Version=3.0.0.0, Culture=neutral,
PublicKeyToken=31BF3856AD364E35" />
    <add assembly="System.Web.WebPages, Version=1.0.0.0, Culture=neutral,
PublicKeyToken=31BF3856AD364E35" />
  </compilation>
```

As you can see, I have in the code above the version 1.0 for **Helpers** and **Routing** and this is problematic because the assembly I have in the project has been converted to version 2.

This leads us to two options: Migrate everything with MVC4 and use version 2, or use MVC3 with version 1.

I hope that if you get this type of 404 error after migrating from Asp.Net 4 to 4.5 you will think to check all references.

HttpCookie and web.config domain

Released Date: 12-Jul-12
Url: http://patrickdesjardins.com/blog/?post_type=post&p=1178

You can set in your Asp.Net web.config file a domain for all your cookies. This is done by setting the **httpcookies** from the system.web.

```
<system.web>
  <httpCookies domain=".domain.com"/>
</system.web>
```

The main goal is to have all your cookies attached to the domain and not set to the subdomain. Also, notice that I have written .domain.com and not domain.com. This is important; it will not work with a subdomain.

So what does it do behind the scene? It simply sets the domain property of the cookie to the domain name. In fact, you could have coded it manually:

```
var cookie = new HttpCookie();
cookie.Domain = ".domain.com";
```

Instead you set it once in the web.config. This is the constructor of HttpCookie. As you can see, it calls SetDefaultsFromConfig().

```
public HttpCookie(String name, String value)
{
    _name = name;
    _stringValue = value;
    SetDefaultsFromConfig();
    _changed = true;
}
```

This method goes into web.config to get the domain:

```
private void SetDefaultsFromConfig()
{
    HttpCookiesSection config = RuntimeConfig.GetConfig().HttpCookies;
    _secure = config.RequireSSL;
    _httpOnly = config.HttpOnlyCookies;
    if (config.Domain != null && config.Domain.Length > 0)
        _domain = config.Domain;
}
```

The variable _domain is changed by the configuration file value.

This variable is also set by the domain property.

```
public String Domain
{
    get {
        return _domain;
    }
    set {
        _domain = value;
        _changed = true;
    }
}
```

Differences between ViewData, ViewBag, Session and TempData

Release Date: 16-Feb-12
Url: http://patrickdesjardins.com/blog/?post_type=post&p=714

ViewData, ViewBag and TempData are three mechanisms to transport information from one page to another. **ViewData** and **ViewBag** can be treated identically because they are both the same thing. The ViewBag is an object that uses ViewData. The main difference is that it is possible to access the values from dynamic properties instead of accessing from an array with a string key.

```
ViewData["Name"] = "Patrick"; //Or ViewBag.Name = "Patrick";
```

So, in fact, we are storing an object value into a dictionary that is defined to have Object type value and string key.

TempData is also a dictionary of string key and object value. The difference is the life cycle of the object. TempData keeps the information for the time of an HTTP Request. This means only from one page to another. This also works with a 302/303 redirection because it is in the same HTTP Request.

```
TempData["Name"] = "Patrick";
```

ViewData and ViewBag will not have any value after a redirection. This is because their goal is to provide a way to communicate between controllers and views. It is a communication mechanism within the server call. The life cycle of the ViewData and ViewBag is shorter than TempData.

The last mechanism is the **Session.** It works like ViewData or like a Dictionary that takes a string for key and an object for value. The session key is stored into the client Cookie and can be used for a much longer time. It also needs more verification to ensure it never has any confidential information.

How to easily update JQuery library with ASP.MVC project

Release Date: 27-Feb-12
Url: http://patrickdesjardins.com/blog/?post_type=post&p=735

It is always a good habit to have the latest framework updated. This way, you have most recent bugs fixed and all the new features available. This can be done manually by changing files, but if you have **NuGet** installed, it is even easier. It removes all manual downloads and also checks for compatibility.

You can use **Update-Package jquery** to update JQuery, which will not only get the latest JQuery version of the main library but also will get the UI, Validation and other JavaScript libraries that are close to JQuery.

To be able to execute **Update-Package jquery** you will need to launch the **Package Manager Console**. This is located in Tools>Library *Package Manager>Package Manager Console*.

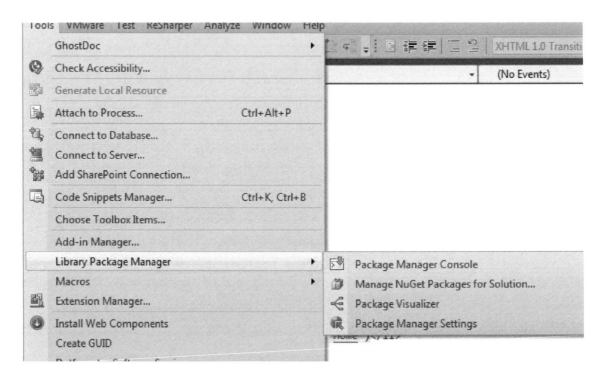

Asp MVC controller return HTML by Jquery Ajax to load dynamically HTML into div

Release Date: 05-Mar-12
Url: http://patrickdesjardins.com/blog/?post_type=post&p=762

When it is time to load HTML from the server side from JavaScript, the best way to do it is with Ajax.

You can use JQuery framework to make the call to the server. This is pretty interesting if you need to get HTML loaded with Model information from the server. A simple way to do it without having to use parameters is to simply call a partial view with the routing url to the information you want.

For example, let's say you want to call an action with an ID.

```
var ajaxCall = $.ajax(
    {        url: 'MyController/MyAction/' + id
        , success: /*...*/
        , dataType: "html"
    }
```

);

This will call the server, get the information of the ID, and render the HTML for it.

In the Success function, you just have to set up with **.html**(contentHere) and you will be fine to load the data from the Model of the server into the HTML without having to do a request with a PostBack.

An important note is that the controller needs to return a **PartialView** and not simply a View. This would cause it to load the whole layout back to the client and that is not what you want.

RenderPartial vs RenderAction

Release Date: 30-Mar-12
Url: http://patrickdesjardins.com/blog/?post_type=post&p=911

The official Asp.Net MVC website describes pretty well the difference between the two. **RenderPartial** is used to display a reusable part from within the same controller and **RenderAction** renders an action from any controller. They both render the HTML and do not provide a String for output.

Here is a picture that illustrates the difference between RenderPartial and RenderAction in Asp Mvc .Net.

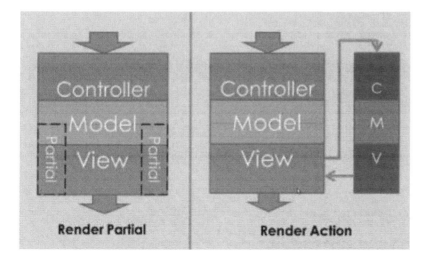

If you need to have a String, which can be the case if you need to return values from an Ajax call in which the content is HTML, you should use Html.Partial or Html.Action. They both create the view but, instead of rendering it directly into the Http Response, will produce an HTML string which could be returned to be loaded into a div with JavaScript or JQuery.

```
$('#result').load('http://localhost/myApp/User/Profile/1');
```

This is a small example where the action Profile of the controller User could return directly a String. To be able to generate this output on the server side, it would require that the Profile action return **ContentResult** type that will be generated by Html.Partial or Html.Action.

MVC cannot have two actions with the same name

Release Date: 10-Apr-12
Url: http://patrickdesjardins.com/blog/?post_type=post&p=966

You can compile any controllers to have the same method name if they have different parameter types or parameter numbers. This is normal in .Net Framework but what the MVC developer must know is that you cannot have two actions (which are class methods) with the same name even if they don't have the same parameter type. That means you cannot have :

```
public ActionResult Edit(int id){   /**/}
```

and in the same controller have:

```
public ActionResult Edit(MyObjectToEdit obj){   /**/}
```

Having these two action methods will fail because the MVC framework does not know which one to use. However, you have two solutions to make MVC routing know which action to use.

First, you can change the name. I think it is obvious that if you have different names the routing will not have any problem knowing which one to choose.

The second solution is to add the attribute POST, GET, PUT, DELETE. The routing is executed correctly depending on the http header type. So you could have:

```
[HttpGet]
public ActionResult Edit(int id)
```

```
{
//...
}

[HttpPost]
public ActionResult Edit(MyObjectToEdit obj)
{
    //...
}
```

From here, you could call them by specifying in the Http Request the type of request you sent (Get or Post) and the MVC's routing system will know which one to choose.

Wait a minute

All right, there is a catch and it is if you return from those methods **Json,** because you cannot return Json from a Get request by default. This is for security purposes. In fact, someone could attack using Json HiJacking and harm you only if:

- You return data into an array. This can be solved by returning into an object that may contain an array.

- You return sensitive information. This can be solved by using SSL.

- You use Get with Json. This can be solved by using Post or having multiple names instead of having the same action with two types of Http call type.

- The browser supports "__defineSetter__" which is where the vulnerability is executed. With this one, you have no control.

So, it is not a big deal if you know what you are doing. In most cases, you can allow Json to return data from Get if you can handle what your action returns. This means you should know what object you return and not return an array directly.

To allow Json to use Get to return data, simply add as a second parameter **JsonRequestBehavior.AllowGet**. This will remove all possible errors.

```
[HttpGet]
public ActionResult Edit(int id)
{
    return Json(new { MyData = 1, MyData2 = "ASD" },JsonRequestBehavior.AllowGet);
}
```

How to validate a model object with Asp.Net MVC correctly

Release Date: 13-Apr-12
Url: http://patrickdesjardins.com/blog/?post_type=post&p=970

There are a lot of ways to validate a model object in the object-oriented world. Most of the time, we see that we can check the information inside the Setter (which in C# is the SET of a property). This is interesting and personally was my favorite way to do it. The main reason is that you never have any model object in a dirty state that could fail in future use. My second reason is that it is easier to control what goes in the model. Everything that goes into the object has to pass through setters, and this way everything is clean inside the model.

In my last two years in development, I had to do development with Silverlight a few times and also had to use Asp.Net MVC, which pushed me to use a different approach. Instead of using validation directly into the setter to validate input, I had to use a custom function to do it. Not that Silverlight forces you to validate outside the setter; in fact, it is still easier in my opinion, with the MVVM pattern, to use setter to handle exceptions and business rules from setter. The other approach has the advantage of validating multiple values that have interdependencies among each of them. For example, let's say that you have a "Car" class that needs to have a special rule concerning the Color depending on the Type of this class. This means that every time you need to set the Type before the Color. Also, with ORM that loads your object directly, you may find some situations where this   does not load your object in the right order for the properties, which will raise an error. Another problem is that you have to validate in several places the same logic depending on what changed, the color or the type.

At the same time, Asp.Net MVC strongly encourages not validating directly with the setter. What motivated me to like more and more the validation outside setter is that Microsoft has implemented since the first version of ASP.Net MVC the **ModelState** that handles all errors from the model binding, from annotation validation in your model to your own business logic error. This is built in. This mechanism is used by the model binding to let you know if something has not been bound correctly if you use the automatic model binding. Here is an example of automatic model binding:

```
public ActionResult Edit(Car car){...
```

.Net Framework lets you add your own error into the model binding. This way, inside the controller you will be able to validate if everything is fine before saving your creation or edition of your model.

```
[HttpPost]
public ActionResult Edit(Car car)
{
    if(ModelState.IsValid)
    {
        //Update code to be placed here
        return RedirectToAction("CarList");
    }
    else
    {
        return View("CarEdit",car);
    }
}
```

The code above demonstrates the addition of a *Car* class. Two things appear in the first line. The **IsValid** function will return true if nothing has been added to the ModelState and will return false if a Model Binding error occurs OR if you have a business logic error. That is right—Asp.Net MVC calls your object business logic validation IF you use a single specific interface called **IValidatableObject**. This interface lets you inherit from a method called **Validate**. Inside this method you need to validate your business logic. Every time an error is found, you need to add it to a collection to return it at the end of this method. This lets you add many errors if desired. Here is an example of the *Car* model object.

```
public class Car : IValidatableObject
{
    public int Id { get; set; }
    public string Name { get; set; }
    public string Type { get; set; }
    public string Color { get; set; }

    public IEnumerable<ValidationResult> Validate(ValidationContext
validationContext)
    {
        if (string.IsNullOrEmpty(Name))
        {
            yield return new ValidationResult("Name is mandatory"
                                            , new[] {"Name"});
        }
        if (string.IsNullOrEmpty(Type))
        {
            yield return new ValidationResult("Type is mandatory"
                                            , new[] {"Type"});
        }
        if (string.IsNullOrEmpty(Color))
```

```
        {
            yield return new ValidationResult("Color is mandatory"
                                       , new[] {"Color"});
        }
    }
}
```

As you can see, we have three errors that are added to the return collection with the yield statement. We could have declared a variable of IEnumerable but for the sake of simplicity we can use yield. This collection of errors is generic. The type is **ValidationResult**. The class ValidationResult lets you add a message that will be to go next to the control that has the erroneous property which is specified in the second parameter. This means that you could set, instead of "Color is mandatory," simply a star symbol and a second generic error message without specifying the property, like the example below.

```
public class Car : IValidatableObject
{
    public int Id { get; set; }
    public string Name { get; set; }
    public string Type { get; set; }
    public string Color { get; set; }

    public IEnumerable<ValidationResult> Validate(ValidationContext
validationContext)
    {
        if (string.IsNullOrEmpty(Name))
        {
            yield return new ValidationResult("Name is mandatory"
                                       , new[] {"Name"});
        }
        if (string.IsNullOrEmpty(Type))
        {
            yield return new ValidationResult("Type is mandatory"
                                       , new[] {"Type"});
        }
        if (string.IsNullOrEmpty(Color))
        {
            yield return new ValidationResult("*", new[] {"Color"});
            yield return new ValidationResult("Color is mandatory");
        }

    }
}
```

From here, you have validation from the Model Binding and from the Model class. What is about validation needs to be done inside the action of the controller. This could be that maybe we do not want anyone to edit a car that is not available. This requires a call to the database and of course won't be inside the model object. The controller can be a good position to check. No problem for the ModelState because this   not only has the IsValid property but also has the method *AddModelError* that lets you add any error message.

```
[HttpPost]
public ActionResult Edit(Car car)
{
    if (IsCarAvailable())
    {
        ModelState.AddModelError(string.Empty
                    , "Car cannot be edited because not available anymore");
    }
    if (ModelState.IsValid)
    {
        //Update code to be placed here
        return RedirectToAction("CarList");
    }
    else
    {
        return View("CarEdit", car);
    }
}
```

Some scenarios remain; for example partial view or **Ajax** call. For partial view, no problem, everything will be stored in the ModelView that contains a dictionary of all errors during the life cycle of the request to the server. The Ajax situation is not really more complex because the Ajax call will call the action method, which will store all errors in the ModelState. The action method will return a JsonResult most of the time, which contains, most of the time, a partial view in a string that will be injected into an HTML div. When you want to get back a positive message only if it is a success, and all errors when it fails, you can always return the collection of errors. Here is the way to retrieve a collection of String that contains all messages of the ModelState.

```
var allErrors = ModelState.Values.SelectMany(e => e.Errors)
                        .Select(gh => gh.ErrorMessage);
```

This can then be used wherever you want.

The final scenario is the one where you need to store all error messages in a session. Since you can have a list of errors, it should not be hard to just store them into a session. But, let's say that you desire to store the whole ModelState into a session. What is a good way to do it? This is another story and it is not only feasible but a good pattern that will be discussed later.

ModelState.Clear() is required to display back your model object

Release Date: 18-Apr-12
Url: http://patrickdesjardins.com/blog/?post_type=post&p=1013

If you are getting your Model from a form and you want to manipulate the data that came from the client form and write it back to a view, you need to call ModelState.Clear() to clean the ModelState values.

The reason is that normally you want to post back to the client the form with all the errors. So, when you put back the parameter that contains your model to the view to be returned, this uses the value of the ModelState.

So, for example, if I change a property and send it back to the client :

```
[HttpPost]
public ActionResult Edit(MyObject objModel)
{
    objModel.Property1 = "NEW VALUE";
    //...return View(objModel)
}
```

This won't put on the UI the new value for the property1 because the ModelState values don't contain this value but the one entered by the user.

To be able to override the model state you need to remove all the data from it.

```
[HttpPost]
public ActionResult Edit(MyObject objModel)
{
    objModel.Property1 = "NEW VALUE";
    //...ModelState.Clear();
    return View(objModel);
```

```
}
```

To clear the memory of the model state you need to use **ModelState.Clear()**. You could also remove only the desired field by using the method of ModelState.

```
ModelState.Remove("Property1");
```

Also, if you always want to not use the ModelState, you also may want to not use HtmlHelper, butdirectly use the model with HTML code.

```
My Property: <input type="text" name="Property1" value="@Model.Property1" />
```

In all situations, what you need to remember is that ModelState is the default mechanism and will by default be the one that will be used to display information back to the form.

How to localize data attributes in MVC3

Release Date: 29-Apr-12
Url: http://patrickdesjardins.com/blog/?post_type=post&p=1042

If you are using the **Data Annotation** with Asp.Net MVC you might need to localize the message from these annotations.

Here is an example:

```
public class Person
{
    [Required(ErrorMessage = "FirstName is required")]
    public string FirstName { get; set; }
    //...
}
```

If you want to have the Data Annotation translated into many languages, you should use two others properties that are:

ErrorMessageResourceType and **ErrorMessageResourceName**. This will let you specify the resource type and the resouce name which is the key to inside the resource file.

```
public class Person
{
  [Required(ErrorMessageResourceType = typeof (MyResourcesNameSpace.ResourcesFile)
```

```
            , ErrorMessageResourceName = "FirstNameRequiredKey")]
    public string FirstName { get; set; }
    //...
}
```

This way, you will have your application localized from the Model to the View without any problem.

How to localize property name

Release Date: 30-Apr-12
Url: http://patrickdesjardins.com/blog/?post_type=post&p=1046

If you are using **Html Helper** to generate your form you may end up with a label with the property name in it. You may also have an error message with the property name. The problem is if your object contains an English term, you would prefer not to show it in English if you write something in French.

```
public class Person
{
    public string Name { get; set; }
}
```

The example above could display the word "Name" in a localized string, which is not what we want. But, if we use the **Display** data annotation attribute, it is possible to localize the property Name.

```
public class Person
{
    [Display(ResourceType = typeof (ResourceFileTypeHere)
            , Name = "NamePropertyKey")]
    public string Name { get; set; }
}
```

This will search inside the resource specified by the key inside the Name attribute. That's it! You have your property localized.

How to get from an ASP.MVC Controller the absolute path for an action

Release Date: 04-May-12
Url: http://patrickdesjardins.com/blog/?post_type=post&p=1063

You may need to have the full url of an action in case you desire to do some JavaScript redirection. You may want to specifiy which url to redirect via Json. Using a not fully constructed url will fail the redirection. The trick is to specify a full url. Asp.Net MVC gives you the possibility of generating a fully formed url with the URL helper. The class that will help you to get the url is called **UrlHelper**.

The class contains many **Action** methods that are loaded with many parameters. The one that interests us has four parameters.

```
public string Action(string actionName, string controllerName, object routeValues,
string protocol)
{
//...
}
```

The first parameter is the action name which you want the url to have. The second one is the controller name. This one can be NULL if you use it inside a controller and want to have the url with the same url. If you are inside the action X or the controller Y and you put NULL, you will get a url for the controller Y. The route values don't interest us in this case. You can pass NULL. The last parameter is the protocol. When you provide a procotol, the url returned by the Action method will contain a full absolute url. A trick is to use **Request.Url.Scheme** that will use the current protocol used by the method that has been called by the controller. That means that if you are using HTTP the url formed will have the same protocol, HTTP. Same thing if the request had been made by an HTTPS request, the formed url would contain HTTPS.

We can take a look inside Asp.Net MVC source code and see that the Action method with four parameters calls *GenerateURL* with a lot of parameters.

```
public string Action(string actionName, string controllerName, object routeValues,
string protocol)
{
    return GenerateUrl(null /* routeName */, actionName, controllerName
        , protocol, null /* hostName */, null /* fragment */
            , new RouteValueDictionary(routeValues), RouteCollection
            , RequestContext, true /* includeImplicitMvcValues */);
}
```

The *GenerateUrl* method checks the protocol and, if not NULL, will build the absolute URL.

```
public static string GenerateUrl(string routeName, string actionName, string
controllerName, string protocol, string hostName, string fragment,
RouteValueDictionary routeValues, RouteCollection routeCollection, RequestContext
requestContext, bool includeImplicitMvcValues)
{
    string url = GenerateUrl(routeName, actionName, controllerName, routeValues,
routeCollection, requestContext, includeImplicitMvcValues);
    if (url != null)
    {
        if (!String.IsNullOrEmpty(fragment))
        {
            url = url + "#" + fragment;
        }
        if (!String.IsNullOrEmpty(protocol) || !String.IsNullOrEmpty(hostName))
        {
            Uri requestUrl = requestContext.HttpContext.Request.Url;
            protocol = (!String.IsNullOrEmpty(protocol)) ? protocol :
Uri.UriSchemeHttp;
            hostName = (!String.IsNullOrEmpty(hostName)) ? hostName :
requestUrl.Host;
            string port = String.Empty;
            string requestProtocol = requestUrl.Scheme;
            if (String.Equals(protocol, requestProtocol,
StringComparison.OrdinalIgnoreCase))
            {
                port = requestUrl.IsDefaultPort ? String.Empty : (":" +
Convert.ToString(requestUrl.Port, CultureInfo.InvariantCulture));
            }
            url = protocol + Uri.SchemeDelimiter + hostName + port + url;
        }
    }
    return url;
}
```

So, that means that if you want to have your action method get an absolute URL you would need to call:

```
return Json(new JsonResponse { url = Url.Action("MyActionOfThisController", null,
null, Request.Url.Scheme) });
```

What is the HandleError attribute goal

Release Date: 09-May-12
Url: http://patrickdesjardins.com/blog/?post_type=post&p=1069

In Asp.Net Mvc, you can add an attribute to your controller or to some actions of your controller to tell Asp that you will take care of errors if they occur. You simply need to add the attribute **HandleError**.

```
[HandleError]
public class MyController : Controller { }
```

You can take care of a specific error by specifying one or many types of exceptions that you want to handle. To do that, simply add the property **ExceptionType** at your HandleError level.

```
[HandleError(ExceptionType = typeof(SqlException))]
public class MyController : Controller { }
```

If you need to handle multiple exceptions, you will need to use multiple attributes.

```
[HandleError(ExceptionType = typeof(SqlException))]
[HandleError(ExceptionType = typeof(NullReferenceException))]
public class MyController : Controller { }
```

You can also in HandleError attribute specify what view to display.

```
[HandleError(ExceptionType = typeof(SqlException), View = "SqlView")]
public class MyController : Controller { }
```

If you do not specify any view, the exception will be viewed in the default error page. At first, it will check for Error.aspx in the **Views folder** associated with the Controller and then go look in the Shared folder.

Now you have the control to display a specific exception to a specific view, other errors to the generic error page, or to not use anything and use the default ASP error page (yellow page of death) by setting the customErrors to off in the web.config file.

Server Error in '/' Application.

Runtime Error

Description: An application error occurred on the server. The current custom error settings for this application prevent the details of the application error from being viewed.

Details: To enable the details of this specific error message to be viewable on the local server machine, please create a <customErrors> tag within a "web.config" configuration file located in the root directory of the current web application. This <customErrors> tag should then have its "mode" attribute set to "RemoteOnly". To enable the details to be viewable on remote machines, please set "mode" to "Off".

```
<!-- Web.Config Configuration File -->

<configuration>
    <system.web>
        <customErrors mode="RemoteOnly"/>
    </system.web>
</configuration>
```

MvcHtmlString.Create to encode HTML with Asp.net MVC

Release Date: 04-Jun-12
Url: http://patrickdesjardins.com/blog/?post_type=post&p=1121

You may want to use a string that contains HTML and display this not with the HTML tag but to execute it. Of course, you would like to do it encoded with HTML (to have secure rendering).

This can be done by using MvcHtmlString.Create.

This method takes a string as parameter and returns an MvcHtmlString.

So, instead of using directly @Model.YourStringProperty, you should use MvcHtmlString.Create(Model.YourStringProperty)

The Create method will check if the property passed by the parameter is inherited from IHtmlString. If so, it won't do anything because a property inherited from IHtmlString does not require encoding. If not, it will encode the HTML output.

From here, you can create your own HTML extension to extend.

```
public static class HtmlHelpers
{
    public static MvcHtmlString HtmlEncode(this string data)
    {
        return MvcHtmlString.Create(data);
    }
}
```

This extension will let you encode any string, so you could use it with your properties.

This is my property: @Model.Name.HtmlEncode()

On the other hand, if you do not want to have the HTML encoded, you could use **Html.Raw()** method which return an **IHtmlString** that will not be encoded by the MVC framework.

If you go inside the source code of Asp.Net you will find that Html.Raw() uses the string and generates a simple IHtmlString from the concrete class HtmlString.

```
public IHtmlString Raw(string value)
{
    return new HtmlString(value);
}

public IHtmlString Raw(object value)
{
    return new HtmlString(value == null ? null : value.ToString());
}
```

This is different from MvcHtmlString.Create()

```
public sealed class MvcHtmlString : HtmlString
{
    public static readonly MvcHtmlString Empty = Create(String.Empty);
    private readonly string _value;

    public MvcHtmlString(string value) : base(value ?? String.Empty)
    {
        _value = value ?? String.Empty;
    }

    public static MvcHtmlString Create(string value)
    {
        return new MvcHtmlString(value);
    }

    public static bool IsNullOrEmpty(MvcHtmlString value)
```

```
    {
        return (value == null || value._value.Length == 0);
    }
}
```

As you can see, this one returns an MvcHtmlString. At the end, both return something similar and encoded in HTML.

In the scenario where you want to display the HTML string you simply need to use the variable:

```
{
    var x = "<b>Test</b>";
}
@x
```

To conclude, if you need to display HTML rendered to the browser, you can use one of the two methods and it will work. The reason is that **MvcHtmlString** inherits from HtmlString which inherits from IHtmlString. If you need to display the content of the string that contains HTML (which will print the HTML string and not the rendered content) simply use directly the variable like: @Model.MyStringWithHtml

How to change the master page for a specific view with Asp.Net MVC

Release Date: 17-Jun-12
Url: http://patrickdesjardins.com/blog/?post_type=post&p=1138

You may want to have a specific master page for a specific page. This can be handled in many ways.

The first way is the simplest and can be good enough for a few pages that need a specific master page. This is done by returning the view with the master page parameter.

```
public ActionResult Index()
{
    return View("Index", "MasterPageCustom");
}
```

You could also use the View object and set the master page name with a setter.

```
public ActionResult SomeOtherPage()
{
    var view = View("Index");
    view.MasterName = "MasterPageCustom";
    return view;
}
```

Generally, if you have a bigger website, you would prefer to handle the master page at a higher level like the controller. This can be done by using the *OnActionExecuted*. Right after the action is executed, the controller can change the master page of the returned view.

```
protected override void OnActionExecuted(ActionExecutedContext filterContext)
{
    var action = filterContext.Result as ViewResult;
    //Verify that nothing has been previously set. This give the possibility to
    //still be able to set the master page at a more atomic position (action).
    if (action != null && String.IsNullOrEmpty(action.MasterName))
    {
        action.MasterName = "MasterPageCustom";
    }
    //Default stuff
    base.OnActionExecuted(filterContext);
}
```

The latter solution is the best one in situations where you have multiple action methods that use the same master page. It also gives the flexibility to change it for specific actions. The first solution should be used if the master page is used for a few actions only.

How to add CSS file or JavaScript file by action of the controller

Release Date: 29-Jun-12
Url: http://patrickdesjardins.com/blog/?post_type=post&p=1161

Wouldn't it be great to specify for a specific action what CSS or JavaScript file to load? With Asp.Net MVC it is possible to do something custom pretty fast and useful with an attribute. An attribute is something that the developer adds at the top of the method (action). The syntax is simple. It uses the square brackets and between the brackets you place the name of the attribute and its parameters.

Below is how to use the JavaScript attribute to get two JavaScript files loaded only when Index is called. We could improve this by also letting the developer add the tag over the controller class which would load the JavaScript for all actions of this controller.

```csharp
public class HomeController : Controller
{
    [JavaScript("MyFile1", "MyFile2")]
    public ActionResult Index()
    {
        ViewBag.Message = "Welcome to ASP.NET MVC!";
        return View();
    }

    public ActionResult About()
    {
        return View();
    }
}
```

The first step is to create an attribute for each of the specific files you want. For example, one for CSS and one for JavaScript . For simplicity, we will only do JavaScript here.

```csharp
[AttributeUsage(AttributeTargets.Class | AttributeTargets.Method)]
public class JavaScript : Attribute
{
    public string[] FileNames { get; set; }

    public JavaScript(params string[] fileName)
    {
        this.FileNames = fileName;
    }
}
```

Then, we need to add to the master page (by default _Layout.cshtml) a code that will read those attributes and add the JavaScript tag in the header of the HTML code.

```html
@<!DOCTYPE html>
<html>
<head>
    <meta charset="utf-8" />
    <title>@ViewBag.Title</title>
    <link href="@Url.Content("~/Content/Site.css")" rel="stylesheet"
type="text/css" />
    <script src="@Url.Content("~/Scripts/jquery-1.5.1.min.js")"
type="text/javascript"></script>
    <script src="@Url.Content("~/Scripts/modernizr-1.7.min.js")"
type="text/javascript"></script>
    @Html.GetJavaScript ();
</head>
```

The GetJavaScript () helper code will loop all attributes to find what has been defined at the controller side.

```
public static MvcHtmlString GetJavaScript (this HtmlHelper helper)
{
    IList<string> fileNames = new List<string>(); //The class may have more than
one JavaScript  file. Need to loop them all and also loop all entries
    MemberInfo controllerInfo = helper.ViewContext.Controller.GetType();
    object[] listOfcontrollerAttributes = controllerInfo
                        .GetCustomAttributes(typeof (JavaScript), true);
    FillUpFileArray(fileNames, listOfcontrollerAttributes);//Method attributes.
First get the method that has been called and loop all possible JavaScript  tag
and entries
    MethodInfo method;
    if (helper.ViewContext.HttpContext.Request.HttpMethod == "POST")
    {
        method = helper.ViewContext.Controller.GetType().GetMethods()
            .FirstOrDefault(t => t.Name ==
                helper.ViewContext.RouteData.GetRequiredString("action")
            && t.GetCustomAttributes(typeof (JavaScript), true).Any()
            && t.GetCustomAttributes(typeof (HttpPostAttribute), true).Any());
    }
    else
    {
        method = helper.ViewContext.Controller.GetType().GetMethods()
            .FirstOrDefault(t => t.Name ==
                helper.ViewContext.RouteData.GetRequiredString("action")
            && t.GetCustomAttributes(typeof (JavaScript), true).Any()
            && !t.GetCustomAttributes(typeof (HttpPostAttribute),true).Any());
    }
    if (method != null)
    {
        object[] methodAttributes = method
                        .GetCustomAttributes(typeof (JavaScript), true);
        FillUpFileArray(fileNames, methodAttributes);
    }
    //Create Html
    if (fileNames.Any())
    {
        var sb = new StringBuilder();
        var url = new UrlHelper(helper.ViewContext.RequestContext);
        const string JS_SCRIPT_FORMAT = "<script src=\"{0}.js\"
type=\"text/javascript\"></script>";
        foreach (string fmt in fileNames
                    .Select(name => string.Format(JS_SCRIPT_FORMAT
                                , url.Content("~/Scripts/") + name)))
        {
            sb.AppendLine(fmt);
        }
```

```
            return new MvcHtmlString(sb.ToString());
    }
    return new MvcHtmlString(string.Empty);
}

private static void FillUpFileArray(ICollection<string> fileNames,
IEnumerable<object> listOfcontrollerAttributes)
{
    if (listOfcontrollerAttributes != null)
    {
        foreach (string name in listOfcontrollerAttributes.OfType<JavaScript>()
                         .SelectMany(classAttributes =>
                                            classAttributes.FileNames
                              .Where(name => !string.IsNullOrEmpty(name)
                                     && !fileNames.Contains(name)))
                         )
        {
            fileNames.Add(name);
        }
    }
}
}
```

Here is the explanation step by step:

```
MemberInfo controllerInfo = helper.ViewContext.Controller.GetType();
    object[] listOfcontrollerAttributes =
controllerInfo.GetCustomAttributes(typeof (JavaScript), true);
    FillUpFileArray(fileNames, listOfcontrollerAttributes);
```

The first section gets everything from the controller that has been called into view to get all possible attributes defined and loop through them. Every time it finds an attribute, it loops through the list of strings that represent a JavaScript file.

```
MethodInfo method;
if (helper.ViewContext.HttpContext.Request.HttpMethod == "POST")
{
    method = helper.ViewContext.Controller.GetType().GetMethods()
        .FirstOrDefault(t => t.Name ==
helper.ViewContext.RouteData.GetRequiredString("action")
            && t.GetCustomAttributes(typeof (JavaScript), true).Any()
            && t.GetCustomAttributes(typeof (HttpPostAttribute), true).Any());
}
else
{
    method = helper.ViewContext.Controller.GetType().GetMethods()
        .FirstOrDefault(t => t.Name ==
helper.ViewContext.RouteData.GetRequiredString("action")
```

```
                && t.GetCustomAttributes(typeof (JavaScript), true).Any()
                && !t.GetCustomAttributes(typeof (HttpPostAttribute), true).Any());
}
if (method != null)
{
    object[] methodAttributes = method
                                .GetCustomAttributes(typeof (JavaScript), true);
    FillUpFileArray(fileNames, methodAttributes);
}
```

It is almost the same with another method, but this time we need to get the better action method. The same method can be good for GET or HTTP so we need to figure out the better one. As you can see, we do not search explicitly for GET because the action's method is implicitly GET.

```
if (fileNames.Any())
{
    var sb = new StringBuilder();
    var url = new UrlHelper(helper.ViewContext.RequestContext);
    const string JS_SCRIPT_FORMAT = "<script src=\"{0}.js\"
type=\"text/javascript\"></script>";
    foreach (string fmt in fileNames
                .Select(name => string.Format(JS_SCRIPT_FORMAT
                                , url.Content("~/Scripts/") + name)))
    {
        sb.AppendLine(fmt);
    }
    return new MvcHtmlString(sb.ToString());
}
return new MvcHtmlString(string.Empty);
```

At the end, we print the list of JavaScript files by adding the extension but referring to the good script folder.

Here is an example of a controller that works pretty well with this kind of scenario:

```
[JavaScript("Controller1", "Controller2")]
public class HomeController : Controller
{
    [JavaScript("MyFileAction1", "MyFileAction2")]
    public ActionResult Index()
    {
        ViewBag.Message = "Welcome to ASP.NET MVC!";
        return View();
    }

    [JavaScript("Integer", "Integer")]
```

```
[HttpGet]
public ActionResult Test(int i, int j)
{
    ViewBag.Message = "Welcome to ASP.NET MVC!" + i + " " + j;
    return View("Index");
}

[JavaScript("PostFile1")]
[HttpPost]
public ActionResult Test(string s)
{
    ViewBag.Message = "Welcome to ASP.NET MVC!" + s;
    return View("Index");
}

public ActionResult About()
{
    return View();
}
}
```

Hope it helps you to get cleaner code!

Make all actions of controller secure with Authorize filter implicit

Release Date: 08-Aug-12
Url: http://patrickdesjardins.com/blog/?post_type=post&p=1234

A few months ago, I had to add Asp.Net membership to an Asp.Net MVC project. Instead of adding the filter [Authorize] on every action that required a valid authentication, I decided to use the technique described here:

http://blogs.msdn.com/b/rickandy/archive/2011/05/02/securing-your-asp-net-mvc-3-application.aspx.

By inverting the normal behavior of the security, which is to mark with a filter which method to protect, and instead mark the one that shouldn't be protected, by default everything is secured. By default everything requires an authenticated user. So, with this new filter, only anonymous methods require the filter.

How do we implement that? First, we need to add a new filter that will authorize only methods that contain a specific filter. This is done by adding three lines of code in the

Global.asax.cs.

```
public static void RegisterGlobalFilters(GlobalFilterCollection filters)
{
    private filters.Add(private new LogonAuthorize());
}
```

Since version 3 of ASP.NET MVC, you can add the AuthorizeAttribute filter to the global.asax file to protect every action method of every controller. Second, we need to create the LogonAuthorize class that inherits from AuthorizeAttribute.

```
public sealed class LogonAuthorize : AuthorizeAttribute
{
    public override void OnAuthorization(AuthorizationContext filterContext)
    {
        bool skipAuthorization = filterContext.ActionDescriptor
                .IsDefined(typeof (AllowAnonymousAttribute), true) ||
            filterContext.ActionDescriptor.ControllerDescriptor
                    .IsDefined(typeof (AllowAnonymousAttribute), true);
        if (!skipAuthorization)
        {
            base.OnAuthorization(filterContext);
        }
    }
}
```

If the base.OnAuthorization() is skipped, than we do not have any protection. If the base.OnAuthorization() is called, then the protection mechanism is called and authentication rules are applied.

So, what is happening in the OnAuthorization method? It simply checks if the method or the class contains the attribute defined (AllowAnonymous). If it does, than we skip the authorization so we do not call the base class (AuthorizeAttribute).

From there, you need to add [AllowAnonymous] to methods that you want to be allowed without having the visitor authenticated. For example, the method for login and creating an account should have this attribute.

```
[AllowAnonymous]
public ActionResult LogOn()
{
    //...
}
```

TempData why you should use bracket instead of .Add

Release Date: 12-Aug-12
Url: http://patrickdesjardins.com/blog/?post_type=post&p=1253

TempDataDictionary (TempData inherits from TempDataDictionary) is useful if you need to keep your data between redirections. I have seen some cases of error with a programmer who used the **TempData** with the**Add** method.

First, the Add method won't let you add more than one of the same key. This means that it will crash if you write:

```
TempData.Add("key1", "value1");

TempData.Add("key1", "value2");
```

You ask why someone would do this. Well, in the scenario of redirection, which should occur if you are using **TempData** instead of **ViewBag,** you may come back into the same path of code where the user set the data. In this case, the values are set twice because the TempData in a redirection keeps its values.

You can add some validation with the ContainsKey method.

```
if (!TempData.ContainsKey("key1"))
{
    TempData.Add("key1", "value1");
}
```

This solves the problem but creates overwhelming code for a simple task. The solution in my opinion is to simply use the bracket overload of the TempDataDictionary.

```
TempData["key1"] = "value1";
```

The code is shorter, cleaner and does what we want. It sets the value and if it is a redirection to the same code that has set the value, it will just reset the same value. That's it! Simple and clean.

If you are curious about the bracket code, here is the source code of the TempData for the property [].

```
private Dictionary<string, object> _data;
```

```
private HashSet<string> _initialKeys = new
HashSet<string>(StringComparer.OrdinalIgnoreCase);
//...
public object this[string key]
{
    get
    {
        object value;
        if (TryGetValue(key, out value))
        {
            _initialKeys.Remove(key);
            return value;
        }
        return null;
    }
    set
    {
        _data[key] = value;
        _initialKeys.Add(key);
    }
}
```

Of course, the real question now is why does this code have redirection that double sets this value, but that is another story.

How to do a custom secured file access with Http Handler and MVC framework

Release Date: 14-Sep-12
Url: http://patrickdesjardins.com/blog/?post_type=post&p=1151

In diverse scenarios you could be required to give your user access to files. You could let them be accessed directly by having a directory of files and give the complete path to the file, but this could lead to a different issue. First of all, this will bind the server folders/files structures to the url that you give the user, which might not be desirable. Second, it does not give you any control over the files shared. Third, you may want to add an algorithm for caching or give an expiry to some files. All those custom codes can't be done by giving direct access to files. The solution? Using Http Handler.

HttpHandler was there in Asp.Net traditional, and in Asp.Net MVC it is even easier because configuration is not required for IIS.

First, you need to add a new route to let the MVC routing system know that the url sent is not going to go to a traditional controller but to your http handler.

```
public class ExternalFileRouteHandler : IRouteHandler
{
    public IHttpHandler GetHttpHandler(RequestContext requestContext)
    {
    }
}
```

Inside the Global.asax.cs you need to add your route. You need to put the new route BEFORE the default route because otherwise it will not see the new route. If you set the default FilesRoute before the new route, the condition will match and FilesRoute will be executed. It takes the first route that matches the routing pattern.

```
public static void RegisterRoutes(RouteCollection routes)
{
    routes.IgnoreRoute("{resource}.axd/{*pathInfo}");
    routes.Add("FilesRoute", new Route("files/{uniqueidentifier}", new
ExternalFileRouteHandler()));
    routes.MapRoute("Default", // Route
    name"{controller}/{action}/{id}",// URL with parameters
    new { controller = "Home", action = "Index", id = UrlParameter.Optional } //
Parameter defaults
    );
}
```

With the route above, the code does not compile because our IRouteHandler does not return anything from the GetHttpHandler. This is why we need to create a class that will inherit from IHttpHandler.

```
public class ExternalFileHandler : IHttpHandler
{
    public void ProcessRequest(HttpContext context)
    {
    }

    public bool IsReusable { get; private set; }
}

public class ExternalFileRouteHandler : IRouteHandler
{
    public IHttpHandler GetHttpHandler(RequestContext requestContext)
    {
        return new ExternalFileHandler();
    }
}
```

At this point, we have nothing to do any more from the perspective of the url. Every call will look like this:

http://yourwebsite.com/files/yourIdenfierHere.abc

Now you need to get the file, but first let's get some information about the request, e.g, the request itself, where we will send back the image, and some information about the server and what file is requested.

```csharp
public class ExternalFileHandler : IHttpHandler
{
    public void ProcessRequest(HttpContext context)
    {
        var response = context.Response;
        var request = context.Request;
        var server = context.Server;
        var uniqueFileIdentifier =
RequestContext.RouteData.Values["uniqueidentifier"].ToString();
    }

    public bool IsReusable { get; private set; }
}
```

If we debug we can see that if the request is sent with a good url the http handler will catch the request with the good value.

```csharp
public class ExternalFileHandler : IHttpHandler
{
    public void ProcessRequest(HttpContext context)
    {

        var response = context.Response;
        var request = context.Request;
        var server = context.Server;
        var uniqueFileIdentifier = request.RequestContext.RouteData.Values["uniqueidentifier"];
    }                uniqueFileIdentifier  Q ▾ "myunique123" ▭

    public bool IsReusable { get; private set; }
}
```

The next step is to check if the file really exists. In fact, we need to check if the unique identifier matches a file. If that is not the case, in a scenario of someone trying to get someone else's file, it should return a message.

File not found

This can be done by simply writing in the **Response** a string.

```
public void ProcessRequest(HttpContext context)
{
    var response = context.Response;
    var request = context.Request;
    var server = context.Server;
    var uniqueFileIdentifier =
request.RequestContext.RouteData.Values["uniqueidentifier"].ToString();
    FileInformation file = GetFromPersistenceStorage(uniqueFileIdentifier);
    if (file == null)
    {
        response.Write("File not found");
    }
}
```

As you can see, the file came from the *GetFromPersistenceStorage* method. This method, in reality, would go into the database and search for the file from the unique file identifier. This field in the database should be indexed and unique.

The next step is to check if the file is really on the server. It might be stored correctly into the database but not available on the server.

```
public void ProcessRequest(HttpContext context)
{
    var response = context.Response;
    var request = context.Request;
    var server = context.Server;
    var uniqueFileIdentifier =
request.RequestContext.RouteData.Values["uniqueidentifier"].ToString();
    FileInformation file = GetFromPersistenceStorage(uniqueFileIdentifier);
//Validate the file exist in the persistence storage
    if (file == null)
    {
        response.Write("File not found");
        return;
    }
```

```
    //Validate the the file exist on the server physically
    string completeFilePath = Path.Combine(file.PathOnServer, file.FileName);
    if (!File.Exists(completeFilePath))
    {
        response.Write("File not on the server");
        return;
    }
    //Prepare to send the fileresponse.Clear();
    response.ContentType = file.FileType;
    response.TransmitFile(completeFilePath);
    response.End();
}
```

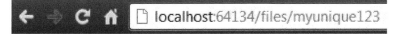

File not on the server

Finally, if the file is present, we will receive its content.

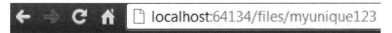

```
Message from the file.
```

You can now secure the file. This can be done in many ways. First, I suppose that the database table that contains every file will have some kind of relation between the user and files. Let's say that every file has the possibility to allow many users; that means you should have three tables: *User, UsersFiles* and *Files. UsersFiles* table contains the ID of the *User* that can access the file and the ID of the file.

So the *FileInformation* class that we have defined earlier would have a List that can access the file. A small modification will be required to get the current user from the session and to check if the file allows the user.

```
public void ProcessRequest(HttpContext context)
{
    var response = context.Response;
    var request = context.Request;
    var server = context.Server;
    var uniqueFileIdentifier =
request.RequestContext.RouteData.Values["uniqueidentifier"].ToString();
    FileInformation file = GetFromPersistenceStorage(uniqueFileIdentifier);
//Validate the file exist in the persistence storage
    if (file == null)
```

```
{
    response.Write("File not found");
    return;
} //Validate if the current logged user can access the file
if (!file.UserIdAuthorized.Contains(SessionUserId))
{
    response.Write("You are not authorized to see this file.");
    return;
} //Validate the the file exist on the server physically
string completeFilePath = Path.Combine(file.PathOnServer, file.FileName);
if (!File.Exists(completeFilePath))
{
    response.Write("File not on the server");
    return;
} //Prepare to send the file
response.Clear();
response.ContentType = file.FileType;
response.TransmitFile(completeFilePath);
response.End();
}

public class FileInformation
{
    public string PathOnServer { get; set; }
    public string FileName { get; set; }
    public string FileType { get; set; }
    public List<int> UserIdAuthorized { get; set; }
}
```

And that is it. You can from here add any other type of validation or expiry or caching. The method **GetFromPersistenceStorage()** could store into the cache the content of the file and if the file is requested again would get it from the cache instead of the server. You could also add an expiry for the file that may be deleted later by setting a timespan on the FileInformation and having a generated DateTime inside the table that contains the file information. A simple validation inside **ProcessRequest** will do the job.

You are now limitless with what you can do with files on your server.

How to render a partial view for an Ajax call in Asp.Net MVC

Release Date: 19-Sep-12
Url: http://patrickdesjardins.com/blog/?post_type=post&p=1409

If you have an Ajax call to perform an action on the server side you may want to answer back with a message, refreshed values, or a portion of the page to be updated. To do that, you need to send back into a JSON object the view (or partial view). In this article, we will create a method that should be placed into every of your controller (maybe in a Base Controller).

The method is this one:

```
/// <summary>
/// Render a PartialView into a string that contain the Html to display to the
browser.
/// </summary>
/// <param name="partialViewName">The name of the partial view to render</param>
/// <param name="model">The model to bind to the partial view</param>
/// <returns>The html rendered partial view</returns>
protected virtual string RenderPartialView(string partialViewName, object model)
{
    if (ControllerContext == null)
    {
        return string.Empty;
    }
    if (model == null)
    {
        throw new ArgumentNullException("model");
    }
    if (string.IsNullOrEmpty(partialViewName))
    {
        throw new ArgumentNullException("partialViewName");
    }
    ModelState.Clear(); //Remove possible model binding error.
    ViewData.Model = model; //Set the model to the partial view
    using (var sw = new StringWriter())
    {
        var viewResult = ViewEngines.Engines
                        .FindPartialView(ControllerContext, partialViewName);
        var viewContext = new ViewContext(ControllerContext
                        , viewResult.View, ViewData, TempData, sw);
        viewResult.View.Render(viewContext, sw);
        return sw.GetStringBuilder().ToString();
    }
}
```

In short, it uses the View Engines of MVC to get the result of the partial view (if found). From there, a view context is generated from the current call (with the current controller context). The model is passed with the ViewData that is required by the ViewContext constructor. Finally, we generated the HTML that is returned.

Here is an example of its use.

```
return Json(new { StatusCode = 1, StatusMessage = "Customer has been created",
ResponseView = RenderPartialView("CustomerPanel", customer) });
```

This could have been otherwise, but you can see the logic behind using Json to have an anonymous object serialized back to the client. From there, you can use JQuery or a plain JavaScript statement to display the ResponseView into an HTML element. The idea of rendering a partial view from a controller came from this other blog http://craftycodeblog.com/2010/05/15/asp-net-mvc-render-partial-view-to-string.

Asp.Net MVC sections are on-the-fly partial defined by view

Release Date: 24-Sep-12
Url: http://patrickdesjardins.com/blog/?post_type=post&p=1433

In Asp.Net MVC we use layout to display common structural HTML structure. If you are in Asp.Net you can see this as the **Master Page**. The layout contains the header, the menu, the main content, the footer, etc. The content itself is not defined inside the layout but uses a Body and Section. It can also use **Partial** to load something that will be static for every page.

The body is the View that will be loaded. If you have a list of customers to display and the controller returns the index view, this will be loaded inside the layout at the RenderBody() statement.

```
//Controller
public ViewResult Index()
{
    var customers = db.Customers.ToList();
    return View(customers);
}
```

The layout will load the View of the Index (Index.cshtml) since no specific view is explicitly defined in the return.

```
<!DOCTYPE html>
<html>
    <head>
        <meta charset="utf-8" />
        <title>@ViewBag.Title</title>
```

```
        <link href="@Url.Content("~/Content/Site.css")" rel="stylesheet"
type="text/css" />
        <script src="@Url.Content("~/Scripts/jquery-1.5.1.min.js")"
type="text/javascript"></script>
        <script src="@Url.Content("~/Scripts/modernizr-1.7.min.js")"
type="text/javascript"></script>
    </head>
<body>
    <div class="page">
        <header>
            <div id="title">
                <h1>My MVC Application</h1>
            </div>
            <div id="logindisplay">
                @Html.Partial("_LogOnPartial")

            </div>
            <nav>
                <ul id="menu">
                    <li>@Html.ActionLink("Home", "Index", "Home")</li>
                    <li>@Html.ActionLink("About", "About", "Home")</li>
                </ul>
            </nav>
        </header>
        <section id="main">
            @RenderBody()
        </section>
        <footer>
        </footer>
    </div>
</body>
</html>
```

Line 17 shows the load of a partial view; that means that the login view is the same for every page. The code of the partial "_LogOnPartial" could have been set directly into the _Layout.cshtml but divides the main structure from details, so it is a good idea to split. Line 27 shows you where the view is loaded. This is done by calling the RenderBody() function.

What about a section that changes in each view but is always at the same location in the _Layout.cshtml? This can be done with the RenderSection("YourSectionName").

RenderSection loads a section that is defined directly inside the View. Let's say you have this view for the customer list :

```
@model IEnumerable<EFCodeFirst.Models.Customer><h2>Index</h2><p>
@Html.ActionLink("Create New", "Create")</p><table>    <tr>        <th>
FirstName        </th>        <th>          LastName        </th>
```

```
<th></th>        </tr>@foreach (var item in Model) {        <tr>            <td>
@Html.DisplayFor(modelItem => item.FirstName)              </td>            <td>
@Html.DisplayFor(modelItem => item.LastName)              </td>            <td>
@Html.ActionLink("Edit", "Edit", new { id=item.Id }) |
@Html.ActionLink("Details", "Details", new { id=item.Id }) |
@Html.ActionLink("Delete", "Delete", new { id=item.Id })              </td>
</tr>}</table>
```

If the Layout is changed for :

```
<!DOCTYPE html>
<html>
<head>
    <meta charset="utf-8" />
    <title>@ViewBag.Title</title>
    <link href="@Url.Content("~/Content/Site.css")" rel="stylesheet"
type="text/css" />
    <script src="@Url.Content("~/Scripts/jquery-1.5.1.min.js")"
type="text/javascript"></script>
    <script src="@Url.Content("~/Scripts/modernizr-1.7.min.js")"
type="text/javascript"></script>
</head>
<body>
    <div class="page">
        <header>
            <div id="title">
                <h1>My MVC Application</h1>

            </div>                <div id="logindisplay">
                @Html.Partial("_LogOnPartial")
            </div>
            <nav>
                <ul id="menu">
                    <li>@Html.ActionLink("Home", "Index", "Home")</li>
                    <li>@Html.ActionLink("About", "About", "Home")</li>
                </ul>
            </nav>
        </header>
        <section id="main">
            @RenderBody()
        </section>
        <footer>
        @if(IsSectionDefined("MySectionName"))
        {
                @RenderSection("MySectionName")
        }
        else
        {
                <p>This is the footer when the View doesn't define a MySectionName
section</p>
        }
        </footer>
```

```
    </div>
  </body>
</html>
```

This produces the main page (not the list of customers):

But if we go inside the customer list view and we define the section with the "section" keyword we will have this section loaded.

In Asp.Net you could have used multiple placeholders. With Asp.Net MVC you have a main placeholder and you can have multiple sections. If the section is not defined, the default is rendered.

How to add JavaScript and CSS dynamically to your view with Asp.Net MVC4

Release Date: 15-Oct-12

Url: http://patrickdesjardins.com/blog/?post_type=post&p=1535

In a previous post concerning "How to add CSS and JavaScript files dynamically" (page 35), depending on the action used, we have found a way to add them by setting a filter to the controller or the action of any controller. The problem with this approach is that it is the controller that chooses client side elements. In fact, the controller should just indicate what view to use and the use itself should be able to determine what CSS or JavaScript to load. Of course, adding CSS/JavaScript directly into the View isn't the best solution because we want to put the CSS at the top of the HTML header and we want to set up the JavaScript at the bottom of the HTML.

This is where Asp.Net MVC **section** can shine.

Named Section

Asp.Net MVC has something called **Named Section**. It lets the developer set up optional placeholders inside the master page and, if required, lets the view inject some HTML code.

```
<html>
<script type="text/javascript"
src="@Url.Content("/Scripts/javascriptAlwaysLoaded.js)">
@RenderSection("scripts", required: false)
</html>
```

The code above shows you some code that could have been written to be in the master page. As you can see, we have one JavaScript file hard coded that will be loaded whatsoever the page. This is good for JQuery or any other JavaScript file that is required to be always there. Then, we have the **RenderSection**. RenderSection works a little bit like **RenderBody()**. We have set the parameter required to false, meaning that this placeholder is not required if no script needs to be registered.

The next step is to go into a view that needs to have a specific script and add the HTML to load it. For example:

```
@section scripts
    {
    <script type="text/javascript" src="@Url.Content("/Scripts/ABC.js")"></script>
}
```

Conclusion

I think this approach is better than the Filter one because it lets you handle the client side directly inside the view without having to modify the controller. It is also not exactly up to the controller to specify what design style (CSS) or script (JavaScript) to display. In fact, the controller role is really to handle the request and give a correct response, not to implement the detail for the view.

Asp.Net MVC4 AllowAnonymous

Release Date: 17-Oct-12
Url: http://patrickdesjardins.com/blog/?post_type=post&p=1566

In Asp.Net MVC3 and before, if we wanted to make by default all actions of the controller secured we had to create an AllowAnonymous filter to authorize the filter implicitly (page 34) and add a global filter to require a valid authentication before accessing the action.

With Asp.Net MVC 4, it is built in. You need to go inside the App_Start folder which contains the FilterConfig.cs file. Inside the FilterConfig.cs you will find what was inside the Global.Asax.cs: The static method *RegisterGlobalFilters*.

You need to add to this method the new folder called "AuthorizeAttribute."

```
public class FilterConfig
{
    public static void RegisterGlobalFilters(GlobalFilterCollection filters)
    {
        filters.Add(new HandleErrorAttribute());
        filters.Add(new AuthorizeAttribute());
    }
}
```

By now, all actions require a valid authentication. If you want to allow an anonymous person to see the action, you need to add the **AllowAuthorize** attribute to the action. In fact, it is already set up for the login and register method of the AccountController.cs.

```
[AllowAnonymous]
public ActionResult Login(string returnUrl)
{
    ViewBag.ReturnUrl = returnUrl;
    return View();
}

[AllowAnonymous]
public ActionResult Register()
{
    return View();
}
```

That's it. Pretty simple and more secure!

How to add ReCaptcha to your Asp.Net MVC4 register form

Release Date: 19-Oct-12
Url: http://patrickdesjardins.com/blog/?post_type=post&p=1572

To prevent a bot (automatic programs that act like a human without being a real one) from registering an account to your website, you can use what we call captcha. Captcha is an image that only a human can read. They have characters that need to be input into a text box when the form is filled out. Today, I'll show you how to implement ReCaptcha, a popular Captcha service that is totally free and owned by Google.

The first step is to register an API key for your website. You can go to http://www.google.com/recaptcha and create a new one. I suggest you do not check "Enable this key on all domains" to be able to debug with localhost. So, after this step, you will have a private and public key that will be required to use the ReCaptcha service.

The second step is to have a library to access ReCaptcha. Inside your project, add the two following NuGet Packages. One is the Recaptcha API service and the other one will give you **HTML helper**.

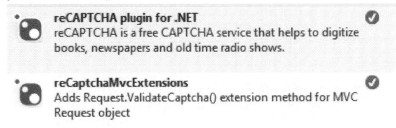

The third step is to configure your project with the public and private key. This can be done by adding two app settings in the web.config.

```
<appSettings>
  <add key="webpages:Version" value="2.0.0.0" />
  <add key="webpages:Enabled" value="false" />
  <add key="PreserveLoginUrl" value="true" />
  <add key="ClientValidationEnabled" value="true" />
  <add key="UnobtrusiveJavaScriptEnabled" value="true" />
  <add key="RecaptchaPrivateKey" value="123nI9cSAAAAALtUefffnLRn2pWb7IpNrtOGQjzz"
/>
  <add key="RecaptchaPublicKey" value="123nI9cSAAAAAOH3eee3t1ZaZ6rRUwHQK4KMimfu"
/>
</appSettings>
```

The fourth step is to let every page know about the new library by adding the name space into the system.web configuration of the web.config.

```
<system.web>
  <pages>
    <namespaces>
      <add namespace="System.Web.Helpers" />
      <add namespace="System.Web.Mvc" />
      <add namespace="System.Web.Mvc.Ajax" />
      <add namespace="System.Web.Mvc.Html" />
      <add namespace="System.Web.Optimization" />
      <add namespace="System.Web.Routing" />
      <add namespace="System.Web.WebPages" />
      <add namespace="Recaptcha" />
    </namespaces>
  </pages>
</system.web>
```

The fifth step is to add the control to the registration form.

```
<li>
```

```
@Html.Raw(Html.GenerateCaptcha())
@Html.ValidationMessage("recaptcha")
</li>
```

The last step is to check if everything is fine from the controller side. This will be validated when the user submits the form to the server.

```
[RecaptchaControlMvc.CaptchaValidator]
public ActionResult Register(RegisterModel model, bool captchaValid, string
captchaErrorMessage)
{
    if (ModelState.IsValid)
    {
        if (!captchaValid)
        {
            ModelState.AddModelError("recaptcha", captchaErrorMessage);
            return View(model);
        }
    }
//...
```

You need first to add the attribute that will call the server and do the validation. Second, you need to add two variables to the action that will tell you if the captcha is valid, and the message. You can then check the value and display the form again if it is wrong.

Nothing has to be done when developing into localhost (or 127.0.0.1) because the ReCaptcha service allows a developer to use any key for the localhost domain.

Behind the library

The first section was enough to let you implement ReCaptcha with your Asp.Net MVC 4 website. Now, let's check a little bit the code behind the library. First, the HTML helper. This helper creates an instance of RecaptchaControl with the ID "recaptcha".

```
public static string GenerateCaptcha(this HtmlHelper helper)
{
    return RecaptchaControlMvc.GenerateCaptcha(helper, "recaptcha", "default");
}

public static string GenerateCaptcha(this HtmlHelper helper, string id, string
theme)
{
    if (string.IsNullOrEmpty(RecaptchaControlMvc.publicKey) ||
string.IsNullOrEmpty(RecaptchaControlMvc.privateKey))
    {
```

```
        throw new ApplicationException("reCAPTCHA needs to be configured with a
public & private key.");
    }
    RecaptchaControl recaptchaControl1 = new RecaptchaControl();
    recaptchaControl1.ID = id;
    recaptchaControl1.Theme = theme;
    recaptchaControl1.PublicKey = RecaptchaControlMvc.publicKey;
    recaptchaControl1.PrivateKey = RecaptchaControlMvc.privateKey;
    RecaptchaControl recaptchaControl2 = recaptchaControl1;
    HtmlTextWriter writer = new HtmlTextWriter((TextWriter) new StringWriter());
    recaptchaControl2.RenderControl(writer);
    return writer.InnerWriter.ToString();
}
```

This is quite interesting because when you validate your Recaptcha you may want to add the error message next to it.

From the same code, we can see that the public and private keys come from RecaptchaControlMvc… Those are two static strings that get their values from the application setting of the web config file.

```
public static class RecaptchaControlMvc
{
    private static string publicKey =
ConfigurationManager.AppSettings["RecaptchaPublicKey"];
    private static string privateKey =
ConfigurationManager.AppSettings["RecaptchaPrivateKey"];
}
```

So far, nothing is very hard to understand and we have two answers concerning the name of the control generated and the name of the setting used for the web.config.

The last interesting part is concerning the filter that we had to add to the action to validate the input of the user. This one is straightforward. It uses the RecaptchaValidator class to access the service and get a response from the ReCaptcha service. It then adds the validation answer to the parameter. We now have our third answer concerning what parameter to add to the action.

```
public override void OnActionExecuting(ActionExecutingContext filterContext)
{
    RecaptchaValidator recaptchaValidator = new RecaptchaValidator();
    recaptchaValidator.PrivateKey = RecaptchaControlMvc.PrivateKey;
    recaptchaValidator.RemoteIP =
filterContext.HttpContext.Request.UserHostAddress;
```

```
    recaptchaValidator.Challenge =
filterContext.HttpContext.Request.Form["recaptcha_challenge_field"];
    recaptchaValidator.Response =
filterContext.HttpContext.Request.Form["recaptcha_response_field"];
    this.recaptchaResponse = !string.IsNullOrEmpty(recaptchaValidator.Challenge) ?
(!string.IsNullOrEmpty(recaptchaValidator.Response) ?
recaptchaValidator.Validate() : RecaptchaResponse.InvalidResponse) :
RecaptchaResponse.InvalidChallenge;
    filterContext.ActionParameters["captchaValid"] = (object) (bool)
(this.recaptchaResponse.IsValid ? 1 : 0);
    filterContext.ActionParameters["captchaErrorMessage"] = (object)
this.recaptchaResponse.ErrorMessage;
    base.OnActionExecuting(filterContext);
}
```

So that's it for using a captcha in the registration form of an Asp.Net MVC 4 application.

An attribute argument must be a constant expression, typeof expression or array creation expression of an attribute parameter type

Release Date: 09-Nov-12
Url: http://patrickdesjardins.com/blog/?post_type=post&p=1643

If you are trying to use a static string in an attribute for an action inside an Asp.Net MVC's controller, you will get a strange error.

An attribute argument must be a constant expression, typeof expression or array creation expression of an attribute parameter type.

This is because you are using a static string instead of a constant.

```
public static string AdministratorRole="admin";
```

The code below works because it is a public **const** string instead of a public **static** string.

```
public const string AdministratorRole="admin";
```

For the final result:

```
[Authorize(Roles = AdministratorRole)]
public ActionResult Creation()
```

```
{
    //...
}
```

How to have a custom role to use with the Authorize attribute of Asp.Net MVC

Release Date: 12-Nov-12
Url: http://patrickdesjardins.com/blog/?post_type=post&p=1650

If you are developing a website with Asp.Net MVC you might use the [Authorize] attribute over actions of your controllers. The Authorize attribute lets you mark the method of access to a user or a group of users (called role).

```
public const string AdministratorRole="admin";
[Authorize(Roles = "groupName1, groupeName2")]
public ActionResult Creation()
{
    //...
}
```

The code in the example above illustrates the authorization of the creation method to the groupeName1 and groupeName2.

The Authorize method uses the IPrincipal to get the current username logged. It uses the "IsInRole" method. Here is a part of the code from the MVC framework.

```
public bool IsInRole(string role)
{
    if (_Identity == null)
    {
        throw new
ProviderException(SR.GetString(SR.Role_Principal_not_fully_constructed));
    }
    if (!_Identity.IsAuthenticated || role == null)
    {
        return false;
    }
    role = role.Trim();
    if (!IsRoleListCached)
    {
        _Roles.Clear();
        string[] roles =
Roles.Providers[_ProviderName].GetRolesForUser(Identity.Name);
        foreach (string roleTemp in roles)
```

```
    {
        if (_Roles[roleTemp] == null)
        {
            _Roles.Add(roleTemp, String.Empty);
        }
    }
    _IsRoleListCached = true;
    _CachedListChanged = true;
    }
    return _Roles[role] != null;
}
```

As we can see, it first checks if the user is authenticated; if not, then there is no need to check anything. Then, it checks with the Roles.Providers[].**GetRolesForUser**(...).

This code calls the RoleProvider to get the complete list of roles for the logged user and check if the role specified by the attribute is inside the collection. If it is, then the access is granted, otherwise, a 401 error will arise.

So, to create a custom role provider, you need to create a new class that inherits from **System.Web.Security.RoleProvider**. This will let you override two important methods:

- bool IsUserInRole(string username, string roleName)

- string[] GetRolesForUser(string username)

The first one will call the second one. The second one, **GetRolesForUser,** is the one used by **IPrincipal** (and by this I mean used by the attribute Authorized).

From here, you can do whatever you want to do. For example, in a project, I had to use the WindowsTokenRoleProvider but to check for a specific suffix. If the user had the suffix "_PROJECTNAME" then it was a possible role; other roles were not checked. That means that if the user ABC has "admin_PROJECT1" and "admin_PROJECT3" and this user logs in to the PROJECT3 it shouldn't be authorized. Fine, but the problem was that I couldn't simply add the attribute over the method with the full name for some reason. I had to use [admin] and not [admin_PROJECT3]. So, the task was to implement a custom RoleProvider, get the list of all available roles for the user and then filter by project to return in fact a list of roles for the project. Of course, I had to also remove the suffix to be able to return a clean list that would be comparable with the role name like "admin".

```csharp
public class MyRoleProvider : System.Web.Security.RoleProvider
{
    private readonly WindowsTokenRoleProvider _windows;

    public MyRoleProvider()
    {
        _windows = new WindowsTokenRoleProvider();
    }

    public override void Initialize(string name, NameValueCollection config)
    {
        base.Initialize(name, config); //config can access attribute specified in
the web.config
    }

    public override bool IsUserInRole(string username, string roleName)
    {
        return GetRolesForUser(username)
            .FirstOrDefault(s => s == roleName) != null;
    }

    public override string[] GetRolesForUser(string username)
    {
        var sufix = "PROJECT1";
        return _windows.GetRolesForUser(username).ToList()
                .Where(s => s.EndsWith(sufix))
                    .Select(s => s.Replace(sufix, string.Empty).ToArray();
    }
}
```

Here is a short example; in fact the suffix was taken from a configuration file. From there, it is possible to use the attribute with the role without having to specify anything about the suffix. The suffix can be set to the configuration file. This could be useful for a different deployment server wherein some server users have a different role. You could set "admin_Testing" and "admin_Production" where you can set developer "Patrick" the role of "admin_Testing" but not to "admin_Production". IN the web.config, you just set "_Testing" for the testing environment and on the production "_Production." So, if Patrick logs in to the testing environment, he should be able to do whatever this role gives him access to, but not when he goes into production.

The MyRoleProvider is specified in the web.config under system.web

```xml
    <roleManager enabled="true" defaultProvider="MyRoleProvider">
  <providers>
    <clear />
```

```
    <add name="MyRoleProvider" type="YourNameSpace.RoleProvider.MyRoleProvider"
/>
  </providers>
</roleManager>
```

The addition of the provider element can have a custom attribute to add information that can be read by the Role Provider inside the Initialize method.

How to localize The value {0} is not valid for {1}

Release Date: 21-Nov-12
Url: http://patrickdesjardins.com/blog/?post_type=post&p=1661

You cannot simply use an attribute like Required to specify the message your want for an invalid value. What you have to do is to change the default model binding resource class. When the model binder tries to convert the input to the type of the model, if it cannot be converted, a message is sent back to the client in the format: The value '{0}' is not valid for {1}. To change the message, you need to go inside the Global.asax.cs, in the Application_Start method.

Server Error in '/' Application.

Could not find any resources appropriate for the specified culture or the neutral culture. Make sure "Resources.MvcFrameworkMessage.resources" was correctly embedded or linked into assembly "App_GlobalResources.lmloxx4z" at compile time, or that all the satellite assemblies required are loadable and fully signed.

Description: An unhandled exception occurred during the execution of the current web request. Please review the stack trace for more information about the error and where it originated in the code.

You need to set the name of a resource file that you will create.

```
DefaultModelBinder.ResourceClassKey = "GlobalErrorMessage"
```

The file (in our case called GlobalErrorMessage) needs to be inside the App_GlobalResources of the assembly that uses the view. Then, you need to add an entry called PropertyValueInvalid. For a French translation, you could use: La valeur '{0}' n'est pas valide pour le champ {1}.

If you mistmatch the name of the resource class key and the file you may receive an error saying that it was incorrectly embedded:

"Could not find any resources appropriate for the specified culture or the neutral culture." Make sure "Resources.MvcFrameworkMessage.resources" was correctly embedded or linked into assembly "App_GlobalResources.lmloxx4z" at compile time, or that all the satellite assemblies required are loadable and fully signed.

To solve this error, just rename the file or change the string. With this solution, you can now have a valid translated error message for invalid data type.

How to load JavaScript for the whole application except a few folders or areas

Release Date: 27-Dec-12
Url: http://patrickdesjardins.com/blog/?post_type=post&p=1770

When you want to load a specific resource like a JavaScript file or a CSS file depending on a view, you can use a **RenderSection** (see page 48 for how to add JavaScript and CSS Dynamically).

On the other hand, if you always want to load this JavaScript file (or CSS) but not in a particular folder, how can you do it? This can be resolved by using _ViewStart.cshtml file. Every folder can have a defined _ViewStart.cshtml which allows you to choose which Layout to use.

```
@{
    Layout = "~/Views/Shared/_MasterPage.cshtml";
}
```

This is an example of a _ViewStart.cshtml page that defines the Layout. If you are using Area within your application, you can have an Area which doesn't use the same Layout. This can be defined by adding this file to the folder of your views and you change the Layout. It can be at the root of the Area's view folder or directly into the folder of a specific view. Asp.Net MVC will execute ALL _ViewStart.cshtml from the root to the view. That means that if you define something at the root, this will remain if not overwritten. It works fine with the Layout property which can be redefined in a folder which will override the default _ViewStart.cshtml value.

So, if you want to load a JavaScript file for all views except one Area, you cannot do it:

```
//_ViewStart.cshtml : At the root for every view
@{
    Layout = "~/Views/Shared/_Layout.cshtml";
    <script src="@Url.Content("~/Scripts/myFile.js")" type="text/javascript">
</script>
}

//_ViewStart.cshtml : Inside the View directory of the Area
@{
    Layout = "~/Views/Shared/_Layout.cshtml";
}
```

This doest not work because the _ViewStart.cshtml will be executed first and add the script.

To solve this issue you can use TempData.

```
//_ViewStart.cshtml : At the root for every views
@{
    Layout = "~/Views/Shared/_Layout.cshtml";
    ViewContext.TempData.Add("MyFileKey", @Url.Content("~/Scripts/MyFile.js"));
}

//_ViewStart.cshtml : Inside the View directory of the Area
@{
    Layout = "~/Views/Shared/_Layout.cshtml";
    ViewContext.TempData.Remove("MyFileKey");
}
```

This requires you to modify the Layout also:

```
<head>
    ...
    @if (ViewContext.TempData.ContainsKey("MyFileKey"))
    {
        <script src="@ViewContext.TempData["MyFileKey"]" type="text/javascript">
</script>
    }
    ...
</head>
```

That's it. You now have the JavaScript file loaded for the whole application except those areas where it removes it from the TempData. Of course, an even better solution would be to use an object that can have multiple resources which are then handled in the Layout. The goal here is just to show you a way to handle JavaScript and CSS files with the perspective of

Area where this removes an additional resource.

How to secure Cookie when using Https

Release Date: 30-Nov-11
Url: http://patrickdesjardins.com/blog/?post_type=post&p=601

By default cookies are not secured when using Https with SSL(TSL) security.

Asp.net security with cookies

You have two choices with **ASP.NET**

The first one is to explicitly mark the cookie as secure.

```
var cookie = new HttpCookie("MyCookieName", "MyValue");
cookie.Secure = true;
Response.Cookies.Add(cookie);
```

The advantage is that even if the page is not accessed with http the cookie will still work. But, the cost is to add more code.

The second choice is to change in the web.config a line that will implicitly make all cookies secure. But, the disadvantage is that the http won't work, only https.

```
<httpcookies requiressl="true" />
```

Asp.Mvc security with cookies

On the other side, with **ASP MVC** if you want to secure you have two ways and it is better to use both of them at the same time.

The first approach is to use the Https attribute to the controller class.

```
[RequireHttps]
public class MyLoginController : Controller
{
    //...
}
```

This will create a 302 redirect to the Https version of this page. If you want to avoid having a call two times to the server (avoid the redirect) you can also use the overloaded method of ActionLink which lets you specify the protocol.

```
@Html.ActionLink("My Login Link", "LogOn", "MyLoginController", "https", null,
null, null, null)
```

So that's it. If you need to have a secured website, do not forget to secure your cookies.

Using the System.Web.Cache object into your MVC3 project

Release Date: 07-Apr-12
Url: http://patrickdesjardins.com/blog/?post_type=post&p=944

Sometimes you may need to store information a few times in the memory without having to compute the data every time a user requests it. This can save time and also processor time. To do this, we can use the System.Web.Cache object.

```
var cc = HttpRuntime.Cache.Get("Test");
DateTime t;
if (cc == null)
{
    t = DateTime.Now;
    HttpRuntime.Cache.Insert("Test", t);
}
else
{
    t = (DateTime) cc;
}
```

The code above sets into the cache the value of the current time and for all subsequent calls will get the value from the cache instead of getting the date itself. This demonstrates that, in fact, it will not do exhaustive calculations (date, in this example).

HttpRuntime.Cache.Get lets you get an object from a key. The key is set when you are using HttpRuntime.Cache.Insert.

The Insert method has many parameters. The first parameter is the key, the second the value. Other parameters are concerning the time the value will stay in cache. The third parameter is by default NULL but could be anything that, if changed, will flush the cache. The fourth parameter is the time when the data must be removed from the cache in absolute time. For example, you can write that you want the data to be removed 20 minutes later by setting the DateTime.Now + 20 minutes (*DateTime.UtcNow.AddMinutes(20)*).

The last possible parameter is the sliding that decides if it gives additional time to the expiration of the cache if the data is accessed. This parameter is a TimeSpan. If you say 1 minute in this parameter you will have the data stored for 1 minute after the last Get is done. This gives you a 1-minute time frame every time a user Gets the value from the time you Inserted it. If at any time nobody accesses the cache, even in the first 1 minute, the cache is reset for this key. You can say that you do not want to use absolute time by setting this to Cache.NoAbsoluteExpiration and only set a TimeSpan.

```
HttpRuntime.Cache.Insert("Test",    t,    null,    Cache.NoAbsoluteExpiration,    new
TimeSpan(0, 0, 1, 0));
```

Or, to set it for 20 minutes

```
HttpRuntime.Cache.Insert("Test",    t,    null,    DateTime.UtcNow.AddMinutes(20),
Cache.NoSlidingExpiration);
```

If you try to use the absolute and sliding at the same time you will get an Argument Exception.

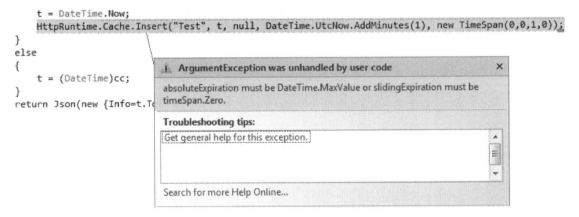

This means you can only use one of the types at the same time. It is also possible to have a callback when the data is removed from the cache. This can be interesting if you need to act differently when something is accessed and removed from the cache. To do this, you need to set the CacheItemRemovedCallback. This method will be called whenever the cache is removed. If you set 1 minute, 1 minute after the callback it will be raised. This is raised whatever happens on the server side, even if no client calls the server.

```
HttpRuntime.Cache.Insert("Test",    t,    null,    DateTime.UtcNow.AddMinutes(1),
Cache.NoSlidingExpiration, CacheItemPriority.Normal, onRemoveCallback);
```

This method will give you also the detail about why it has been removed. Your item might have been set to stay 30 minutes but because there is low memory the cache system will remove it. You will get the reason with the enumerator **CacheItemRemovedReason**.

```
DateTime t;
if (cc == null)
{
    t = DateTime.Now;
    HttpRuntime.Cache.Insert("Test", t, null, DateTime.UtcNow.AddMinut
}
else
{
    t = (DateTime)cc;
}
return Json(new {Info=t.ToLongTimeString()});
}

private void onRemoveCallback(string key, object value, CacheItemRemovedRe
{
    //Call back when removed
    CacheItemRemovedReason.
}
```

```
DependencyChanged
Expired
Removed
TryParse
Underused                        Enum member CacheItemRemovedReas
                                 The item is removed from the cache bec
⚠ 0 Warnings    ⓘ 0 Messages
```

That's pretty much it about the Cache for basic use. Do not forget that the data is cached into the memory of the process and is not shared across multiple servers if you have multiple Web Servers. You should use a server with affinity to be able to reuse the cache for the same client; otherwise, the cache will be good only for the Web Server that has inserted the values.

ASP.Net MVC Model Binding

Release Date: 10-Sep-12
Url: http://patrickdesjardins.com/blog/asp-net-mvc-model-binding

ASP.Net MVC Model Binding is one of the powerful "in-the-box" features that make the life of a developer easier.

The primary goal is to let you get information from the http request without having to map manually all strings to your objects. This can be the case for any http request type like POST after a form is submitted or a GET where information is requested. In fact, it will get a query string with many values or values in JSON format and take the information to instantiate the object specified with the good values. Of course, this is possible only if some conventions are followed.

Without Model Binding

Without model binding the code of loading an object from an HTML form would look like the following code:

```
public ActionResult Create()
{
    var product = new User() {
                        BirthDay = DateTime.Parse(Request["birthdate"])
                        , UserId = Int32.Parse(Request["userid"])
                        , Name = Request["name"]
    };
}
```

As you can see, we directly go to the Http Request to get every parameter that corresponds to the name of the input of the HTML form.

Binding simple value with Model Binding

With Asp.Net MVC you can let the model binding automatically parse every parameter to the parameter type specified in the signature of the method. For example, if you have a method with two parameters, and one is an integer and one a string, if the method (which is called "action" in the MVC world) detects a request parameter name that fits with the action parameter name, it will get by reflection the time required and will automatically parse it. If the parameter is not provided, the null value is used, or the default value if one is provided. The code above will now look like this:

```
public ActionResult Create(DateTime birthdate, int userid, string name)
{
    var product = new User()
    {
        BirthDay = birthdate,
        UserId = userid,
        Name = name
    };
}
```

This is not bad! In fact, the MVC model binding can do even better, which is to create the user object itself. This is called Binding Complex Object.

Asp.Net MVC Binding Complex Object

Complex objects will need to have a scalar property that has the same name as the form input's name and if the complex object contains more than only a scalar object (like having sub object) it will need to receive a JSON object. .Net will be able to transform this JSON object into C# object if every JSON variable has its property called the same way. With the example that we have used since the beginning, this means that we could have:

```
public ActionResult Create(User user)
{
    //User user here
}
```

This is very strong, isn't it? The only thing we require is to have the signature of the method with User and then the view to have input names that are similar to the model properties name. What is even more powerful is that if you use the framework to generate the form, let's say to bind the model User to the Razor view, the name used will be automatically the property name. The reason is that the Razor view can use **HTML extension** which will reflect the name when bound to property.

```
@Html.TextBoxFor(model => model.userId);
```

This will generate something like:

```
<input name="userId" value="" />
```

When the user enters a value, let's say for example 123, and submits the form, this will put in the http request, inside the http post data in the http header. The format looks like this: "userId=123". If you have many parameters, every one will be separated by the ampersand (&) symbol. Asp.net MVC will receive the information and will check the type of the parameter that is a User and check all public property to find a match. In our example, it will find the property userId. Since it is an integer type, it will try to parse and convert the string.

Note that you need to have an empty constructor to be able to let the model binding instantiate the object.

If you ask yourself "what about a wrong type value? How does it handle error?" don't worry, you can check if the model binding has an error. You can see this in a previous post (page

16, How to validate a model object…)

MVC Model Binding Example

Let's imagine a really simple model object: *Customer.*

```
public class BaseEntity
{
    public int Id { get; set; }
}

public class Customer : BaseEntity
{
    public string FirstName { get; set; }
    public string LastName { get; set; }
}
```

To be able to create a new customer, the view created needs to bind input fields to the name of the property.

```
@using (Html.BeginForm())
{
    @Html.ValidationSummary(true)
    <fieldset>
        <legend>Customer</legend>
        <div class="editor-label">
            @Html.LabelFor(model => model.FirstName)
        </div>        <div class="editor-field">
            @Html.EditorFor(model => model.FirstName)
            @Html.ValidationMessageFor(model => model.FirstName)
        </div>        <div class="editor-label">
            @Html.LabelFor(model => model.LastName)
        </div>        <div class="editor-field">
            @Html.EditorFor(model => model.LastName)
            @Html.ValidationMessageFor(model => model.LastName)
        </div>
        <p>
            <input type="submit" value="Create" />
        </p>
    </fieldset>
}
```

These HTML helpers create the HTML with good names to be able to read them back from the controller once posted (the create is a POST Http method).

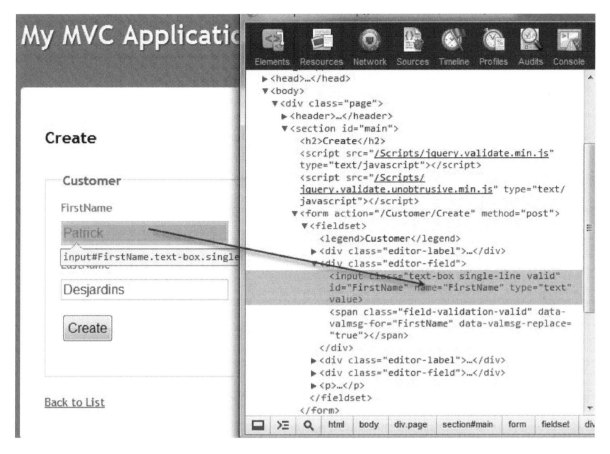

When the user hits "Save" the server will receive:

"FirstName=Patrick&LastName=Desjardins".

We can save the new customer:

```
[HttpPost]
public ActionResult Create(Customer customer)
{
    if (ModelState.IsValid)
    {
        db.Customers.Add(customer);
        db.SaveChanges();
        return RedirectToAction("Index");
    }
    ViewBag.Id = new SelectList(db.Licenses, "Id", "Name", customer.Id);
    return View(customer);
}
```

but we could have simply used:

```
[HttpPost]
public ActionResult Create(string firstName, string lastName)
{
    var customer = new Customer {FirstName = firstName, LastName = lastName};
    if (ModelState.IsValid)
    {
        db.Customers.Add(customer);
        db.SaveChanges();
        return RedirectToAction("Index");
    }
    ViewBag.Id = new SelectList(db.Licenses, "Id", "Name", customer.Id);
    return View(customer);
}
```

or

```
[HttpPost]
public ActionResult Create(FormCollection inputs)
{
    var customer = new Customer {FirstName = inputs["FirstName"], LastName =
inputs["LastName"]};
    if (ModelState.IsValid)
    {
        db.Customers.Add(customer);
        db.SaveChanges();
        return RedirectToAction("Index");
    }
    ViewBag.Id = new SelectList(db.Licenses, "Id", "Name", customer.Id);
    return View(customer);
}
```

All three ways are correct, but the first one uses the power of MVC to automatically bind input values to the object.

Complex object

Complex objects are instanced classes that contain another object. Let say that we change the *Customer* class to have a 1 to 1 relation with the *Avatar* class.

```
public class Customer : BaseEntity
{
    public string FirstName { get; set; }
    public string LastName { get; set; }
    public Avatar Avatar { get; set; }
}
```

```
public class Avatar : BaseEntity
{
    public string Name { get; set; }
}
```

How can we modify the View to have it receive the *Avatar* name and save it when the form is submitted to the controller?

The only thing that needs to be done is to modify the view.

```
@using (Html.BeginForm())
{    @Html.ValidationSummary(true)
    <fieldset>
        <legend>Customer</legend>
        <div class="editor-label">
            @Html.LabelFor(model => model.FirstName)
        </div>          <div class="editor-field">
            @Html.EditorFor(model => model.FirstName)
            @Html.ValidationMessageFor(model => model.FirstName)
        </div>
        <div class="editor-label">
            @Html.LabelFor(model => model.LastName)
        </div>
        <div class="editor-field">
            @Html.EditorFor(model => model.LastName)
            @Html.ValidationMessageFor(model => model.LastName)
        </div>
        <div class="editor-label">
            @Html.LabelFor(model => model.Avatar.Name)
        </div>
        <div class="editor-field">
            @Html.EditorFor(model => model.Avatar.Name)
            @Html.ValidationMessageFor(model => model.Avatar.Name)
        </div>
        <p>
            <input type="submit" value="Create" />
        </p>
    </fieldset>
}
```

This will automatically load the *Customer* object in the controller. Let's see the generated HTML.

```
<form action="/Customer/Create" method="post">
    <fieldset>

        <legend>Customer</legend>
```

```
    <div class="editor-label">
        <label for="FirstName">FirstName</label>
    </div>
    <div class="editor-field">
        <input class="text-box single-line" id="FirstName" name="FirstName"
type="text" value="" />
        <span class="field-validation-valid" data-valmsg-for="FirstName" data-
valmsg-replace="true"></span>
    </div>
    <div class="editor-label">
        <label for="LastName">LastName</label>
    </div>
    <div class="editor-field">
        <input class="text-box single-line" id="LastName" name="LastName"
type="text" value="" />
        <span class="field-validation-valid" data-valmsg-for="LastName" data-
valmsg-replace="true"></span>
    </div>
    <div class="editor-label">
        <label for="Avatar_Name">Name</label>
    </div>
    <div class="editor-field">
        <input class="text-box single-line" id="Avatar_Name"
name="Avatar.Name" type="text" value="" />
        <span class="field-validation-valid" data-valmsg-for="Avatar.Name"
data-valmsg-replace="true"></span>
    </div>
    <p>
        <input type="submit" value="Create" />
    </p>
</fieldset>
</form>
```

As you can see, the name of the input is the property of *Customer* followed by a dot and the name of the property of the *Avatar* object. This is how the **Model Binding** can figure out that the value inside the text box belongs to the Avatar object of Customer.

How to save the ModelState into a session following a good practice

Release Date: 20-Apr-12
Url: http://patrickdesjardins.com/blog/?post_type=post&p=1032

Tim Barcz, Matt Hawley, Stephen Walther and Scott Guthrie (VP at Microsoft and lead for many projects like Entity Framework, Asp.Net, etc) have already discussed this problem and created the PRG (Post, Redirect, Get) pattern to solve it. In fact, to solve this problem you should not handle manually the ModelState but simply use Import and Export attributes like the following example.

```
[AcceptVerbs(HttpVerbs.Get), ImportModelStateFromTempData]
public ActionResult MyAction(ModelObject myObject) { return View(); }

[AcceptVerbs(HttpVerbs.Post), ExportModelStateToTempData]
public ActionResult MyActionSubmit(ModelObject myObject) { return View(); }
```

These attributes are not from the .Net framework and you need to have them inside your project by creating them. Once it is done once, it is done for the lifetime of your project.

First, you need to create the attributes. To do so, you need to create a class that inherits the class **ActionFilterAttribute**. Since we are using two attributes that share the same information, we will create three classes. The first one will contain the sharing key for the session and the two others will be for the Import and Export.

```
public abstract class ModelStateTempDataTransfer : ActionFilterAttribute
{
    protected static readonly string Key
                            = typeof (ModelStateTempDataTransfer).FullName;
}
```

Then, create the class to export. Here you can add more custom code for your project. This version will call the ModelState only if this one contains errors.

```
public class ExportModelStateToTempData : ModelStateTempDataTransfer
{
    public override void OnActionExecuted(ActionExecutedContext filterContext)
    {
        //Only export when ModelState is not valid
        if (!filterContext.Controller.ViewData.ModelState.IsValid)
        {
            //Export if we are redirecting
            if ((filterContext.Result is RedirectResult) || (filterContext.Result
is RedirectToRouteResult))
            {
                filterContext.Controller.TempData[Key] =
filterContext.Controller.ViewData.ModelState;
            }
        }
        base.OnActionExecuted(filterContext);
    }
}
```

The last class will import the ModelState. In fact, it will merge the new one with the old one in the session.

```
public class ImportModelStateFromTempData : ModelStateTempDataTransfer
{
    public override void OnActionExecuted(ActionExecutedContext filterContext)
    {
        ModelStateDictionary modelState
                = filterContext.Controller.TempData[Key] as ModelStateDictionary;
        if (modelState != null)
        {
            //Only Import if we are viewing
            if (filterContext.Result is ViewResult)
            {
                filterContext.Controller.ViewData.ModelState.Merge(modelState);
            }
            else
            {
                //Otherwise remove it.
                filterContext.Controller.TempData.Remove(Key);
            }
        }
        base.OnActionExecuted(filterContext);
    }
}
```

As you can see, we do not use the session directly but we store everything into the TempData which uses the session but handles the life cycle for us. This mean that it will not stay for 20 minutes (default value of a session life). It will stay until the next postback and be there if the request is redirected.

You can see it in the MVC open source project called MVCContrib, http://mvccontrib.codeplex.com, (slightly modified version of this one). You can also find the source of the code in this blog post at this http://bit.ly/1jwPVRJ.

HTML Extension Helper with generic access to object property

Release Date: 24-Apr-12
Url: http://patrickdesjardins.com/blog/?post_type=post&p=1036

It is possible to create a custom generic **HTML Extension Helper** with the use of Expression Helper and, if required, the ModelMetadata to get the value.

```
public static string MyExtensionFor<TModel, TProperty>(this HtmlHelper<TModel>
htmlHelper, Expression<Func<TModel, TProperty>> property)
{
    var meta =
          ModelMetadata.FromLambdaExpression(property, this.HtmlHelper.ViewData);
    string fullPropertyName = HtmlHelper.ViewContext.ViewData.TemplateInfo
          .GetFullHtmlFieldName(ExpressionHelper.GetExpressionText(property));
    //Do what you need to do here
}
```

The variable **fullPropertyName** meta data contains the value of the property, if required.

```
@Html.MyExtensionFor(x => x.MyClassProperty1)
```

With little or no code you can set up HTML Helper that is strongly typed. This has the advantage of not writing string. This, of course, is better to reduce the chance to write a wrong string but also helps the refactoring because all refactoring tools work with a property name change.

How to create an HttpHandler with Asp Mvc

Release Date: 28-Jun-12
Url: http://patrickdesjardins.com/blog/?post_type=post&p=1157

With traditional Asp.Net, doing an http handler required without a doubt adding a new Http Handler in IIS to handle a specific extension and then doing some work to get the request and to send back a response. This is about the same with Asp.Net MVC but you have the leverage to do everything in code with routing.

In this article, we will do an Http Handler for an image. This will allow us, instead of using directly a server path for our image in our website, to call this image http handler to get the image. This can be useful if you want to protect who accesses the image. Direct linking from outside of the website won't be allowed, for example. You could also decide to implement a special algorithm that returns an image depending on who is logged in to the website, etc.

First of all, you need to create a new class that will inherit from **IRouteHandler**.

```
public class ImageHandler : IRouteHandler
{
    public IHttpHandler GetHttpHandler(RequestContext requestContext)
    {
    }
```

```
}
```

Once created, you need to specify to the website that this routing handler exists. This is done with global.asax.cs You need to add the route into the Application_Start().

```
RouteTable.Routes.Add("ImagesRoute"
                , new Route("privateImage/{uniqueIdentifier}"
                , new ImageHandler()));
```

As you can see, I have decided that any url that has privateImage/#### will be routed to the new http handler.

Let's go back to the Http handler. Now we need to verify that the uniqueIdentifier is present when the handler is called. Otherwise, we will return a 404 Http error. This is done by returning null.

```
public IHttpHandler GetHttpHandler(RequestContext requestContext)
{
    var routeValues = requestContext.RouteData.Values;
    if (routeValues.ContainsKey("UniqueIdentifier"))
    {
    }
    else
    {
        return null;
    }
}
```

Now we need to get the image and send it back to the user. This is done by opening the file one the server via a stream and writing it back to the response stream which will go to the client via http.

```
public class ImageHandler : IRouteHandler
{
    public IHttpHandler GetHttpHandler(RequestContext requestContext)
    {
        var routeValues = requestContext.RouteData.Values;
        if (routeValues.ContainsKey("UniqueIdentifier"))
        {
            //Do something with the parameter (UniqueIdentifier) to get the image
on the server
            string serverPathToImageToOutput = //What ever you want like database
call or file server algo;
            //Start a new Response
            requestContext.HttpContext.Response.Clear();
```

```
            //Response type will be the same as the one requested
            requestContext.HttpContext.Response.ContentType =
GetContentType(requestContext.HttpContext.Request.Url.ToString());
            //We buffer the data to send back until it's done
            requestContext.HttpContext.Response.BufferOutput = true;
            Image image = Image.FromStream(new
FileStream(serverPathToImageToOutput, FileMode.Open));
            image.Save(requestContext.HttpContext.Response.OutputStream,
ImageFormat.Png);
            requestContext.HttpContext.Response.End();
        }
        else
        {
            return null;
        }
    }
}
```

As you may notice, nothing is yet written for security purposes. In fact, it is quite simple. What we need to do is to check from where the request has been sent. Since we are the only one who should use the http handler, we can authorize only a server request by checking the referer variable.

```
request.ServerVariables["HTTP_REFERER"]
```

This can be added at the beginning of the GetHttpHandler method and returns a static image that says "Image is not authorized".

How to unit test a method that returns an anonymous type

Release Date: 02-Apr-12
Author : Patrick Desjardins

It is really easy to have in ASP.NET MVC a function that returns an anonymous type. I say in ASP.NET MVC but this could be also in ASP.NET. In fact, when you have an action inside a controller that returns a JsonResult you can simply return an anonymous type and JavaScript will be able to handle it as simply as using the same syntax that you would use with an object in C#.

```
public JsonResult Update(MyObject o)
{
    //...
    return Json(new { IsSaved = false, Id = 123});
```

```
}
```

In JavaScript you would use:

```
//...Ajax call
success: function (data)
{
    var x = data.IsSaved;
    var xx = data.Id;
}
```

To unit test this scenario, you need to do two things. First, you need to use the **dynamic** keyword of .Net to be able to receive from the controller the response of the action which is anonymous.

```
dynamic returnedData = myController.Update(new MyObject());
```

The problem is that everything that has been generated as anonymous in a DLL stays internal. If you are doing your unit testing in a separated assembly (DLL) you will need to explicitly say that you want to share internal values with another assembly. This can be done by modifying the assembly configuration by editing **AssemblyInfo.cs**. You need to open the file AssemblyInfo.cs of the tested controller and add the following statement.

```
[assembly: InternalsVisibleTo("Tests.Unit")]
```

This will give the permission to see the internal to the unit testing project called "Tests.Unit".

How to have a localized string with MVC and Entity Framework

Release Date: 17-Sep-12
Url: http://patrickdesjardins.com/blog/?post_type=post&p=1419

In some situations, you may have a string that will need to be localized and be displayed differently depending on the current culture.

This can be the case of a specific name or description. You may want to display the name of the product in French if the user is logged in in French but be able to display it in English for other users.

You have a lot of different ways to handle this situation. The one proposed here is simple, it respects the SOC (separation of concern), and doesn't change the database drastically. By not changing the database drastically I mean that I do not have to have a table with association to multiple languages.

First, let's create some model classes. To have a relatively useful example that is near to a real life example I will reuse the *Customer* and *Avatar* classes defined in the previous blog post.

```
public class Customer : BaseEntity
{
    public string FirstName { get; set; }
    public string LastName { get; set; }
    public Avatar Avatar { get; set; }
}
```

The *Customer* class contains two strings that won't be localized and a property of type *Avatar*. This class contains two fields—name and Description—that require translating into multiple languages.

```
public class Avatar : BaseEntity
{
    public string Name { get; set; }
    public string Description { get; set; }
}
```

Right here, we see something wrong. The Name and Description properties are a type of string which can only have one value. So, we need to have Name in two languages (or more).

```
public class Avatar : BaseEntity
{
    public string NameFrench { get; set; }
    public string DescriptionFrench { get; set; }
    public string NameEnglish { get; set; }
    public string DescriptionEnglish { get; set; } //And so on...
}
```

The problem with this solution is that it goes really out of proportion if you have, let's say, 10 languages to support. It is also a problem when it is time to bind to the view. Which one is the best one to display depends on the user language and you couldn't simply bind to one property.

This leads us to think that maybe the problem is that we are using a wrong approach. In fact, what we want to use is not a string but a **LocalizedString**. What we would like is to have the Avatar having only two properties, one for the Name and one for the Description.

```
public class Avatar : BaseEntity
{
    public LocalizedString Name { get; set; }
    public LocalizedString Description { get; set; }
}
```

The **LocalizedString** is a class that we will create that will handle all different languages that we have. Let's say we want French and English. The class could look like the above with two properties. If we need 10 languages, we would have 10 properties. I choose to have one property per language because I want to have in the database one column per language and not have a table with multiple languages. The reason is that I do not want the overhead of multiple join tables.

```
[ComplexType]
public class LocalizedString
{
    public string French { get; set; }
    public string English { get; set; }

    public override string ToString()
    {
        return English;
    }

    [NotMapped]
    public string Current
    {
        get
        {
            switch (Thread.CurrentThread.CurrentUICulture
                        .TwoLetterISOLanguageName.ToUpperInvariant())
            {
                case "FR":
                    return French;
                case "EN":
                    return English;
            }
            return ToString();
        }
        set
        {
            switch (Thread.CurrentThread.CurrentUICulture
                        .TwoLetterISOLanguageName.ToUpperInvariant())
            {
```

```
                case "FR":
                    French = value;
                    break;
                case "EN":
                    English = value;
                    break;
            }
        }
    }
}
```

Much information is in the **LocalizedString**. First, the attribute **ComplexType** is added to the class. The reason is that I do not want to have a new class for each Model that will use the new type of string. In fact, what I want is to have *Avatar* having all properties automatically generated for me. From the database point of view, it is the same thing—I do not want to have a table Customer with a 1 to1 association to the table Avatar and from there have 10 relations for 10 different languages. I would like to have Customer have a relation to Avatar that contains all names and descriptions. This is the reason for the **Complex Type**.

The second attribute is the NotMapped over the Current property. The Current property is there to display the string in the active language. I could have directly put the code of Current into the ToString() but I didn't because I want to be able to bind to a property from the view.

From here, we are almost done. The last step is to create templates. We need one **EditorTemplates** and one **DisplayTemplates**. Both of them are used to let Asp.Net MVC know how to display the new type **LocalizedString**.

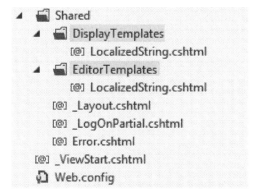

Both DisplayTemplates and EditorTemplates must be in the Shared folder. You need to create one file per folder with the name of your new type. In our case, it is **LocalizedString**.

Both of them are very simple. This is for the DisplayTemplates:

```
@model EFCodeFirst.General.LocalizedString<p>@Model.Current</p>
```

And this is for the EditorTemplates:

```
@model EFCodeFirst.General.LocalizedString
@Html.TextBoxFor(s => s.Current)
```

If we go into the view, the code used **EditorFor** for the Name and Description of the Avatar. This will trigger MVC to use the correct template for the type **LocalizedString**.

```
<fieldset>
    <legend>Customer</legend>
    <div class="editor-label">
        @Html.LabelFor(model => model.FirstName)
    </div>          <div class="editor-field">
        @Html.EditorFor(model => model.FirstName)
        @Html.ValidationMessageFor(model => model.FirstName)
    </div>          <div class="editor-label">
        @Html.LabelFor(model => model.LastName)
    </div>          <div class="editor-field">
        @Html.EditorFor(model => model.LastName)
        @Html.ValidationMessageFor(model => model.LastName)
    </div>          <div class="editor-label">
        @Html.LabelFor(model => model.Avatar.Name)
    </div>          <div class="editor-field">
        @Html.EditorFor(model => model.Avatar.Name)
        @Html.ValidationMessageFor(model => model.Avatar.Name)
    </div>
    <div class="editor-label">
        @Html.LabelFor(model => model.Avatar.Description)
    </div>
    <div class="editor-field">
        @Html.EditorFor(model => model.Avatar.Description)
        @Html.ValidationMessageFor(model => model.Avatar.Description)
    </div>
    <p>
        <input type="submit" value="Create" />
    </p>
</fieldset>
```

The generated HTML contains a valid name that links to the Current property of *Avatar.*

```
<input id="Avatar_Name_Current" name="Avatar.Name.Current" type="text" value="" />
```

The controller will use the model binding to be able to set the Current value to the appropriate language. This is automatically done because of the setting of Current that checks the current language and sets the value into the correct property.

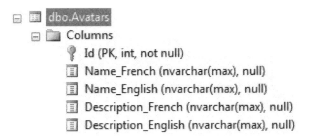

Once saved, the data is inserted into the avatar table.

- dbo.Avatars
  - Columns
    - Id (PK, int, not null)
    - Name_French (nvarchar(max), null)
    - Name_English (nvarchar(max), null)
    - Description_French (nvarchar(max), null)
    - Description_English (nvarchar(max), null)

And the data :

	Id	Name_French	Name_English	Description_French	Description_English
1	1	NULL	English Avatar Name	NULL	English Avatar Description
2	2	Current1	NULL	Current2	NULL
3	3	Avatar Name French	NULL	Avatar Name English	NULL

That's it. The model is clean with one property; the view is clean because it uses a template so it is a one-liner like normal string; the controller is clean because it does not have any logic for the language; the database is clean because the information is stored in whatever class will use **LocalizedString**. Those additional rows are automatically created by Entity Framework and do not require any additional work on your part.

To conclude, an alternative solution like using a ViewModel could have been a solution but would add a lot of additional overhead like having to auto-map most of the field, having to redo mapping for localized string for every new model, and for that would have to have additional testing because you would have a ViewModel with a condition which could have led to possible error. I suggest you use this approach which is simple, object oriented and works fine with Entity Framework.

Edit: Reflection

Instead of using a **Switch** case, you can use **reflection** to get the correct property depending on the thread language. Here is the version with reflection:

```
[ComplexType]
public class LocalizedString
{
    public string French { get; set; }
    public string English { get; set; }

    [NotMapped]
    public string Current
    {
        get { return (string) LanguageProperty().GetValue(this, null); }
        set { LanguageProperty().SetValue(this, value, null); }
    }

    public override string ToString()
    {
        return Current;
    }

    private PropertyInfo LanguageProperty()
    {
        string currentLanguage =
                Thread.CurrentThread.CurrentUICulture.DisplayName;
        return GetType().GetProperty(currentLanguage);
    }
}
```

Entity Framework 4.3 Update a complex object from Asp.Mvc controller

Release Date: 27-Mar-12
Url: http://patrickdesjardins.com/blog/?post_type=post&p=898

Having to update an object from an edit action is pretty standard. In fact, it is also very straightforward with a basic object (one not containing an other object).You could use the FormCollection way to do it:

```
[AcceptVerbs(HttpVerbs.Post)]
public ActionResult Edit(FormCollection form)
{
    // Get movie to update
    var id = Int32.Parse(form["id"]);
    var movieToUpdate = _db.MovieSet.First(m => m.Id == id);
    // Deserialize (Include white list!)
    TryUpdateModel(movieToUpdate, new string[] {"Title", "Director"},
form.ToValueProvider());
    // If valid, save movie to database
    if (ModelState.IsValid)
    {
        _db.SaveChanges();
        //...
    }
}
```

Or, you could use the ability of auto binding each http parameter:

```
[HttpPost]
public ActionResult Edit(Course course)
{
    if (ModelState.IsValid)
    {
        db.Entry(course).State = EntityState.Modified;
        db.SaveChanges();
        //...
    }
}
```

However, the problem remains that these two examples are only good for objects with scalar properties. This means that it works fine until you have an object that references another object. In real life, there are a lot of chances that you will handle complex objects that contain reference to many other objects or to optional objects or to a 1 to 1 object.

To be able to handle those scenarios, you need to handle scalar data and reference objects separately. Here is an example of saving a complex object and its reference:

```
public void Update(MyObject obj)
{
    //Update all but not relationship (scalar properties are updated)
```

```
var fromDatabase = Database.Customers.Where(p => p.Id == customer.ID);
Database.Entry(fromDatabase).CurrentValues.SetValues(obj);
//Update reference
if (obj.OtherObject != null)
{
    Database.OtherObjects.Attach(obj.OtherObject);
}
fromDatabase.OtherObject = obj.OtherObject;
return Database.SaveChanges();
}
```

This checks if the reference is null from the form. If yes, it means that we need to save NULL to be able to have NULL in the foreign key of the database. If not, you need to attach to the Database Context the object (even if this object is not fully loaded, we just need the primary key to be available).

How to handle many users editing the same object with Asp.Net MVC and Entity Framework

Release Date: 03-Oct-12
Url: http://patrickdesjardins.com/blog/?post_type=post&p=1456

The web is stateless and has the ability to have many users. In some applications, a single piece of information can or could be modified by more than one person. This has the side effect that conflicts could occur.

Let say that user A wants to edit the product 123 and a few seconds later user B edits the same product. By the time user A saves the product, user B might have changed some information. If user A saves it and later user B saves it, this could create some conflict.

In the normal web situation, user B would have overridden the user A changes. In fact, this is totally acceptable in a lot of situations. This is called *"Client Wins"* By this, I mean that if user B decided that the product 123 name should be called "product 12345" and if this user is the last to edit the product, he should be the one with the latest information about what should be the name of this product. If many users want to change something and change it to a different value, (let's say user A wanted to called it "prod 12345" and user B "product 12345") then it is more a logic problem by the enterprise than a software problem.

Nevertheless, in some situations, the first user must have the privilege to be not overridden. Since we cannot lock the entry, another approach is to simply signal the second user that someone has changed the information since the load of the entity. This situation is called *"Server Wins"* and solves the problem of **concurrency conflict**.

How to handle concurrency conflict with Entity Framework and Asp.Net MVC with Server Wins approach

We do not want to lock an entry from the database because some entries could be locked when the system crashes and that also causes performance problems. The best way is to use an optimistic approach. With Microsoft SQL Server, we can use a column of type TimeStamp or RowVersion. In both cases, it will contains an incremental sequential number that will increase every time the entry is modified. This approach lets you know that if you load an entity with the number 23, and when you save you are at 24, someone has done something to the entity because it should remain at 23.

To be able to apply this strategy to your entities, you need to configure your BaseEntity.cs class (a class that every model will inherit). You need to add a **TimeStamp** property with the TimeStamp and ConcurrencyCheck attribute.

```
public class BaseEntity
{
    public int Id { get; set; }

    [ConcurrencyCheck]
    [Timestamp]
    public Byte[] Timestamp { get; set; }
}
```

To be able to use this value we need to add it into the view in a hidden field. This hidden field will give back the Timestamp to the server and will be used to compare with the database version when saving.

```
@Html.HiddenFor(model => model.Timestamp)
```

So, the whole view looks like this:

```
@using (Html.BeginForm())
{    @Html.HiddenFor(model => model.Timestamp)
    @Html.ValidationSummary(true)<fieldset>
    <legend>Customer</legend>
    <div class="editor-label">
        @Html.LabelFor(model => model.FirstName)
    </div>
    <div class="editor-field">
```

```
    @Html.EditorFor(model => model.FirstName)
    @Html.ValidationMessageFor(model => model.FirstName)
</div>
<div class="editor-label">
    @Html.LabelFor(model => model.LastName)
</div>
<div class="editor-field">
    @Html.EditorFor(model => model.LastName)
    @Html.ValidationMessageFor(model => model.LastName)
</div>
@Html.HiddenFor(model => model.Id)
<p>
    <input type="submit" value="Save" />
</p>
</fieldset>}
```

The model looks like:

```
public class Customer : BaseEntity
{
    public string FirstName { get; set; }
    public string LastName { get; set; }
}

public class BaseEntity
{
    public int Id { get; set; }

    [ConcurrencyCheck]
    [Timestamp]
    public Byte[] Timestamp { get; set; }
}
```

And the controller that contains the compare code looks like:

```
[HttpPost]
public ActionResult Edit(Customer customer)
{
    if (ModelState.IsValid)
    {
        db.Entry(customer).State = EntityState.Modified;
        try
        {
            db.SaveChanges();
        }
        catch (DbUpdateConcurrencyException ex)
        {
            var entry = ex.Entries.Single();
            var databaseValues = (Customer) entry.GetDatabaseValues().ToObject();
```

```
            var clientValues = (Customer) entry.Entity;
            if (databaseValues.FirstName != clientValues.FirstName)
            {
                ModelState.AddModelError("Name", "Current value: " +
databaseValues.FirstName);
            }
            if (databaseValues.LastName != clientValues.LastName)
            {
                ModelState.AddModelError("Budget", "Current value: " +
databaseValues.LastName);
            }
            ModelState.AddModelError(string.Empty, "The record you attempted to
edit " + "was modified by another user after you got the original value. The " +
"edit operation was canceled and the current values in the database " + "have been
displayed. If you still want to edit this record, click " + "the Save button
again. Otherwise click the Back to List hyperlink.");
            customer.Timestamp = databaseValues.Timestamp;
        }
        return RedirectToAction("Index");
    }
    ViewBag.Id = new SelectList(db.Licenses, "Id", "Name", customer.Id);
    return View(customer);
}
```

As you can see, if you open two tabs of a single entity and if you save in the first tab and try to save in the second you will see the error message. The exception message is from Asp.net website(http://bit.ly/1iHAbi2).

Edit

* The record you attempted to edit was modified by another user after you got the original value. The edit operation was canceled and the current values in the database have been displayed. If you still want to edit this record, click the Save button again. Otherwise click the Back to List hyperlink.

If we go check in the database, we will see that the table contains a hexadecimal value inside the TimeStamp.

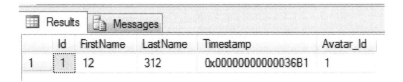

Conclusion

You can have a quick and easy way to control concurrency conflicts with a timespan field located inside every entity. You only need to add this field in a base model class, modify your controller to handle the exception, and add a hidden field into the view.

Edit February 2, 2013

In the Workout website I have used concurrency and I have found a few details that were not included in the above blog article. First of all, you must have the **ConcurrencyCheck** attribute and not just the **Timestamp** attribute over the property that will take care of the concurrency. If you do the modification, do not forget to regenerate the database so that the database has this field (which should be not nullable). Entity Framework will take care to compute the correct value to set into this field automatically. Second, you need to not load the entity from the database just before using SetValues (to update the scalar property of your object). This would result in altering the Timestamp and overriding the one that came from the form (ViewModel to Model) to the value of the one from the database. This will cause the mechanism to not detect the concurrency. Here is what I had previously, which works to update the scalar value but doesn't work with the concurrency. Following that will be the new code which works in both cases.

Replace:

```
public int Update(Muscle entity)
{
    Muscle fromDatabase = Get(entity.Id);
    DatabaseContext.Entry(fromDatabase).CurrentValues.SetValues(entity);
    DatabaseContext.Entry(fromDatabase).State = EntityState.Modified;
}
```

With this:

```
public int Update(Muscle entity)
{
    this.Set<Muscle>().Attach(entity);
    this.ChangeTracker.Entries<Muscle>().Single(d => d.Entity == entity).State =
EntityState.Modified;
}
```

I hope this detail will help someone else who is struggling with Asp.Net MVC concurrency with Entity Framework.

Asp.Net MemberShip with MVC4

Release Date: 10-Oct-12
Url: http://patrickdesjardins.com/blog/?post_type=post&p=1533

MVC4 does not use the same tables and infrastructure of MemberShip that Asp.Net or Asp.NET MVC3 used. You can see that just by creating a new MVC4 project. You will notice that inside the **Model** folder you have a class "AccountModel.cs". Also, inside the AccountController.cs you will see the use of WebSecurity that came from **WebMatrix** namespace.

The default configuration is not a problem until you want to remove the DbContext from the Model folder (which should not be there but inside the DAL layer). Also, it is not a problem until you you want to autogenerate the table inside the database with some data in it. Creating a user is pretty easy with WebSecurity but it is not easy when you try to seed the database with it. In fact, you will get an error message saying that WebSecurity needs to be initialized before use, and if you initialize it the database might not be created by Entity Framework and then it crashes.

The solution is to use the Package Manager Console and to generate the database with some command lines. This processes is called "**Migration.**"

Removing default code

The first step is to clean up some code that does not have its place. The first code to delete is inside *AccountModels.cs* inside the Models folder. You will see at the top of the file a class called *UsersContext*. This needs to be removed.

```
namespace WorkoutPlanner.Models
{
    /*public class UsersContext : DbContext
    {
        public UsersContext()
            : base("DefaultConnection")
        {
        }

        public DbSet<UserProfile> UserProfiles { get; set; }
    }*/

    [Table("UserProfile")]
    public class UserProfile : ICurrentUser
```

The second code that needs to be deleted is the filter *InitializeSimpleMembershipAttribute*. This filter creates the tables for Membership if not already created. Since we do not want to create on the fly but when the application starts (or with the commands line) we can delete this filter. It is a good idea because it uses the UsersContext that we just deleted. This file is located inside the *Filters* folder.

The third code to remove is the filter that is above the *AccountController* class inside *AccountController.cs* file.

```
namespace WorkoutPlanner.Controllers
{
    [Authorize]
    //[InitializeSimpleMembership]
    public class AccountController : BaseController
    {
```

Of course, now you have to set up your *DbContext* to be able to do what *UsersContext* was doing. If you compile now, it won't compile because we have deleted the *UsersContext*. But, two lines of code are required inside *AccountController*.cs to be able to compile. The first one is to create in your *DbContext* a method to get the user by name, and one to create a new user. Here is an example that uses a "Service layer" to access the repository that will use a *DbContext* later.

```
if (ModelState.IsValid)
{

    UserProfile user = _service.GetByUserName(model.UserName.ToLower());
    // Check if user already exists
    if (user == null)
    {
        // Insert name into the profile table
        _service.CreateUserProfile(new UserProfile { UserName = model.UserName });


        OAuthWebSecurity.CreateOrUpdateAccount(provider, providerUserId, model.UserName
        OAuthWebSecurity.Login(provider, providerUserId, createPersistentCookie: false)
```

Configure Entity Framework Migration

The next step is to make sure the the web.config contains the right provider for the role and membership. Inside web.config, in the system.web section be sure that you have the code below. If it is not already there, add it.

```
<roleManager enabled="true" defaultProvider="SimpleRoleProvider">
  <providers>
    <clear/>
    <add name="SimpleRoleProvider" type="WebMatrix.WebData.SimpleRoleProvider,
WebMatrix.WebData"/>
  </providers>
</roleManager>
<membership defaultProvider="SimpleMembershipProvider">
```

```
<providers>
  <clear/>
  <add name="SimpleMembershipProvider"
type="WebMatrix.WebData.SimpleMembershipProvider, WebMatrix.WebData"/>
  </providers>
</membership>
```

This will specify that we are using the **SimpleRoleProvider** and the **SimpleMembershipProvider**. To be honest, I think with MVC4 it is the default configuration so you are not required to do this but this website (http://bit.ly/MokVd5) suggests having it.

Once done, you need to build the Migration Configuration. This is automatically done if you are using the **Package Manager Console**. This tool can be opened by going inside VIEW>Other Windows>Package Manager Console.

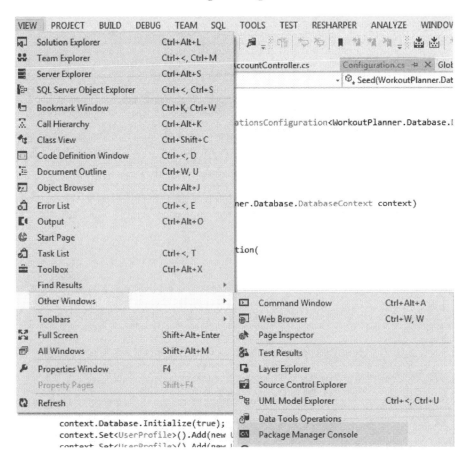

The next step is to use the command below that will force the creation of the configuration file. This will be required only once. Do not forget to use "EnableAutomaticMigration." This will let you update the database later according to changes you made to your model and entity configuration.

Enable-Migrations –EnableAutomaticMigrations -Force

Since we have removed the *UsersContext* we won't have any conflict using the command above. Otherwise, we would have needed to specify to which DbContext we want the migration to occur. Also, if you already had a database initializer (IDatabaseInitializer) like a "DropCreateDatabaseIfModelChanges," this will not work with the **DbMigrationsConfiguration.** In fact, you need to remove any initializer because we are switching to the Migration configuration. Nevertheless, this will give us additional control, more manual control but at least the possibility to generate the database automatically and also seed the database with Membership and custom tables.

The command creates a folder called *Migrations* with a *Configuration.cs.* Inside the Seed method, you will be able to create all the data you want inside the database. Here is a small snippet of code that creates a role, a user and some entities.

```csharp
internal sealed class Configuration :
DbMigrationsConfiguration<WorkoutPlanner.Database.DatabaseContext>
{
    public Configuration()
    {
        AutomaticMigrationsEnabled = true;
    }

    protected override void Seed(WorkoutPlanner.Database.DatabaseContext context)
    {
        base.Seed(context);
        WebSecurity.InitializeDatabaseConnection("DefaultConnection",
"UserProfile", "UserId", "UserName", autoCreateTables: true);
        if (!Roles.RoleExists("Administrator"))
        {
            Roles.CreateRole("Administrator");
        }
        if (!WebSecurity.UserExists("123123"))
        {
            WebSecurity.CreateUserAndAccount("123123", "123123");
        }
        if (!((IList<string>)
Roles.GetRolesForUser("123123")).Contains("Administrator"))
```

```
    {
        Roles.AddUsersToRoles(new[] {"123123"}, new[] {"Administrator"});
    }
    context.Database.Initialize(true);
    context.Set<UserProfile>().Add(new UserProfile {UserId = 1, UserName =
"123123"});
    context.Set<Workout>().Add(new Workout {Id = 1, Name = "My First workout
user1", StartTime = DateTime.Now.Add(TimeSpan.FromDays(-10)), Goal = "Increase
body mass"});
    context.Set<Workout>().Add(new Workout {Id = 2, Name = "My Second workout
user1", StartTime = DateTime.Now, Goal = "Increase chest muscle, lower fat around
abs"});
    }
}
```

The last step is to create table schema and insert those values from the seed configuration. This is done by this command:

update-database -verbose -force

The verbage will show you the SQL statement executed, and the force will regenerate the table even if data already exist in those tables.

Conclusion

Any time you change your model or the configuration of your entities, you need to run *update-database* command. This will drop tables, create them again, create FK and insert seed data.

Circular reference with Entity Framework and JSON when developing with Asp.Net MVC

Release Date: 29-Oct-12
Url: http://patrickdesjardins.com/blog/?post_type=post&p=1415

A circular reference was detected while serializing an object of type …

Here comes the problem of serializing. First of all, this occurs because a parent object references a child object and the child object references back to its parent. Sound familiar? Well, if you are working with Entity Framework and Code First, it should. Why? Because most of the Entities are cross referencing with each other. This way, it is convenient for many operations. For example, if you are a Team entity that has a list of Players, won't it be convenient to have the User having a Team property to access his team name? It is also interesting to do myPlayer.Team.Id = 1 and save the myPlayer. This way you do not have to instantiate the Team 1 object and add the player and save the team. Anyway, that's how Entity Framework works, and when it is time to serialize to JSON, it can cause this behavior.

The second problem is concerning the object itself. When trying to serialize, you are in fact serializing the Proxy also, which is not what you want. In fact, you will get this error:

The RelationshipManager object could not be serialized. This type of object cannot be serialized when the RelationshipManager belongs to an entity object that does not implement IEntityWithRelationships.

This is why you should disable the proxy creation and handle the state of your POCOPOCO with the DbContext instead of relying on a proxy. Disabling the proxy is a matter of setting to false your DbContext's property **ProxyCreationEnabled**.

```
_dbContext.Configuration.ProxyCreationEnabled = false;
```

Let's come back to the main purpose of this article. The problem with circular reference can be fixed by two solutions.

The first one is to break those references when we send the information to JSON. That means that in your controller, before sending back the ActionResult, you loop the problematic property to remove the reference. If we take the example with Player and Team, we could simply loop the Team array of Player and set to Null all Player[i].Team.

The second solution is to use the attribute **ScriptIgnore** over the property of Team, for example. So, it will serialize only from one side. I have not tried this solution, which I found at StackOverflow.com (http://bit.ly/1idvhos) because I do not think that anyone should alter the Model for the View this way. The serialization process shouldn't impact the model and for sure not make something work only half the time. At the end, we lose the reference on one side which will require to us to rebind it later on.

A better solution is to use a different library of JSON which can handle reference, and by that I mean the **Newton King Library** (http://james.newtonking.com/projects/json-net.aspx). This library supports circular reference by adding ID to the object serialized.

First, you need to remove the serialization from the default JSON serializer and use the JSON Newton King Library. This can be done in the *Global.asax.cs* file. with the following code:

```
GlobalConfiguration.Configuration.Formatters.Clear();
GlobalConfiguration.Configuration.Formatters
                    .Add(new JsonNetFormatter(new JsonSerializerSettings()));
var jsonSerializerSettings =
        new JsonSerializerSettings
            {PreserveReferencesHandling = PreserveReferencesHandling.Objects};
```

As you can see, we are setting up the PreserveReferencesHandling.Ojects. This will add the reference to the object when circular dependencies are found.

This setting adds values into the JSON structure that are in the format "$id": "1" and instead of copying the object over and over (and creating a stack overflow), will use the syntax "$ref": "1" to refer to the object. For example, if we have an object Player that contains the Team and the Team contains the players, than we could have a circular reference. The serialization with the library and the PreserveReferencesHandling will produce something similar to the code below if we serialize a single player.

The C# code:

```
public Program()
{
    var t1 = new Team() {TeamName = "MyTeam"};
    var p1 = new Player {PlayerName = "Patrick", PlayerTeam = t1};
    var p2 = new Player() {PlayerName = "Melodie", PlayerTeam = t1};
    t1.Players.Add(p1);
    t1.Players.Add(p2);
    var settings = new JsonSerializerSettings()
            {PreserveReferencesHandling = PreserveReferencesHandling.Objects};
    string json = JsonConvert.SerializeObject(p1, settings);
    Console.WriteLine(json);
    Console.ReadLine();
    //Product deserialized
    Product = JsonConvert.DeserializeObject<Player>(json);
}
```

The result:

```
{
    "$id":"1",
    "PlayerName":"Patrick",
```

```
    "PlayerTeam":{
        "$id":"2",
        "TeamName":"MyTeam",
        "Players":[
            {
                "$ref":"1"
            },
            {
                "$id":"3",
                "PlayerName":"Melodie",
                "PlayerTeam":{
                    "$ref":"2"
                }
            }
        ]
    }
}
```

If instead your serialize the team you will get:

```
{
    "$id":"1",
    "TeamName":"MyTeam",
    "Players":[
        {
            "$id":"2",
            "PlayerName":"Patrick",
            "PlayerTeam":{
                "$ref":"1"
            }
        },
        {
            "$id":"3",
            "PlayerName":"Melodie",
            "PlayerTeam":{
                "$ref":"1"
            }
        }
    ]
}
```

To conclude, you have to remember two things with Asp.Net MVC and Entity Framework. First, if you have not disabled proxy, then you will have this object serialized and it will cause a problem when serializing. Second, you need to break those circular references to stop the possibility of stack overflow. Using **JSON Newton library** is simple and powerful when it comes to handling references.

Returning a JSONResult within the Error function of JQuery Ajax

Release Date: 04-Apr-12
Url: http://patrickdesjardins.com/blog/?post_type=post&p=926

Let's say that you have an exception on the server side and you want to specify this error to the client. What could you do?

The easiest way is to return the error into the return value directly:

```
public JsonResult Create(MyObject myObject)
{
    //AllFine
    return Json(new {IsCreated = True, Content = ViewGenerator(myObject));
    //Error
    return Json(new { IsCreated = false,Content = ViewGenerator(myObject),
                    ErrorMessage = 'Could not save because XYZ'});
}
```

In JavaScript, we just need to take the error message and display it.

```
$.ajax({
    type: "POST"
    , dataType: "json"
    , url: "MyObjectController/Create"
    , data: JSON.stringify(myObjectJson)
    , success: function (result)
    {
        if (result.IsCreated)
        {
            //...
        }
        else
        {
            alert(result.ErrorMessage);
        }
    }
});
```

This is a correct way to do it. But sometimes you may want to return a handled error this way because you "control" the situation, and do something else for an unhandled error. This could be the case with any error that you do not catch with precision but you still need to return something to the client. Since you are using Ajax you may not want to redirect your user to another page but just to display an alert that the operation was unsuccessful.

This can be done by changing the Response Header with an Http Code that is different from the normal 200.

```
public JsonResult Create(MyObject myObject)
{
    //AllFine
    return Json(new {IsCreated = True, Content = ViewGenerator(myObject)});
    //Use input may be wrong but nothing crashed
    return Json(new { IsCreated = False, Content = ViewGenerator(myObject)});
    //Error
    Response.StatusCode = (int)HttpStatusCode.InternalServerError;
    return Json(new { IsCreated = false,Content = ViewGenerator(myObject),
ErrorMessage = 'Could not save because XYZ'});
}
```

The JavaScript can then go in three different directions:

```
$.ajax({
    type: "POST"
    , dataType: "json"
    , url: "MyObjectController/Create"
    , data: JSON.stringify(myObjectJson)
    , success: function (result)
    {
        if(result.IsCreated)
        {
            //... ALL FINE
        }   else
        {
            //... Use input may be wrong but nothing crashed
        }
    }
    , error: function (jqXHR, textStatus, errorThrown)
    {
        alert("Error:" + jQuery.parseJSON(jqXHR.responseText).Info);//Error
    }
});
```

This way, you handle in a clear way how to display an error to the user or to display a problem with his inputs. It also gives you the possibility to do it in a clean way at the server side and also to the client side.

For your curiosity, if you want to play with different statuses you can see in **System.Net** the enumeration **HttpStatusCode of** all different possible values.

Here it is:

```
namespace System.Net
{
    public enum HttpStatusCode
    {
        Continue = 100,
        SwitchingProtocols = 101,
        OK = 200,
        Created = 201,
        Accepted = 202,
        NonAuthoritativeInformation = 203,
        NoContent = 204,
        ResetContent = 205,
        PartialContent = 206,
        Ambiguous = 300,
        MultipleChoices = 300,
        Moved = 301,
        MovedPermanently = 301,
        Found = 302,
        Redirect = 302,
        RedirectMethod = 303,
        SeeOther = 303,
        NotModified = 304,
        UseProxy = 305,
        Unused = 306,
        RedirectKeepVerb = 307,
        TemporaryRedirect = 307,
        BadRequest = 400,
        Unauthorized = 401,
        PaymentRequired = 402,
        Forbidden = 403,
        NotFound = 404,
        MethodNotAllowed = 405,
        NotAcceptable = 406,
        ProxyAuthenticationRequired = 407,
        RequestTimeout = 408,
        Conflict = 409,
        Gone = 410,
        LengthRequired = 411,
        PreconditionFailed = 412,
        RequestEntityTooLarge = 413,
        RequestUriTooLong = 414,
        UnsupportedMediaType = 415,
        RequestedRangeNotSatisfiable = 416,
        ExpectationFailed = 417,
        InternalServerError = 500,
        NotImplemented = 501,
        BadGateway = 502,
```

```
        ServiceUnavailable = 503,
        GatewayTimeout = 504,
        HttpVersionNotSupported = 505,
    }
}
```

Asp.Net MVC with JQuery DatePicker and default custom format date

Release Date: 26-Nov-12
Url: http://patrickdesjardins.com/blog/?post_type=post&p=1676

If you want to use a date picker I suggest you use JQuery UI **Date Picker**. It is simple, does not require a lot of configuration and it is localized for you in several languages.

The whole process of adding JQuery Date Picker result to download JQuery UI and to create an editor template that will add a class that will let you bind the date picker into it is described below.

Using JQuery UI DatePicker with a default date format in Asp.Net MVC

First step, in the layout you need to add JQuery UI. If you are using Asp.Net MVC 4.0+ you can use the Bundles. This should be located inside the App_Start folder of the project. The configuration is inside BundleConfig.cs.

```
bundles.Add(new ScriptBundle("~/bundles/jqueryui")
                    .Include("~/Scripts/jquery-ui-{version}.js"));
```

If you are getting JQuery UI with NuGet package, this will be automatically set up for you. Do not forget to add inside your masterpage (by default : _layout.cshtml) the use of this bundle.

```
@Scripts.Render("~/bundles/jqueryui")
```

The second step is to create a template that will be used for the binding of a DateTime type. You can put the template for DateTime into the Views/Shared folder. You just need to create (if not already there) a folder called **EditorTemplates** and create a .cshtml with the name of "DateTime".

```
@model DateTime?
@if(Model.HasValue)
{
    @Html.TextBox(string.Empty,Model.Value.Date.ToString("yyyy-MM-dd"), new
{@class = "ui-date-picker"})
}
else
{
    @Html.TextBoxFor(m => m, new {@class = "ui-date-picker"})
}
```

Here is an example. You could use instead of a hard coded format the format you want. In fact, if you do not define here with a ToString() the format you want, you will get the time. This way to proceed lets you use JQuery date picker but **lets you have a default value** for your date without the section. If you do not format, you will not only have a default value with date time but when the user selects a date with the date picker, it will be formatted. Indeed, this would be very strange to have the date formatted half of the time. The first parameter of the TextBox helper is an empty string. This is because the view has a context that is aware of what the field prefix is and we do not need to specify it. Since we do not know which property will use the template, it is better to keep it empty. We could not use the *TextBoxFor* method because it doesn't let us bind on a method like the *ToString*.

If you go into the MVC framework we can see that it will check the *TemplateInfo* to get the current bound property and will assign the name property to the control:

```
private static MvcHtmlString InputHelper(HtmlHelper htmlHelper, InputType
inputType, ModelMetadata metadata, string name
    , object value, bool useViewData, bool isChecked
```

```
        , bool setId, bool isExplicitValue, string format
        , IDictionary<string, object> htmlAttributes)
{
    string fullHtmlFieldName =
htmlHelper.ViewContext.ViewData.TemplateInfo.GetFullHtmlFieldName(name);
    //...
}
```

StartTime

2012-09-30 00:00:00

As you can see, the time section is bound but does not have a format.

The last step is to bind **JQuery DatePicker** to the class *ui-date-picker* that we have set in the template.

```
$(document).ready(function ()
{
    $(".ui-date-picker").datepicker({ dateFormat: 'yy-mm-dd' });
}
```

This is set in the document "ready." This will hook the date picker to all elements that have the ui-date-picker class.

How to register a class that needs a connection string with Unity and Asp.Net MVC

Release Date: 05-Oct-12
Url: http://patrickdesjardins.com/blog/?post_type=post&p=1524

Microsoft Unity (http://unity.codeplex.com) is on the inside of Microsoft patterns and practices library (since 2009) as a **dependency injection container**. It can be used with a configuration file or with a fluent API directly inside your .Net project. It supports constructor injection, property injection and also method injection.

With the help of UnityMVC3 library (http://unitymvc3.codeplex.com), it can be really easy to set up your dependency injection container to be unique for each http request and to automate the injection of all your controllers automatically without having to map every controller interface to your concrete implementation.

Unity Mvc 3 includes a bespoke DependencyResolver that creates a child container per HTTP request and disposes of all registered IDisposable instances at the end of the request.

First of all, you need to get both libraries, the Unity and Unity MVC3 (which work perfectly with MVC4).

Then, you need to configure the dependency to your container. This needs to be done in the start of the application which is inside Global.ascx.cs.

```
protected void Application_Start()
{
    AreaRegistration.RegisterAllAreas();
    WebApiConfig.Register(GlobalConfiguration.Configuration);
    FilterConfig.RegisterGlobalFilters(GlobalFilters.Filters);
    RouteConfig.RegisterRoutes(RouteTable.Routes);
    BundleConfig.RegisterBundles(BundleTable.Bundles);
    AuthConfig.RegisterAuth();
    var connectionString =
System.Configuration.ConfigurationManager.ConnectionStrings["DefaultConnection"].C
onnectionString;
    UnityConfiguration.Initialize(connectionString);
}
```

Line 13 initializes Unity. This class is a custom one that takes the connection string that will be injected for the database. If we go inside the UnityConfiguration class we will see that all my interfaces are mapped to concrete types.

```
public static class UnityConfiguration
{
    public static void Initialize(string connectionString)
    {
        IUnityContainer container = new UnityContainer()
                .RegisterType<IDatabaseContext, DatabaseContext>(
                        new InjectionConstructor(connectionString))
                .RegisterType<IRepositoryFactory, RepositoryFactory>()
                    .RegisterType<IWorkoutService, WorkoutService>()
                    .RegisterType<IWorkoutRepository,
WorkoutRepository>();
        DependencyResolver.SetResolver(new UnityDependencyResolver(container));
```

```
        }
}
```

You can see that the DatabaseContext has a parameter. To pass the connection string to my DatabaseContext I used the **InjectionConstructor** object and passed the connection string. The latest stable version of Unity, version 2.1, doesn't require you to write anything more to have all your controllers injected. In fact, I have an IWorkoutController and you do not see it inside this configuration.

The last step is to register the resolver to be used for the http request of each user. This is done by using the DependencyResolver.SetResolver method.

How to access Session information from HttpHandler (Ashx file)

Release Date: 18-Oct-12
Url: http://patrickdesjardins.com/blog/?post_type=post&p=486

You may pass manually the information but wouldn't it be easier if the http handler could read the session information?

This can be done with .Net Framework easily. In theory, this should not be a problem because the handler is in the server. It only needs to provide the session of the current user. To do this, you need to use a special interface that will allow you to reach this information.

This interface is called *IReadOnlySessionState* or *IRequiresSessionState*.

Here is an example:

```
<% @ webhandler language="C#" class="MyClass" %>
using private System ;
using private System.Web ;
using private System.Web.SessionState ;

public class MyClass : IHttpHandler, IReadOnlySessionState
{
    public bool IsReusable
    {
        get { return true; }
    }
```

```
    public void ProcessRequest(HttpContext ctx)
    {
        ctx.Response.Write(ctx.Session["ID"]);
    }
}
```

This example shows you how to get the ID session's variable from the HttpHandler.

The second interface *IRequiresSessionState* is the same but will let you also write in the session.

How to step in (debug) Asp.Net MVC source code

Release Date: 09-Apr-12
Url: http://patrickdesjardins.com/blog/?post_type=post&p=958

If you need to go inside ASP MVC code, which can be very instructive, you just need to mark three checkboxes inside Visual Studio and you will be ready to go.

First of all, you need to go to **Debug>Options and Settings**. This will open the Options of Visual Studio. From the Debug menu, you should already be in the correct menu, which is **Debugging**.

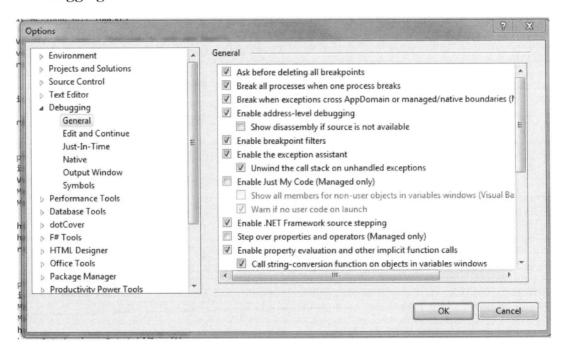

Select the first sub-menu which is called "General" and uncheck **"Enable Just my code (managed only)"**. Check **"Enable .Net Framework source stepping"** and check **"Enable source server support."** That's it. You will be able to step into the .Net source code and also set a breakpoint inside the Microsoft code.

Import JSON object from JavaScript into C# with a Dynamic keyword

Release Date: 23-Oct-11
Url: http://patrickdesjardins.com/blog/?post_type=post&p=511

I never really used the **dynamic** keyword in a real application. I did some tutorials but not much.

This week, I got a situation where I was getting from Silverlight a JSON object that I did not want to create an object for.

```
string response = HtmlPage.Window.Invoke("GetMyJson").ToString();
MyObject data = (MyObject)JsonConvert.DeserializeObject(response);
```

But, I did not want to create the MyObject because it was just for transferring data, a simple DTO object. Instead, I used the **dynamic** keyword provided by .Net framework 4.0.

The **dynamic** keyword will be resolved in runtime and this gives us the leverage to access a property that might not exist. For example, "GetMyJson" function was returning a simple object with two properties "Abc" and "Def".

```
{'Abc':'123','Def':'456'}
```

So, in the C# code, I simply called those properties from the **dynamic** object.

```
string response = HtmlPage.Window.Invoke("GetMyJson").ToString();
dynamic data = JsonConvert.DeserializeObject(response);
string s1 = data.Abc;
string s2 = data.Def;
```

This is pretty useful for accessing quickly some data from a JSON object.

Asp.Net MVC HTTP Error 401.0 - Unauthorized

Release Date: 16-Nov-12
Url: http://patrickdesjardins.com/blog/?post_type=post&p=1654

You do not have permission to view this directory or page.

When an unauthorized action is triggered, the HttpUnauthorizedResult result is called. It produces a 401 error. By default, a 401 error can be handled only by IIS and not directly like a 404 error with Asp. This would be easy if we could set a 401 error page in the web.config, but that is not the case.

HTTP Error 401.0 - Unauthorized

You do not have permission to view this directory or page.

Most likely causes:
- The authenticated user does not have access to a resource needed to process the reque

Things you can try:
- Check the failed request tracing logs for additional information about this error. For mor

Detailed Error Information:

| **Module** | ManagedPipelineHandler | **Requested URL** | http: |

```
namespace System.Web.Mvc
{
    public class HttpUnauthorizedResult : HttpStatusCodeResult
    {
        // HTTP 401 is the status code for unauthorized access. Other code might
        // intercept this and perform some special logic. For example, the
        // FormsAuthenticationModule looks for 401 responses and instead redirects
        // the user to the login page.
        private const int UnauthorizedCode = 401;

        public HttpUnauthorizedResult() : this(null)
        {
        }

        public HttpUnauthorizedResult(string statusDescription) :
base(UnauthorizedCode, statusDescription)
        {
```

```
        }
    }
} // File provided for Reference Use Only by Microsoft Corporation (c) 2007.
// Copyright (c) Microsoft Corporation. All rights reserved.
```

What can be done is to transform the 401 error code into a standard code, like the 200 code. This response header code indicates that the webpage has been found. This will let us counter the 401 behaviors and redirect to a specific action.

```csharp
public abstract class HttpUnauthorizedWithRedirectToResultBase :
HttpUnauthorizedResult
{
    protected ActionResult _result;

    public override void ExecuteResult(System.Web.Mvc.ControllerContext context)
    {
        if (context == null)
        {
            throw new ArgumentNullException("context");
        }
        if (context.HttpContext.Request.IsAuthenticated)
        {
            context.HttpContext.Response.StatusCode = 200;
            InitializeResult(context);
            _result.ExecuteResult(context);
        }
        else
            base.ExecuteResult(context);
    }

    protected abstract void InitializeResult(ControllerContext context);
}
```

We will create a new http unauthorized that will set area and view name. This will let us set the default page if we do not want to specify every time which action to use. If nothing is defined, we will be able to simply put in the shared folder a view with the error.

```csharp
public class HttpUnauthorizedWithRedirectToViewResult :
HttpUnauthorizedWithRedirectToResultBase
{
    private readonly string _area;
    private readonly string _viewName;

    public HttpUnauthorizedWithRedirectToViewResult(string viewName, string area)
    {
        _viewName = viewName;
        _area = area;
```

```
    }

    protected override void InitializeResult(ControllerContext context)
    {
        if (!string.IsNullOrWhiteSpace(_area))
        {
            context.RequestContext.RouteData.DataTokens["area"] = _area;
        }
        _result = new ViewResult {ViewName = _viewName};
    }
}

[AttributeUsage(AttributeTargets.Class | AttributeTargets.Method, Inherited =
true, AllowMultiple = false)]
public class AuthorizeWith401Support : AuthorizeAttribute
{
    private const string VIEW_NAME = "NoAccess401";
    private string _actionName;

    public string ActionName
    {
        get { return string.IsNullOrWhiteSpace(_actionName) ? VIEW_NAME :
_actionName; }
        set { _actionName = value; }
    }

    public string Controller { get; set; }
    public string Area { get; set; }

    protected override void HandleUnauthorizedRequest(AuthorizationContext
filterContext)
    {
        if (filterContext.IsChildAction)
        {
            base.HandleUnauthorizedRequest(filterContext);
        }
        else
        {
            if (string.IsNullOrWhiteSpace(ActionName))
            {
                throw new ArgumentException("You must set an ActionName");
            }
            if (string.IsNullOrWhiteSpace(controller))
            {
                filterContext.Result = new
HttpUnauthorizedWithRedirectToViewResult(ActionName, area);
            }
        }
    }
}
```

Now, you need to use it as you would use the AuthorizeAttribute. It is the same behavior because the *AuthorizeWith401Support* inherits from *AuthorizeAttribute*. However, you have the additional "ActionName,", "Area" and "Controller" properties that let you specify the error action. Of course, if nothing is specifieD, the action 'NoAccess401' will be used.

```
[AuthorizeWith401Support(Roles = "admin")]
public ActionResult Index()
{
    //...
}
```

How to enable CGI extension on IIS7 server

Release Date: 21-Oct-11
Url: http://patrickdesjardins.com/blog/?post_type=post&p=502

I had to install Mercurial Server on IIS 7 recently. One of the prerequisites is to have Python installed on IIS with a CGI extension.

For this, you need to add a handler on IIS to map .cgi to Python. Unfortunately, this operation is not straightforward. If you try to add the Handlers Mapping for CGI you will get this error message.

Handler Mappings

Use this feature to specify the resources, such as DLLs and managed code, that handle responses for specific request types.

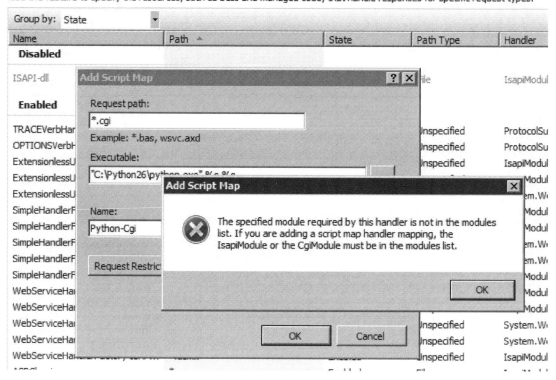

The specified module required by this handler is not in the modules list. If you are adding a script map handler mapping, the IsapiModule or the CgiModule must be in the modules list.

To fix that, you need to open the **Server Manager** (%SystemRoot%\system32\CompMgmtLauncher.exe) and go to **Roles** and **Web Server (IIS)**. From here you may have to wait a few minutes and you will be able to add the CGI extension.

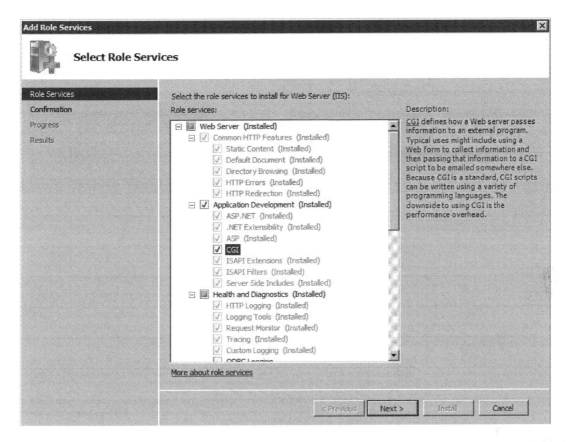

Then, the last step is to Install. This also takes a few minutes. Once done, restart IIS and you will be able to add the Http Handler for Python (or what ever CGI you need).

IIS does not start, the site binding is already taken

Release Date: 08-Nov-11
Url: http://patrickdesjardins.com/blog/?post_type=post&p=561

The IIS service starts well, but all websites sent a 404 error. This behavior is strange because if you go into the IIS Manager you can see that the Sites property displays that the Default Web Site is not started. If you try to start the Default Web Site, an error message tells you that it is already taken by another process.

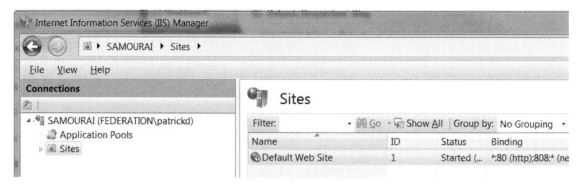

To know which process is using the port, a DOS console needs to be open and the use of netstat.exe is required.

netstat -a -n -p tcp -b

This will list the IP/PORT and under this information the name of the process.

In my case, Skype was running on 127.0.0.1:80. I had to close Skype, start the Default Web Site and then restart Skype and all was back to normal.

To conclude, I have no idea why Skype.exe hooked up to port 80, but for sure if you want to use IIS or Apache with port 80 while Skype is running, you have to start it after your web server.

Kill all instances of IIS web server with a single Command Line

Release Date: 20-Nov-11
Url: http://patrickdesjardins.com/blog/?post_type=post&p=588

When developing with Visual Studio, when you attach to the process or use the inner server (Cassini) a new process is launched. This process doesn't always stop when you stop debugging. You can have a list of process that are running and sometimes this can cause a problem when debugging because you are not accessing the right one.

To close those servers, you can check in the task bar, at the right side, in the tray, and you will notice a little icon with a paper and a mechanism wheel. This is what you need to kill. You can right click and close. The problem is that if you forget to do it every time, after a while you will have a lot of them.

To be quick, you can use a command line that will close them all for you.

```
taskkill /f /im WebDev.*
```

```
t:\>taskkill /f /im WebDev.*
SUCCESS: The process "WebDev.WebServer40.EXE" with PID 6588 has been terminated.
SUCCESS: The process "WebDev.WebServer40.EXE" with PID 9704 has been terminated.
SUCCESS: The process "WebDev.WebServer40.EXE" with PID 8844 has been terminated.
SUCCESS: The process "WebDev.WebServer40.EXE" with PID 12888 has been terminated.
SUCCESS: The process "WebDev.WebServer40.EXE" with PID 12224 has been terminated.
SUCCESS: The process "WebDev.WebServer40.EXE" with PID 896 has been terminated.
SUCCESS: The process "WebDev.WebServer40.EXE" with PID 7408 has been terminated.
SUCCESS: The process "WebDev.WebServer40.EXE" with PID 12792 has been terminated.
SUCCESS: The process "WebDev.WebServer40.EXE" with PID 4360 has been terminated.
SUCCESS: The process "WebDev.WebServer40.EXE" with PID 8552 has been terminated.
SUCCESS: The process "WebDev.WebServer40.EXE" with PID 8576 has been terminated.
```

This command line gives to Windows the right to kill a process by forcing it (/f) to close all process names (/im) that start with WebDev.

2. ENTITY FRAMEWORK AND ADO.NET

This chapter groups every post written during 2011 and 2012 about Entity Framework and Ado.Net. Most of them are still coherent and effective two years later, at the time I published this book. If some information is outdated, I still believe it can provide some positive insight to you by providing the evolution of the Entity Framework.

Mastering SqlConnection

Release Date: 25-Sep-11
Url: http://patrickdesjardins.com/blog/?post_type=post&p=313

The **SqlConnection** object is an object that derives from *DbConnection*. It opens the connection between the application and the database. It inherits from *IDisposable* because of *DbConnection*.

```
var connection = new SqlConnection();
connection.ConnectionString = @"Data Source=PATRICK-PC\SQLEXPRESS;Initial
Catalog=Northwind;Integrated Security=True";
connection.Open();
connection.Close();
```

or

```
using (var connection = new SqlConnection())
{
    connection.ConnectionString = @"Data Source=PATRICK-PC\SQLEXPRESS;Initial
Catalog=Northwind;Integrated Security=True";
    connection.Open();
    connection.Close();
}
```

These two snippets of code illustrate the creation of a connection. Both of them were using connection string from a string but the value can be directly loaded from the app.config or web.config.

```
ConnectionStringSettings connectionStringSettings =
ConfigurationManager.ConnectionStrings["ApplicationServices"];
using (var connection = new
SqlConnection(connectionStringSettings.ConnectionString))
{
    connection.Open();
    connection.Close();
}
```

```
<configuration>
  <connectionStrings>
    <add name="ApplicationServices"
         connectionString="Data Source=PATRICK-PC\SQLEXPRESS;Initial
Catalog=Northwind;Integrated Security=True"
         providerName="System.Data.SqlClient" />
  </connectionStrings>
```

DbCommand under the microscope

Release Date: 26-Sep-11
Url: http://patrickdesjardins.com/blog/?post_type=post&p=316

DbCommand uses the **DbConnection** to be able to send an SQL query or call a stored procedure. It can also execute a DDL (Data Definition Language) query to create a table or to modify the table structure.

Here is an example of updating a row with the SqlCommand that inherits from DbCommand.

```
ConnectionStringSettings connectionStringSettings =
ConfigurationManager.ConnectionStrings["ApplicationServices"];
using (var connection = new
SqlConnection(connectionStringSettings.ConnectionString))
{
    connection.Open();
    using (var command = new SqlCommand())
    {
        command.Connection = connection;
        command.CommandType = System.Data.CommandType.Text;
        command.CommandText = "UPDATE Region SET RegionDescription = 'Estern Yes!'
WHERE RegionID=1";
        command.ExecuteNonQuery();
        connection.Close();
    }
}
```

So, from this example you must have guessed that an SqlCommand that inherits from DbCommand derives also from IDisposable. This is why the *using* statement is still used in this example. The command got the connection that was opened previously and then the CommandType is set to *Text* to execute directly the SQL query.

From there the ExecuteNonQuery method is executed. This method is perfect to call a stored procedure or SQL statement that does not return data. Also, this command can return the number of rows affected.

```
int amountOfRowAffected = command.ExecuteNonQuery();
```

To execute the stored procedure, the command type needs to be changed and the command text must have the stored procedure name. To make a test let's create for the Northwind database the stored procedure.

```
ALTER PROCEDURE [dbo].[UpdateRegion](@id INT,@txt VARCHAR(50)) AS BEGIN
UPDATE region  SET RegionDescription = @txt  WHERE RegionID = @id
END
```

To execute let's use this code:

```
ConnectionStringSettings connectionStringSettings =
ConfigurationManager.ConnectionStrings["ApplicationServices"];
using (var connection = new
SqlConnection(connectionStringSettings.ConnectionString))
{
    connection.Open();
    using (var command = new SqlCommand())
    {
        command.Connection = connection;
        command.CommandType = System.Data.CommandType.StoredProcedure;
        command.CommandText = "UpdateRegion";
        command.Parameters.Add(new SqlParameter("id", "1"));
        command.Parameters.Add(new SqlParameter("txt", "Est"));
        command.ExecuteNonQuery();
        connection.Close();
    }
}
```

Not only the **CommandType** and **CommandText** have changed, but a new addition appears with the parameter. Since the stored procedure takes the ID of the region and the text to display as a new description, the command must be aware of what to pass to the stored procedure.

The creation of the parameter can also be performed with the use of the command. So that's it, you can create a parameter with the CreateParameter method of the DbCommand class.

```
ConnectionStringSettings connectionStringSettings =
ConfigurationManager.ConnectionStrings["ApplicationServices"];
using (var connection = new
SqlConnection(connectionStringSettings.ConnectionString))
```

```
{
    connection.Open();
    using (var command = new SqlCommand())
    {
        command.Connection = connection;
        command.CommandType = System.Data.CommandType.StoredProcedure;
        command.CommandText = "UpdateRegion";
        SqlParameter param1 = command.CreateParameter();
        param1.ParameterName = "id";
        param1.Value = "1";
        command.Parameters.Add(param1);
        command.Parameters.Add(new SqlParameter("txt", "Estern"));
        command.ExecuteNonQuery();
        connection.Close();
    }
}
```

The DbParameter, in the few examples above, was of type SqlParameter. The class SqlParameter derives from DbParameter and contains additional specifications for SQL Server. For example, the Db Type is more specific to SQL Server. Also, you can find multiple additional methods to specify the direction of the parameter, the type, the direction, etc.

```
SqlParameter param1 = command.CreateParameter();
param1.ParameterName = "id";
param1.Value = "1";
param1.Direction = System.Data.ParameterDirection.Input;
param1.SqlDbType = System.Data.SqlDbType.Int;
param1.IsNullable = false;
```

To conclude, the DbCommand is the class to use when you need to execute a query that does not return any data.

DataReader and DataAdapters to read from the database

Release Date: 29-Sep-11
Url: http://patrickdesjardins.com/blog/?post_type=post&p=325

To read data from the database you need to use something else from the DbCommand that was returning no data. Two options are available. The first one is the DataReader, the second is the DataAdapters.

DataReader

This is the fastest way to read data from the database. To create a *DataReader* object, the use of *ExecuteReader* from the *DbCommand* class is required. It is required because you will still need to give them the type of query you want and the SQL statement (or the stored procedure name). Then, the method ExecuteReader() returns a DataReader. In the example below, the reader is an SqlDataReader. This derives from DataReader and is more specialized for Microsoft SQL Server. The latest solution is really not performant.

```
ConnectionStringSettings connectionStringSettings =
ConfigurationManager.ConnectionStrings["ApplicationServices"];
using (var connection = new
SqlConnection(connectionStringSettings.ConnectionString))
{
    connection.Open();
    using (var command = new SqlCommand())
    {
        command.Connection = connection;
        command.CommandText = "SELECT CustomerID, CompanyName FROM Customers WHERE
country LIKE 'canada' ";
        command.CommandType = System.Data.CommandType.Text;
        using (SqlDataReader reader = command.ExecuteReader())
        {
            while (reader.Read())
            {
                System.Diagnostics.Debug.WriteLine(string.Format("{0}:{1}",
reader["CustomerID"], reader["CompanyName"]));
            }
        }
    }
    connection.Close();
}
```

The DataReader acts like a cursor. It can only go forward. You can access the value of each row by using the square brackuet []. You can use the name of the field or an integer that represents the index of the position of the field. For example, we could have replaced

```
System.Diagnostics.Debug.WriteLine(string.Format("{0}:{1}",reader["CustomerID"],
reader["CompanyName"]));
```

with

```
System.Diagnostics.Debug.WriteLine(string.Format("{0}:{1}",reader[0], reader[1]));
```

The problem with the latest version is the maintainability. It is harder to know what will be displayed. Also, it can be problematic if the order of the returned data changes. Let's say that you get data from a stored procedure and for an unknown reason the database administrator changes the order of the returned field. This would create a problem, but not if the name were used.

You can also load the whole data set in one shot using the *Load* method. The data is loaded into a *DataTable*.

```
ConnectionStringSettings connectionStringSettings =
ConfigurationManager.ConnectionStrings["ApplicationServices"];
DataTable datas = new DataTable();
using (var connection = new
SqlConnection(connectionStringSettings.ConnectionString))
{
    connection.Open();
    using (var command = new SqlCommand())
    {
        command.Connection = connection;
        command.CommandText = "SELECT CustomerID, CompanyName FROM Customers WHERE
country LIKE 'canada' ";
        command.CommandType = System.Data.CommandType.Text;
        using (SqlDataReader reader = command.ExecuteReader())
        {
            datas.Load(reader, LoadOption.Upsert);
        }
    }
    connection.Close();
    System.Diagnostics.Debug.WriteLine("Number of rows loaded : " +
datas.Rows.Count);
}
```

One problem with *DataReader* is that it uses a cursor on the server and it keeps the connection to the server open while looping. The second problem is that while looping you won't be able to execute another query within the loop. To solve that problem you can load all the data and loop after or use the Load method. Another option is to use a **DbConnection** with a special connection string. This connection string will require the attribute "MultipleActiveResultSets=True". This lets it have multiple commands but at the cost of performance. It has to be used with caution.

Scalar

Sometimes, we want to have just a single value. This can be an ID from a username, but more often it will be to get a value from an aggregate function, like a count. We could use the DataReader but this gives some over complexity for a single value.

```
ConnectionStringSettings connectionStringSettings =
ConfigurationManager.ConnectionStrings["ApplicationServices"];
using (var connection = new
SqlConnection(connectionStringSettings.ConnectionString))
{
    connection.Open();
    using (var command = new SqlCommand())
    {
        command.Connection = connection;
        command.CommandText = "SELECT count(CustomerID) FROM Customers WHERE
country LIKE 'canada' ";
        command.CommandType = System.Data.CommandType.Text;
        int countValue = (int) command.ExecuteScalar();
        System.Diagnostics.Debug.WriteLine("Count value:" + countValue);
    }
    connection.Close();
}
```

As you can see, line 10 uses the *ExecuteScalar* from the DbCommand to return an Object. In our case, we return an integer.

DbDataAdapter

The *DbDataAdapter* is the reader that gives you more leverage in data functionality. Not only does it let you get the data but it lets you update it.

The *DbDataAdapter* class derives from *DataAdapter*. As the other command, a Microsoft SQL Server exists and it is called *SqlDataAdapter*.

The *DbDataAdapter* contains a *SelectCommand* that uses an *ExecuteReader*. Internally the data is loaded into a *DataTable*. This lets the developer change the value inside the *DataTable* and, if desired, update them to the database or insert new rows and also delete those which are not in the *DataTable* anymore. The *DbDataAdapter* is wise enough to open and close the connection. On the other hand, it lets the user open the connection if desired. In that case, the user will also need to close it. This can be useful when multiple calls are required because it will not open-close repetitively, which is costly in performance. Here is an example of how to load data from the database into a *DbDataAdapter*.

```
ConnectionStringSettings connectionStringSettings =
ConfigurationManager.ConnectionStrings["ApplicationServices"];
DataSet returnedValuesSet = new DataSet();
using (var connection = new
SqlConnection(connectionStringSettings.ConnectionString))
{
```

```
    connection.Open();
    using (var command = new SqlCommand())
    {
        command.Connection = connection;
        command.CommandText = "SELECT CustomerID, CompanyName FROM Customers WHERE
country LIKE 'canada' ";
        command.CommandType = System.Data.CommandType.Text;
        using (var dataAdapter = new SqlDataAdapter(command))
        {
            dataAdapter.Fill(returnedValuesSet);
        }
    }
    connection.Close();
    System.Diagnostics.Debug.WriteLine("Number of rows loaded : " +
returnedValuesSet.Tables[0].Rows.Count);
}
```

So, now the *DataSet* is filled up with the query data. It is a non-connected object but will still be able to do an update later on. From this example, we can see that the *SqlDataAdapter* filled up with the *Fill* method. This *Fill* method can also take a second argument that is the name of the table. This means we can modify the previous example with this argument and instead of referring to the data in the *DataSet* with an index, we will be able to use the string as a key.

```
ConnectionStringSettings connectionStringSettings =
ConfigurationManager.ConnectionStrings["ApplicationServices"];
DataSet returnedValuesSet = new DataSet();
using (var connection = new
SqlConnection(connectionStringSettings.ConnectionString))
{
    connection.Open();
    using (var command = new SqlCommand())
    {
        command.Connection = connection;
        command.CommandText = "SELECT CustomerID, CompanyName FROM Customers WHERE
country LIKE 'canada' ";
        command.CommandType = System.Data.CommandType.Text;
        using (var dataAdapter = new SqlDataAdapter(command))
        {
            dataAdapter.Fill(returnedValuesSet, "Customers");
        }
    }
    connection.Close();
    System.Diagnostics.Debug.WriteLine("Number of rows loaded : " +
returnedValuesSet.Tables["Customers"].Rows.Count);
}
```

The table name is important if you want to use other features like insert, update and delete because the SqlAdapter will use this table to do the desired task. If you use a fake table name, you will get an exception. This exception is:

"Update unable to find TableMapping['Table'] or DataTable 'Table'.".

```
command.CommandType = System.Data.CommandType.Text;
using (var dataAdapter = new SqlDataAdapter(command))
{
    dataAdapter.Fill(returnedValuesSet, "NotARealName");

    returnedValuesSet.Tables["NotARealName"].Rows.Add("-1", "My Company Name");

    dataAdapter.Update(returnedValuesSet);
}
}
connection.Close();
```

InvalidOperationException was unhandled by user code

Update unable to find TableMapping['Table'] or DataTable 'Table'.

Troubleshooting tips:

Invalid Operation with DataSet Update

The correct code would be to provide in the *InsertCommand* property of the *SqlDataAdapter* an SQL statement with an *Insert* statement or a stored procedure. If you do not want to create the Insert, Update, Delete and Select statement every time, it is possible to use the *SqlCommandBuilder*.

```
ConnectionStringSettings connectionStringSettings =
ConfigurationManager.ConnectionStrings["ApplicationServices"];
DataSet returnedValuesSet = new DataSet();
using (var connection = new
SqlConnection(connectionStringSettings.ConnectionString))
{
    connection.Open();
    using (var command = new SqlCommand())
    {
        command.Connection = connection;
        command.CommandText = "SELECT CustomerID, CompanyName FROM Customers WHERE
country LIKE 'canada' ";
        command.CommandType = System.Data.CommandType.Text;
        using (var dataAdapter = new SqlDataAdapter(command))
        {
            dataAdapter.Fill(returnedValuesSet, "Customers");
            var builder = new SqlCommandBuilder(dataAdapter);
            dataAdapter.InsertCommand = builder.GetInsertCommand();
            returnedValuesSet.Tables["Customers"].Rows.Add("-1", "My Company
Name");
            dataAdapter.Update(returnedValuesSet, "Customers");
        }
    }
```

```
        connection.Close();
}
```

This will generate the *InsertCommand* as you can see in this screenshot:

Automatically creates SQL statement with DbCommandBuilder

The created SQL statement uses parameter style and is SQL injection protected.

So far the *DbDataAdapter* committed one change at a time. This is because the *DbDataAdapter* has by default its *UpdateBatchSize* to 1. You can select the size you want or set it to 0 to let the *DbDataAdapter* use the largest batch size. This will increase the performance of the application.

In practice

When using an SQL statement, stored procedure or direct SQL you should always use parameters. In practice, in your data access layer when you have a method that returns data from the database it should query with a *DataReader* and return a *DataSet*. The reason is the *DataSet* lets you close the connection and the *DataReader* is justified by its speed.

```
ConnectionStringSettings connectionStringSettings =
ConfigurationManager.ConnectionStrings["ApplicationServices"];
DataSet returnedValuesSet = new DataSet();
DataTable returnedTable = new DataTable();
using (var connection = new
SqlConnection(connectionStringSettings.ConnectionString))
{
    connection.Open();
    using (var command = new SqlCommand())
    {
        command.Connection = connection;
        command.CommandText = "SELECT CustomerID, CompanyName FROM Customers WHERE
country LIKE @country";
        command.CommandType = System.Data.CommandType.Text;
        SqlParameter paramCountry = new SqlParameter("country", "canada");
        command.Parameters.Add(paramCountry);
        using (var reader = command.ExecuteReader())
```

```
    {
        returnedTable.Load(reader, LoadOption.Upsert);
        returnedValuesSet.Tables.Add(returnedTable);
    }
  }
  connection.Close();
}
```

For inserting, updating and deleting, parameters must be used too. Here is a good example of code that could be used in data access layer methods. Your method should return the number of rows and accept as a parameter your model object of the Customer.

```
ConnectionStringSettings connectionStringSettings =
ConfigurationManager.ConnectionStrings["ApplicationServices"];
DataSet returnedValuesSet = new DataSet();
DataTable returnedTable = new DataTable();
int rowsAffected;
using (var connection = new
SqlConnection(connectionStringSettings.ConnectionString))
{
    connection.Open();
    using (var command = new SqlCommand())
    {
        command.Connection = connection;
        command.CommandText = "INSERT INTO customers (CustomerID, CompanyName)
VALUES (@id, @name)";
        command.CommandType = System.Data.CommandType.Text;
        command.Parameters.Add(new SqlParameter("id", "P1"));
        command.Parameters.Add(new SqlParameter("name", "MyName"));
        rowsAffected = command.ExecuteNonQuery();
    }
    connection.Close();
}
```

Do not forget to handle the *DbAdapter's UpdateBatchSize* when you have a collection that you are going to update. Let's say that you pass to your data access layer a collection (for example an IList), then your method should check the *Count* of items and adjust the *UpdateBatchSize* to the *Count*. This way, your performance will increase by a lot.

The last important thing is the use of **Transaction**. Usually when something goes wrong you would like to know about it and to cancel the current batch edition to restart it once the problem is fixed. SQL Transaction will be discussed in a future article but should be there for insert, update and delete queries.

How to encrypt connection string in .Net

Release Date: 03-Oct-11
Url: http://patrickdesjardins.com/blog/?post_type=post&p=241

It is always more secure to not have the user and password in clear text. This is true for applications but also for web applications.

Microsoft .Net Framework comes with a tool to encrypt the connection string. This tool is **aspnet_regiis.exe** and you can find it at C:\Windows\Microsoft.NET\Framework\v2.0.50727\ if you are working on .Net 2.0 or at C:\Windows\Microsoft.NET\Framework\v4.0.30319 if you are working with .Net 4.0.

Two providers come with the .Net Framework - the **RSAProtectedConfigurationProvider** and the **DataProtectionConfigurationProvider**.

How to use aspnet_regiis.exe

You can get help by using the /? parameter but you will rapidly see that this tool has a lot of parameters.

To encrypt the connection string, you will need to use these parameters:

aspnet_regiis.exe -pef "connectionStrings" "c:\myProject\myFolder\web.config"

But, what about the provider? You can also add "-prov DataProtectionConfigurationProvider" to use DataProtectionConfigurationProvider provider.

What to code to decrypt inside the application?

Nothing. .Net Framework automatically decrypts configuration sections, therefore you do not need to write any additional decryption code.

Possible errors

You could get this error message while executing this command: "The configuration for physical path cannot be opened." If you have this error you should be sure that the file is not in read-only. Also, check if you have permission to edit this file. Then, be sure that the file is not used by any program that may lock the file.

SSPI

This option lets you use the Windows credential instead of using username and password directly in the connection string. To use it, modify the connection string to have **Integrated Security=SSPI** or **Integrated Security=True** and remove the username and password. Of course, this means that the database must let the user connect. This is a good practice to handle the security of your web application with the web Windows credential.

Conclusion

For more information about security you should visit Microsoft MSDN documentation (http://bit.ly/1f0YpF5).

C# Transaction for SQL query

Release Date: 30-Sep-11
Url: http://patrickdesjardins.com/blog/?post_type=post&p=345

Transaction lets you roll back if a problem occurs. If you insert 100 entries into the database and one of them is wrong, the whole list of entries will not be saved in persistent storage. Most of the time you want to have your action to be atomic. An atomic transaction is a series of database operations either all occur, or nothing occurs.

This is an example of a good practice method that should be in a data access layer. To simplify, all will be written in the same file and the database used is the *Northwind* database.

```
public int SaveCustomers(IEnumerable<Customer> customers)
{
    ConnectionStringSettings connectionStringSettings =
ConfigurationManager.ConnectionStrings["ApplicationServices"];
    int rowsAffected = 0;
    using (var connection = new
SqlConnection(connectionStringSettings.ConnectionString))
    {
        connection.Open();
        var transaction = connection.BeginTransaction();
        using (var command = new SqlCommand())
        {
            command.Transaction = transaction;
            command.Connection = connection;
            try
            {
                foreach (var customer in customers)
```

```
            {
                if (customer.IsNew)
                {
                    command.CommandText
    = "INSERT INTO customers (CustomerID, CompanyName) VALUES (@id, @name)";
                }
                else
                {
                    command.CommandText
    = "UPDATE customers SET CompanyName = @name WHERE CustomerID = @id";
                }
                command.CommandType = System.Data.CommandType.Text;
                command.Parameters.Clear(); //Remove
                command.Parameters.Add(new SqlParameter("id", customer.Id));
                command.Parameters.Add(new SqlParameter("name",
                                                        customer.Name));

                rowsAffected += command.ExecuteNonQuery();
            }
            transaction.Commit();
        }
        catch
        {
            transaction.Rollback();
        }
    }
    connection.Close();
    }
    return rowsAffected;
}
```

This code contains some interesting things. First, to create a transaction you must have a connection already open. This is required. Otherwise you will have an exception that will tell you that the connection is closed.

Second, you must know that if you forget to commit once you are done querying, even if all queries were legitimate, the database won't have your data. That's right. Even if the *rowsAffected += command.ExecuteNonQuery();* adds a number in the rowAffected, this will not be real until you commit. The code above works because all customers have *IsNew* set to true. If you run this code and change one to False you will tell the Save method to use the Update statement. The command will Update but the database won't find the customer and will throw an exception. What it means is that the code will go in the catch and Roll Back the transaction. Even if the rowsAffected is at 1, you will have 0 rows added or updated in the database.

Type of isolation

To create a transaction you need to get it from the *DbCommand*. The reason is simple - a transaction is different among database providers. So, when using the *SqlDbCommand*, you will have more options of transactions for the Microsoft SQL Server Database. Also, transaction codes will do isolation on the database. SQL Server lets you do different types of transactions.

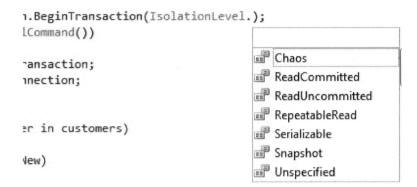

ReadUncommitted

This is a very weak transaction and should not be used. In fact, this type doesn't lock anything in the database. It is possible that the data could change or be deleted by the time the commit is done. This can lead to an unpredictable reaction. This type of isolation will produce for a Select statement this query:

```
SELECT * FROM CUSTOMERS WITH (NOLOCK)
```

ReadCommitted

This tries to have a share-lock on the data. If it succeeds, it will protect any external change to those values.

RepeatableRead

All the data implicated in the transaction are locked.

Serializable

All of the table is locked. This prevents adding other rows to the table. This is the best isolation but it comes with the cost of being not performant. Locking more value than desired can lead to reducing the speed to all other connections that need to read or edit these rows.

Snapshot

If your database is SQL Server 2005 and higher you can use this type of transaction that will make a copy of the affected row. To be more accurate, rows are versioned and when other connections want to access these rows, instead of locking a copy is made. This keeps the system in good shape without creating any slow time for anyone.

Transaction Type

This type of transaction is known as **Lightweight Transaction Manager (LTM)** because only one connection is required. Sometimes, you may use one connection to read and while it is looping you could open another connection to update. Anytime you have two connections open, the transaction type becomes **Distributed Transaction (DT)**. Microsoft Windows operating system has a Distributed Transaction Coordinator (DTC) that is a service that runs in the background of your computer. The Distributed Transaction Coordinator (DTC) requires either the use of *System.Transactions,* that will be discussed in a later article, or the use of explicit code to execute the code under DTC. To use DTC developers have to create classes that inherit from the *ServicedComponent* class in the System.EnterpriseServices namespace. This will not be discussed because it is easier now to simply use the System.Transactions that handles it implicitly if it really requires DTC or LTM.

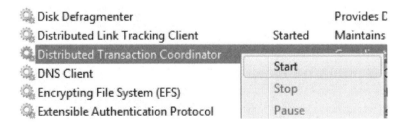

You can activate the Distributed Transaction Coordinator inside Windows Services.

Entity SQL Query (ESQL)

Release Date: 02-Oct-11
Url: http://patrickdesjardins.com/blog/?post_type=post&p=379

Entity SQL Query (ESQL) is not like Linq to Entity. The latter uses the Linq query while the former does not. However, they serve the same purpose and they are both in the Entity Framework.

ESQL looks more like an SQL query. Even if ESQL is not SQL, it will let the developer use an SQL query to the database. So, there are two ways to use ESQL - using *EntityCommand* or using the generic*ObjectQuery* class.

The first thing to do is to create an EDMX file like we would do with Linq to Entity. The generated connection string that it will provide in the web.config (or app.config) will be used after that with the **EntityConnection**. For that, you will need to use the *System.Data.EntityClient* namespace (Add System.Data.Entity).

The connection string will look like this:

```
<add name="NorthwindEntities1"
connectionString="metadata=res://*/NorthwindModel.csdl|res://*/NorthwindModel.ssdl
|res://*/NorthwindModel.msl;provider=System.Data.SqlClient
    ;provider connection string=&quot;Data Source=PATRICK-PC\SQLEXPRESS;Initial
Catalog=Northwind
    ;Integrated Security=True;MultipleActiveResultSets=True&quot;"
    providerName="System.Data.EntityClient" />
</connectionStrings>
```

You need to have this syntax with the metadata and provider connection. The traditional ADO.NET connection string won't work.

To try your connection string for ESQL you can use this kind of code:

```
    string connectionString =
ConfigurationManager.ConnectionStrings["NorthwindEntities1"].ConnectionString;
    using (EntityConnection conn = new EntityConnection(connectionString))
    {
        conn.Open();
        System.Diagnostics.Debug.WriteLine("Connected");
        conn.Close();
    }
```

In the code above, we can see the use of EntityConnection. This derives from DbConnection like SqlConnection does with ADO.NET. It will use an EntityCommand that also inherits from an ADO.NET object - the DbCommand.

ESQL is more error prone than Linq to Entity because the query is in a string. You do not have Intellisense or the compiler to tell you that you have an error. Here is an example of showing with ESQL all regions of the Northwind database.

```
string connectionString =
ConfigurationManager.ConnectionStrings["NorthwindEntities1"].ConnectionString;
using (EntityConnection conn = new EntityConnection(connectionString))
{
    conn.Open();
    string sqlQuery = @"SELECT reg.RegionId
                        , reg.RegionDescription
                        FROM NorthwindEntities1.Region as reg";
    using (EntityCommand command = new EntityCommand(sqlQuery, conn))
    {
        var reader =
command.ExecuteReader(System.Data.CommandBehavior.SequentialAccess);
        while (reader.Read())
        {
            System.Diagnostics.Debug.WriteLine(reader["RegionId"] + " : " +
reader["RegionDescription"]);
        }
    }
    conn.Close();
}
```

This code uses an *EntityDataReader* that derives from *DbDataReader*. Like its inherited class, it can only be used to read forward. The major change is in the sqlQuery variable. As you can see, it does not make the query against the table but against the Entity Model. You have to use the *Entity Container Name*.

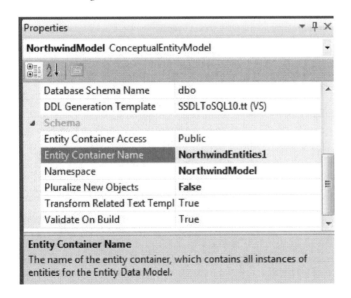

Also, in SELECT, it is not the name of the column in the table that you have to use but the name of the property of the entity. So, people with an SQL background may feel comfortable with the syntax.

Object Context

The previous section showed that **ESQL** lets you have very tight control over the query by using an SQL type of statement. But, on the other hand, it is not very interesting because we could just use an ADO.NET object to do almost the same thing. But ESQL has more under the hood.

ESQL can use Object Context to retrieve an Entity Object without having to build them like with the ADO.NET. This starts to be interesting. Let's check an example.

```
using System.Data.Objects;
//...
string connectionString =
ConfigurationManager.ConnectionStrings["NorthwindEntities1"].ConnectionString;
using (EntityConnection conn = new EntityConnection(connectionString))
{
    using (ObjectContext objectContext = new ObjectContext(connectionString))
    {
        objectContext.Connection.Open();
        string sqlQuery = @"SELECT  reg.RegionId
                , reg.RegionDescription
              FROM NorthwindEntities1.Region as reg";
        var allRegions = new ObjectQuery<DbDataRecord>(sqlQuery,
objectContext).ToList();
        foreach (var region in allRegions)
        {
            System.Diagnostics.Debug.WriteLine(region.GetInt32(0) + " : " +
region.GetString(1));
        }
        objectContext.Connection.Close();
    }
}
```

Line 12 and line 15 contain new code. Line 12 executes the query and returns a *DbDataRecord*. A *DbDataRecord* inherits *IDataRecord* and can only access elements by index. This is not very convenient and from my personal perspective does not give an effective way to get data from the database. However, some extensions let you handle *ObjectQuery* more easily, but at the end you will still need to non typed object.

Linq to SQL vs Entity Framework: What are the differences

Release Date: 13-Sep-11
Url: http://patrickdesjardins.com/blog/?post_type=post&p=172

I have seen in many websites the differences between Linq to SQL and Entity Framework but the most effective summary I saw is from the book "MCTS Self Paced Training Kit Exam 70-516." Here is the table, without their explanation, which can be found in the MCTS book.

CATEGORY	LINQ TO SQL	ENTITY FRAMEWORK
Complexity	Less complex	More complex
Model	Domain model	Conceptual data model
DB Server	SQL Server	Variety of database products
Development Time	Rapid application development	More time required but has mode features
Mapping Type	Class to single table	Class to multiple tables
Inheritance	Difficult to apply	Simple to apply
File Types	DBML files	EDMX, CDSL, MSL, SSDL files
Complex Type Support	No	Yes
Query Capability	LINQ to SQL through *DataContext*	LINQ to Entities, ESQL, Object Services, Entity Client
Performance	Slow for first query	Slow for first query but over-all better than LINQ to SQL
Future Enhancements	No	Yes
Generate DB from Model	No	Yes

Connection pooling means to reuse database connection

Release Date: 21-Sep-11
Url: http://patrickdesjardins.com/blog/?post_type=post&p=233

Connection Pooling is handled by the **Connection Manager** to reuse available connections instead of creating a new one. This is wise performance because the system won't create and kill a connection every time a database is required. This is also very true for web applications so that the same user may not only call the database multiple times per page but also go in multiple pages, and this is done by many users. To activate Pooling, add in the collection string "Pooling=True;" and that's it.

To use connection pooling suffices to change the connection string. From there you can select the size of the pool and many other options. For example, you can change the default value for the pool size to 100

The way pooling works does not involve any modification or special behavior for the database. It is all code handled. All ADO.NET providers can use this mechanism.

Also, pooling does not have any huge disadvantage and so should always be activated. The only moment it makes sense to turn it off is when debugging a connection problem.

How to use a POCO object with Entity Framework 4

Release Date: 15-Sep-11
Url: http://patrickdesjardins.com/blog/?post_type=post&p=199

I have put in the title Entity Framework 4 because since version 4 it has a great new addition. This new feature is that POCO objects do not require the use of any interface inheritance. Also, no meta attribute is required to be added to your classes. So, how do the entities map to your POCO classes? Well, the mapping is done with the name of the entity and the class. These two must be the same. If you have a class named *Region* then you need an entity named *Region*. So, this means that you still need to have a conceptual model with an .edmx file. Also, you do not want the entity model to create the classes since you already have them. To do this, you need to clear in the entity file (.edmx) the **Custom Tool** property. As said previously, the mapping is done with the name. If you have in your project two classes with the same name but with a different namespace, this will confuse the mapper and an exception will be thrown. It is a good practice to put all your POCOPOCO classes in the same project with the Entity Framework file.

Example

Create a new project and add a new Entity Framework Model file. You could choose to create your entities manually, but to be faster let's create them from the database. Let's just select the *Region* table. Do not forget to go into the entity framework model's properties to remove the **Custom Tool**.

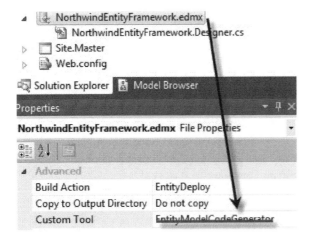

By turning this off, no classes generation will be done.

The last step is to create the Object Context, which is required because we have removed previously the generation of it. To do this, you need to create a new class that inherits the base class *ObjectContext*. Do not forget to add "using System.Data.Objects" at the top of the file to be able to see ObjectContext.

So, here is the code.

Region class:

```
public class Region
{
    public Int32 RegionID { get; set; }
    public string RegionDescription { get; set; }
}
```

The Object Context class:

```
public class NorthwindObjectContext : ObjectContext
{
    private ObjectSet<Region> _Region;

    public NorthwindObjectContext()
                : base("name=NorthwindEntities", "NorthwindEntities")
    {
```

```
        this.ContextOptions.LazyLoadingEnabled = true;
    }

    public ObjectSet<Region> Regions
    {
        get
        {
            if ((_Region == null))
            {
                _Region = base.CreateObjectSet<Region>("Region");
            }
            return _Region;
        }
    }
}
```

Finally, to test, I added a page with a paragraph and showed the first region description:

```
NorthwindObjectContext db = new NorthwindObjectContext();
TextBlock.InnerText = db.Regions
                        .Where(region => region.RegionID == 1)
                        .FirstOrDefault().RegionDescription;
```

There are two errors that can appear if you try this code:

Mapping and metadata information could not be found for EntityType

This message indicates that you have not removed the **Custom Tool** of the entity framework model properties. Or the second error:

The specified default EntityContainer name 'NorthwindEntities1' could not be found in the mapping and metadata information. Parameter name: defaultContainerName

This means that the container name is not the name of the container generated by the entity model. If your model is from the database, it should be the same as the connection string name. If you want to know exactly where the container name is, you need to go into the csdl file. This is inside the entity model. To see it, open the .edmx file with an XML editor and go to the CSDL section. You will see an EntityContainer element.

```
NorthwindEntityFramework.edmx  ×
        </edmx:StorageModels>
        <!-- CSDL content -->
        <edmx:ConceptualModels>
          <Schema Namespace="NorthwindModel" Alias="Self" xmlns:annotat:
            <EntityContainer Name="NorthwindEntities" annotation:LazyLo;
              <EntitySet Name="Region" EntityType="NorthwindModel.Regio|
            </EntityContainer>
            <EntityType Name="Region">
```

There are two other details that you must know when using a POCO object with Entity Framework and that is concerning a complex object. As you know, complex objects are in fact an object inside an object instead of a CLR type. Those complex objects must be built as a class and not as a struct. Also, you cannot use inheritance with a complex type. For example, if your *Company* class contains a list of *Employee* you cannot have the *Employee* derive from *Person*.

From here you should be all good to use Entity Framework and POCOPOCO objects!

POCO Proxy and Lazy Loading

Release Date: 05-Oct-11
Url: http://patrickdesjardins.com/blog/?post_type=post&p=270

POCO objects using Entity Framework as ORM require the creation of a proxy. Once the proxy is created, the rest is exactly the same as if you were using a standard entity from the object context.

Creating the proxy

In fact, the proxy will be generated by the Entity Framework (in runtime). To be more accurate, each of the POCO classes has a proxy. This proxy will derive from your POCO classes. This will let the Entity Framework keep track of the state change and enable the use of lazy loading. Since the proxy class derives from POCO classes, these must not be sealed, private or abstract.

We have said that the proxy is created in the runtime and this is a good thing because we can enable and disable the proxy. If you desire to enable the proxy, you must set the *ProxyCreationEnabled* to true. This property resides inside the context object, inside the context option.

```
var db = new NorthWindContext();
db.ContextOptions.ProxyCreationEnabled=true;//Enable the proxy creation in runtime
```

This is not always enabled because in some cases, like while using serialization with WCF, only *[known]* class can be serialized. This won't be the case with the runtime-generated proxy.

From here, you need to make some changes in your POCO class, and the change varies depending on whether you want only the lazy loading or also the change tracking.

Lazy Loading

To have lazy loading enabled, the navigation properties (the ones that link to another object that needs to be loaded or a collection to be loaded) must be public and virtual and not sealed. This way, it is possible for the proxy to change some calls to add the lazy loaded statement.

Change Tracking

The first step is to make you POCO class legitimate for lazy loading. So, all information in the previous paragraph must remain true. Each collection of objects must return a type that derives from a generic ICollection. It is also required to use the *CreateObject* method instead of using *new* to create your class.

```
var db = new NorthWindContext();
var myPOCO = db.CreateObject<MyPOCOObject>();
```

You can find further information on MSDN (http://bit.ly/1kYxAkB).

Complete example

Let's see this theory in practice. We are going to use the Northwind database and the tables Customers and Orders.

Lets create a new ADO.NET entity data model and use the generator creating the model for us. Do not forget to remove the **Custom Tool** text on the Edmx file.

After that, let's create the two POCO classes.

```
namespace POCOAndLazy.POCO
```

```
{
    public class Customer
    {
        public string CustomerID { get; set; }
        public string CompanyName { get; set; }
        public string ContactName { get; set; }
        public string ContactTitle { get; set; }
        public string Address { get; set; }
        public string City { get; set; }
        public string Region { get; set; }
        public string PostalCode { get; set; }
        public string Country { get; set; }
        public string Phone { get; set; }
        public string Fax { get; set; }
        public virtual List<Order> Orders { get; set; } //Virtual + ICollection<T>
    }
}
```

and

```
namespace POCOAndLazy.POCO
{
    public class Order
    {
        public int OrderID { get; set; }
        public string CustomerID { get; set; }
        public int EmployeeID { get; set; }
        public DateTime? OrderDate { get; set; }
        public DateTime? RequiredDate { get; set; }
        public DateTime? ShippedDate { get; set; }
        public int? ShipVia { get; set; }
        public decimal? Freight { get; set; }
        public string ShipName { get; set; }
        public string ShipAddress { get; set; }
        public string ShipCity { get; set; }
        public string ShipRegion { get; set; }
        public string ShipCountry { get; set; }
        public string ShipPostalCode { get; set; }
    }
}
```

After the ObjectContext class.

```
namespace POCOAndLazy
{
    public class ModelContext : ObjectContext
    {
        private ObjectSet<Customer> customers;
        private ObjectSet<Order> orders;
```

```
        public ModelContext() : base("name=NorthwindEntities",
"NorthwindEntities")
        {
            customers = CreateObjectSet<Customer>();
            orders = CreateObjectSet<Order>();
        }

        public ObjectSet<Customer> Customers
        {
            get { return customers; }
        }

        public ObjectSet<Order> Order
        {
            get { return orders; }
        }
    }
}
```

And let's do a quick test.

```
ModelContext db = new ModelContext();
var bigCustomers = db.Customers.Where(c => c.Orders.Count > 20);
foreach (var customer in bigCustomers)
{
    Debug.WriteLine("Customer#" + customer.CustomerID);
}
```

Output:

Customer#ERNSHCustomer#QUICKCustomer#SAVEA

This displays the list of customers that have over 10 orders. I have not given the explanation of how to create POCO objects with Entity Framework here because this is covered in another article. The important information is that we now have a stable structure to continue to the core of the goal: lazy loading.

Currently, no order can be shown if we loop through the list of orders of each of these three clients. The reason is that the default value is *eager loading* which use the *Include* keyword that is missing and no explicit loading with *Load* is provided.

```
ModelContext db = new ModelContext();
var bigCustomers = db.Customers.Where(c => c.Orders.Count > 20);
foreach (var customer in bigCustomers)
{
```

```
        Debug.WriteLine("Customer#" + customer.CustomerID);
        foreach (var order in customer.Orders)
        {
            Debug.WriteLine("---Order#" + order.OrderID);
        }
    }
}

namespace PocoAndLazy
{
    public partial class _Default : System.Web.UI.Page
    {
        protected void Page_Load(object sender, EventArgs e)
        {
            ModelContext db = new ModelContext();
            var bigCustomers = db.Customers.Where(c => c.Orders.Count > 20);
            foreach (var customer in bigCustomers)
            {
                Debug.WriteLine("Customer#" + customer.CustomerID);
                foreach (var order in customer.Orders)
                {
                    Debug.WriteLine("---Order#" + order.OrderID);
                }
            }
        }
    }
}
```

> ⓘ **NullReferenceException was unhandled by user code**
>
> Object reference not set to an instance of an object.
>
> **Troubleshooting tips:**

POCO Eager Loading

Of course we can add to the constructor of the Customer the initialization of the Orders collection.

```
public Customer()
{
    Orders = new List<Order>();
}
```

But, you and I understand that it still does not load the list of orders. Let's for fun just enable the **Lazy Loading**.

```
ModelContext db = new ModelContext();
db.ContextOptions.LazyLoadingEnabled = true;
var bigCustomers = db.Customers.Where(c => c.Orders.Count > 20);
foreach (var customer in bigCustomers)
{
    Debug.WriteLine("Customer#" + customer.CustomerID);
    foreach (var order in customer.Orders)
```

```
    {
        Debug.WriteLine("---Order#" + order.OrderID);
    }
}
```

We can see in the output:

Customer#ERNSH---Order#10258---Order#10263---Order#10351---Order#10368---
...Customer#QUICK---Order#10273---Order#10285---Order#10286---
...Customer#SAVEA---Order#10324---Order#10393---Order#10398--- ...

If we check the SQL profiler we see N+1 calls to the database (one to get all customers and three to get each of their orders).

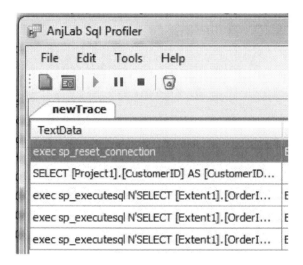

SQL profiler is showing the 1+3 call.

With the use of eager loading, a single query is made.

```
protected void Page_Load (object sender, EventArgs e)
{
    ModelContext db = new ModelContext();
    db.ContextOptions.LazyLoadingEnabled = false;
    var bigCustomers = db.Customers.Include("Orders").Where(c => c.Orders.Count >
20);
    foreach (var customer in bigCustomers)
    {
        Debug.WriteLine("Customer#" + customer.CustomerID);
        foreach (var order in customer.Orders)
        {
```

```
                Debug.WriteLine("---Order#" + order.OrderID);
            }
        }
}
SELECT [Project2].[C1] AS [C1]
        , [Project2].[CustomerID] AS [CustomerID]
        , [Project2].[CompanyName] AS [CompanyName]
        , [Project2].[ContactName] AS [ContactName]
        , ...
FROM (
    SELECT [Project1].[CustomerID] AS [CustomerID]
    , [Project1].[CompanyName] AS [CompanyName]
    , [Project1].[ContactName] AS [ContactName]
    , [Project1].[ContactTitle] AS [ContactTitle]
    , ...1 AS [C1]
    , [Extent3].[OrderID] AS [OrderID], [Extent3].[CustomerID] AS [CustomerID1]
    , [Extent3].[EmployeeID] AS [EmployeeID]
    , [Extent3].[OrderDate] AS [OrderDate]
    , [Extent3].[RequiredDate] AS [RequiredDate]
    , [Extent3].[ShippedDate] AS [ShippedDate]
    , ...
    FROM
        (SELECT [Extent1].[CustomerID] AS [CustomerID]
        , [Extent1].[CompanyName] AS [CompanyName]
        , [Extent1].[ContactName] AS [ContactName]
        , [Extent1].[ContactTitle] AS [ContactTitle]
        , ...
        (SELECT COUNT(1) AS [A1]FROM [dbo].[Orders] AS [Extent2]WHERE
[Extent1].[CustomerID] = [Extent2].[CustomerID]) AS [C1]
        FROM [dbo].[Customers] AS [Extent1] ) AS [Project1]
        LEFT OUTER JOIN [dbo].[Orders] AS [Extent3]
            ON [Project1].[CustomerID] = [Extent3].[CustomerID]
        WHERE [Project1].[C1] > 20) AS [Project2]
        ORDER BY [Project2].[CustomerID] ASC, [Project2].[C2] ASC
```

So without Lazy Loading, nothing is shown until explicit load is called; with Lazy Loading N+1 query is made to the database, and with Eager Loading a single query is made to the database.

How to log with Entity Framework 4.0

Release Date: 26-Aug-11
Url: http://patrickdesjardins.com/blog/?post_type=post&p=26

Logging with Entity Framework is not the same as logging with Linq to SQL. First, you need to have an .edx file with at least one entity declared on it because, to be able to log, a query must be executed. Like the Linq to SQL, to have a log the query needs to be run, and for that it needs to be executed. Here is a snippet of code showing how to log with Entity Framework.

```
NorthwindEntities db = new NorthwindEntities();
var source = db.Customers.Where(c => c.CustomerID.StartsWith("A"));
this.gridEF.DataSource = source;
this.gridEF.DataBind();
sqlEF.Text = (source as ObjectQuery).ToTraceString();
```

The first line contains the Entity Framework ObjectContext that needs to be created first. This is done by adding with Visual Studio a new Item of ADO.NET Entity Data Model. To get the log file, after the execution a call to ToTraceString() is required. This requires a cast to ObjectQuery to the Query. The reason is that the Where clause returns an IQueryable. The ObjectQuery inherits the IQueryable and also a lot of other interface:

```
public class ObjectQuery<T> : ObjectQuery,IOrderedQueryable<T>, IQueryable<T>,
IEnumerable<T>, IOrderedQueryable, IQueryable,IEnumerable, IListSource
```

The ToTraceString() comes from the inherited class ObjectQuery.

The output of ToTraceString() is the SQL statement executed. Here is an example:

```
SELECT [Extent1].[CustomerID] AS [CustomerID]
    , [Extent1].[CompanyName] AS [CompanyName]
FROM [dbo].[Customers] AS [Extent1]
WHERE [Extent1].[CustomerID] LIKE N'A%'
```

This is interesting if we compare the generated SQL from the Entity Framework and from the Linq to SQL. The main difference is that Linq to SQL will use parameters substitution instead of directly adding the value to the query. You can see it in the Where clause of the SQL query. The Linq to SQL code looks like:

```
WHERE [Extent1].[CustomerID] LIKE @p0
```

and the Entity Framework looks like:

```
WHERE [Extent1].[CustomerID] LIKE N'A%'
```

To conclude, if you want to log an Entity Framework generated SQL Query do not forget to add a condition statement when you move into your production environment.

How to convert an Entity Framework that uses file database to server database

Release Date: 05-Sep-11
Url: http://patrickdesjardins.com/blog/?post_type=post&p=155

Entity Framework creates a copy of the database when generating from the database and creates an .mdf for the project, and uses this database. This is good for a small project but once you want to use SQL Profiler or to use the real database, it is not.

To do the switch, only one place needs to be changed and it is the app.config or, if you are in a web environment, the web.config.

Here is the generated connection string generated, and after the modification.

```
<add name="NorthWindContainer"

connectionString="metadata=res://*/FromNorthWind.csdl|res://*/FromNorthWind.ssdl|r
es://*/FromNorthWind.msl;
    provider=System.Data.SqlClient;
    provider connection string='Data Source=.\SQLEXPRESS;
    AttachDbFilename=|DataDirectory|\northwnd.mdf;
    Integrated Security=True;
    Connect Timeout=30;
    User Instance=True;
    MultipleActiveResultSets=True'"
    providerName="System.Data.EntityClient" />
<add name="NorthWindContainer"

connectionString="metadata=res://*/FromNorthWind.csdl|res://*/FromNorthWind.ssdl|r
es://*/FromNorthWind.msl;
    provider=System.Data.SqlClient;
    provider connection string='Data Source=.\SQLEXPRESS;
    Initial Catalog=Northwind;
    Integrated Security=True;
    Connection Timeout=60;
    multipleactiveresultsets=true'"
    providerName="System.Data.EntityClient" />
```

This simple modification does the trick and you are ready to go.

Entity Framework Visual Designer

Release Date: 08-Sep-11
Url: http://patrickdesjardins.com/blog/?post_type=post&p=76

The visual designer is inside Visual Studio. It is a tool that gives you the opportunity to change the Data Model visually. To be able to take a tour of it, let's create a new Console Project and add a new Entity Framework Data Model.

Once the Console project is created, add a new item to the project.

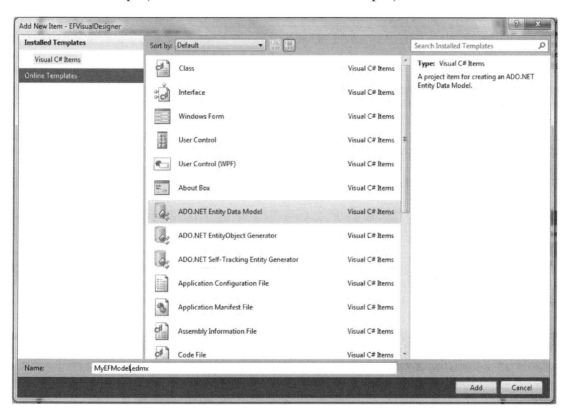

From there, the second wizard step will be to select what the model will contain. We can start from a blank model or from a database. Because we want to see some functionality of the Visual Designer, let's select to load the Entity Model from an existing database. For this example, I will select Microsoft's AdventureWorks 2008R2 SR1 database (http://msftdbprodsamples.codeplex.com/).

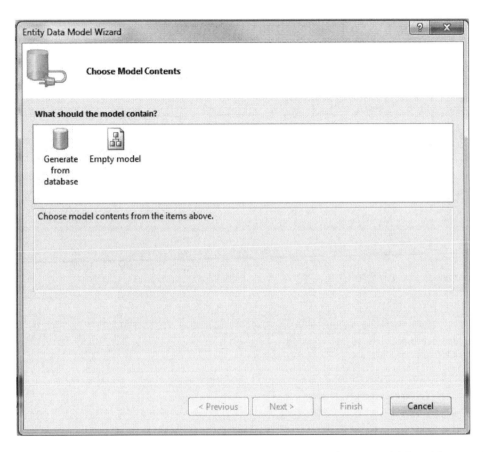

For the purpose of this exercise, when the Wizard asks you which table you desire to import into your Entity Model file, select them all. For the moment, let's just add tables and not Views or Stored Procedures. After that you will see a file in your project called "MyEFModel.edmx". This file, if you double click on it, will open the Visual Designer.

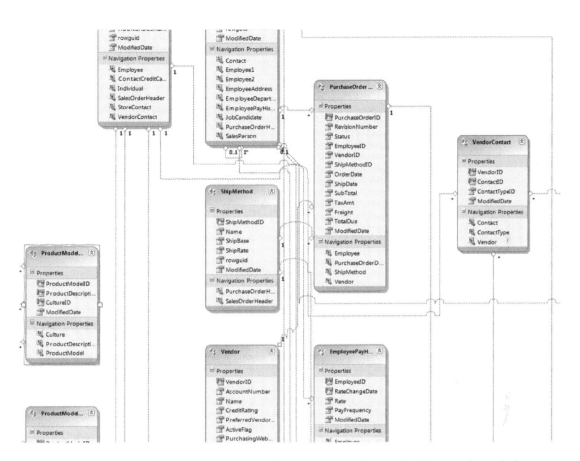

When the Visual Designer is open, it is important to have the Properties windows open (View>Properties Window / F4).

Entity Properties

Let's see available properties of an Entity. To see them, click on an Entity from the Visual Designer. You should see some properties like the screenshot below.

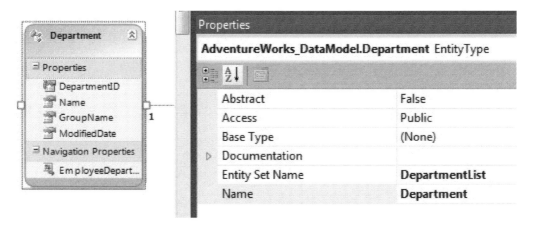

The two most important properties are the **Name** and the **Entity Set Name**. The name represents the Entity single unit. It is usually the table name. For the Department, the name is Department. So data that come from this Entity will be "Department." If a list of departments is required it will be an IEnumerable<**Department**>. The Entity Set Name is identified inside the Object Context to retrieve the department. A metaphor could be a bag of items. The bag name is the Entity Set Name and items inside that bag are the Name. So, if I want to have 10 departments with a unique identifier under 10, I will need to go in the bag called "DepartmentList" to get a collection of "Department." By the way, the DepartmentList name is a modification of mine. Initially, the Entity Set Name was the same as the name: department.

```
var db = new AdventureWorks_DataEntities();
var listOfDepartement = db.DepartmentList.Where(dept => dept.DepartmentID <= 10);
foreach (var d in listOfDepartement)
{
    Console.WriteLine(string.Format("{0}:{1}",d.DepartmentID,d.Name));
}
```

file:///C:/Users/patrick/documents/visual studio 2010/Projects/EFVisualDesigner/EFVisualDesigner...

```
1:Engineering
2:Tool Design
3:Sales
4:Marketing
5:Purchasing
6:Research and Development
7:Production
8:Production Control
9:Human Resources
10:Finance
```

All departments with a unique identifier under 10.

The second line that has a variable named listOfDepartment is in fact an IQueryable collection where the T is Department (the Name of the Entity).

```
var db = new AdventureWorks_DataEntities();
var listOfDepartment = db.DepartmentList.Where(dept => dept.DepartmentID <= 10);
foreach (var d in listOfDepartment)
{
    Console.WriteLine(string.Format("{0}:{1}", d.DepartmentID, d.Name));
}
```

Line 2 could have been:

```
IQueryable listOfDepartment = db.DepartmentList.Where(dept => dept.DepartmentID <= 10);
```

Entity Attributes Properties

It is also possible to set properties on an attribute. When the model is generated from the database, all the hard work is already done. When you do it the other way, by creating the model objects first, you will need to create those attributes by hand and they will be converted into table columns. Depending on the type of the attribute, property options will vary.

If the attribute is the **Entity Key**, this will have a special option like StoreGeneratedPattern.

If the attribute is a relationship attribute called **Navigation Property,** other properties like the association are required. Furthermore, the association's multiplicity is set within this attribute.

Another type of attribute is a simple value. The Value Designer calls them Scalar property. This kind of entity attribute contains a value that will later be a simple column without any key.

The last kind of attribute that an entity can have is **Complex Property**. Complex Property is a way to organize multiple attributes together. Behind, it is like having multiple attributes, but from the object perspective it will be inside a sub-object.

Association Properties

Association attributes contain the multiplicity of each endpoint, it also contains whether cascade delete is required, and so on.

This is a small wrapup of the Visual Designer of Entity Framework 4.0.

Entity Framework XML file: CSDL, SSDL, and MSL

Release Date: 10-Sep-11
Url: http://patrickdesjardins.com/blog/?post_type=post&p=126

Entity Framework is built around three XML files - the CSDL, the SSDL, and the MSL.

The **CSDL** acronym is for "Conceptual schema definition language." This file describes the model object.

The **SSDL** acronym is for "Store schema definition language" and defines the storage model.

The **MSL** acronym is for "Mapping specification language" and is the bridge between CSDL and SSDL, or in other words maps the model and the storage.

Theses files are handled by Entity Framework and most of the time will not be required to be edited by hand. Visual Studio 2010 has a create Visual Designer that lets the developer go through a graphical user interface to create the model, to edit it and also to map everything.

Nevertheless, it is always good to know what's going on under the hood. To get those three files, the project with the entity model must have been compiled with the option to display the metadata of the conceptual model into the Bin folder. By default, these three metadata files are embedded in the assembly. To change the embedded to an external output, you need to open the Visual Designer of the Entity model. Click anywhere in a blank spot (not an entity or an association) and open the Properties window. One property of the ConceptualEntityModel is called "Metadata Artifact Processing" and by default is set to "Embed in Output Assembly." You need to change this to "Copy to Output Directory."

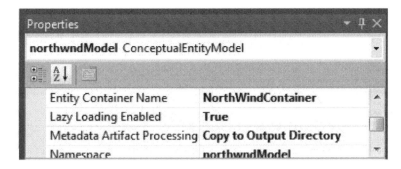

This will output the CSDL, SSDL and MSL files in the bin folder.

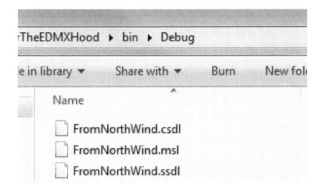

For more information about the CSDL, SSDL and MSL XML files, wait a few days.

Conceptual schema definition languague (CSDL)

Release Date: 11-Sep-11
Url: http://patrickdesjardins.com/blog/?post_type=post&p=131

The Conceptual Schema Definition Language (CSDL) is an XML file generated while compiling a conceptual entity model (EDMX). If you do not see the .csdl file in your output folder (bin folder), it might be because the conceptual entity model is set to embed this file. This can be easily changed.

The CSDL file is in fact an XML with three distinct sections. If we open the NorthWind database .csdl file (the conceptual entity model has been generated from the Microsoft Northwind database) we can see these three sections:

```
FromNorthWind.csdl
  1      <?xml version="1.0" encoding="utf-8"?>
  2     <Schema Namespace="northwndModel" Alias="Self" xmlns:annotation="http://schemas.mi
  3        <EntityContainer Name="NorthWindContainer" annotation:LazyLoadingEnabled="true">
 61        <EntityType Name="Categories">
 71        <EntityType Name="CustomerDemographics">         Section #1 (Entity Container)
 79        <EntityType Name="Customers">
 97        <EntityType Name="Employees">
124        <EntityType Name="Order_Details">
137        <EntityType Name="Orders">                       Section #2 (Entity Type)
160        <EntityType Name="Products">
178        <EntityType Name="Region">
186        <EntityType Name="Shippers">
195        <EntityType Name="Suppliers">
213        <EntityType Name="sysdiagrams">
223        <EntityType Name="Territories">
233        <Association Name="FK_Products_Categories">
245        <Association Name="FK_Orders_Customers">
257        <Association Name="FK_Employees_Employees">
269        <Association Name="FK_Orders_Employees">
281        <Association Name="FK_Order_Details_Orders">
293        <Association Name="FK_Order_Details_Products">   Section #3 (Association)
305        <Association Name="FK_Orders_Shippers">
317        <Association Name="FK_Products_Suppliers">
329        <Association Name="FK_Territories_Region">
341        <Association Name="CustomerCustomerDemo">
345        <Association Name="EmployeeTerritories">
349      </Schema>
```

The three parts of a CSDL file:

The first section is the **Entity Container**. This section contains some information concerning the global container. In the example I created with the NorthWind database, I had chosen to call the NorthWind Conceptual Model "NorthWinContainer." This is the name that we would use inside the project to get the Object Context.

```
<EntityContainer Name="NorthWindContainer" annotation:LazyLoadingEnabled="true">
```

Inside, the code would have been called this way:

```
var db = new NorthWindContainer();
var collectionData = db.Territories;
```

The second attribute of the XML is the **LazyLoading** that is enabled in that case. This option in code can be found in the ContextOption.

```
var db = new NorthWindContainer();
Console.WriteLine("Lazy loading : " + db.ContextOptions.LazyLoadingEnabled);
```

This value can be set also in the Conceptual Entity Model.

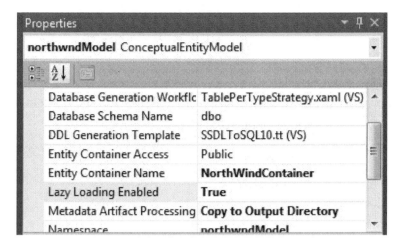

This first part of the CSDL file also contains all entities and association definitions. It is not in this part of the files that properties of these entities are defined. In fact, it contains only the name and namespace. For the associations, it also only contains the two entities related.

```
<EntitySet Name="Categories" EntityType="northwndModel.Categories" />
<EntitySet Name="CustomerDemographics"
EntityType="northwndModel.CustomerDemographics" />
<EntitySet Name="Customers" EntityType="northwndModel.Customers" />
......
<AssociationSet Name="FK_Products_Categories"
Association="northwndModel.FK_Products_Categories">
  <End Role="Categories" EntitySet="Categories" />
  <End Role="Products" EntitySet="Products" />
</AssociationSet>
........
```

The second section of the CSDL file contains more meat about the entity. The unique identifier (key) of the entity is defined there and also all properties. Each property contains its metadata like the type, if the value can be nullable, and other metadata depending on the type. For example, an integer does not have a MaxLength attribute but a String does.

```
  <EntityType Name="Categories">
  <Key>
    <PropertyRef Name="CategoryID" />
  </Key>
  <Property Name="CategoryID" Type="Int32" Nullable="false"
annotation:StoreGeneratedPattern="Identity" />
  <Property Name="CategoryName" Type="String" Nullable="false" MaxLength="15"
Unicode="true" FixedLength="false" />
```

```
  <Property Name="Description" Type="String" MaxLength="Max" Unicode="true"
FixedLength="false" />
  <Property Name="Picture" Type="Binary" MaxLength="Max" FixedLength="false" />
  <NavigationProperty Name="Products"
Relationship="northwndModel.FK_Products_Categories" FromRole="Categories"
ToRole="Products" />
</EntityType>
<EntityType Name="CustomerDemographics">
  <Key>
    <PropertyRef Name="CustomerTypeID" />
  </Key>
  <Property Name="CustomerTypeID" Type="String" Nullable="false" MaxLength="10"
Unicode="true" FixedLength="true" />
  <Property Name="CustomerDesc" Type="String" MaxLength="Max" Unicode="true"
FixedLength="false" />
  <NavigationProperty Name="Customers"
Relationship="northwndModel.CustomerCustomerDemo" FromRole="CustomerDemographics"
ToRole="Customers" />
</EntityType>
```

The last section of the file contains detail about the association previously described in the first section. The association name concords with the AssociationSet_FK's name of the first section. This will define both the ending point and their multiplicity. Also, the property reference is defined.

```
<Association Name="FK_Products_Categories">
  <End Role="Categories" Type="northwndModel.Categories" Multiplicity="0..1" />
  <End Role="Products" Type="northwndModel.Products" Multiplicity="*" />
  <ReferentialConstraint>
    <Principal Role="Categories">
      <PropertyRef Name="CategoryID" />
    </Principal>
    <Dependent Role="Products">
      <PropertyRef Name="CategoryID" />
    </Dependent>
  </ReferentialConstraint>
</Association>
```

To conclude, this file should not really be modified by hand. Visual Studio 2010 visual designer is easier to use, less error prone and can save you a lot of time. Also, if your database is already defined, all the schemas can be pulled from it.

Persistence-ignorant Object

Release Date: 16-Sep-11
Url: http://patrickdesjardins.com/blog/?post_type=post&p=208

What is a persistence-ignorant object?

It is an object that is not aware of any persistence. It does not know if it will persist with a database (or which one), or if it will be saved in an XML file or a binary one. It is ignorant of that information. A POCO object is a persistence-ignorant class.

POCO means "Plain Old CLR Object"

You can have POCO or peristence-ignorant objects with Entity Framework.

Model Defined Function with Entity Framework

Release Date: 17-Sep-11
Author: Url: http://patrickdesjardins.com/blog/?post_type=post&p=211

Entity Framework lets you create a **Model Defined Function** that is a function that will be executed server side on SQL server.

Let's say that you you have a table with three columns: idProduct, Quantity, Price. You want to have the total amount for each row. In SQL you would have done something like

```
SELECT idProduct, Quantity, Price, Quantity*Price as Total
FROM Product
```
You could also get this total with a Linq to Entity query like

```
var allRows = db.Products
               .Select(prod=>new Product(prod.idProduct
                               , prod.Quantity
                               , prod.Price
                               , prod.Quantity * prod.Price);
```

The problem is that with bigger mathematics functions that may require more than two fields on a lot of objects, this would require you to get a lot of data for the calculation. If you just need the total, instead of returning the price, quantity, etc you just need to use the model-defined function and you are ready.

Defining the Model-Defined Function

The first step is to open the Entity Model (.edmx) file in XML. The second step is to search for the CSDL section (you can search for "edmx:ConceptualModels"). Inside this, you need to add your function inside the schema tag.

Here is an example:

```
<Function Name="Total" ReturnType="Decimal">
  <Parameter Name="p" Type="NorthwindModel.Product" />
  <DefiningExpression>(p.Price * p.Quantity) </DefiningExpression>
</Function>
```

The **Parameter Name** is the name used in the calculus and the **Type** is the type of this parameter. This must be a type of the Entity Model. The mapping will be done to the table in the database later. In the DefiningExpression you could use some SQL function like CAST.

The third step is to add some C# code to be able to call this new function. This is where the EDMFunction attribute comes into action. This attribute needs to be placed over a static method that will have the same return type as the one defined in the function attribute ReturnType. Also, the parameter needs to be of the same type defined in the parameter element of the function.

```
[EdmFunction("Northwind", "Total")]
public static decimal Total(Product product)
{
    throw new NotSupportedException("Totalcan only be used in a LINQ to Entities
query");
}
```

This static method can be placed wherever you want. You can insert this method in a class that holds all those EDMFunctions but the best practice is to partial class the related class. This is perfect for a class generated by the Entity Framework because even if you synchronize it won't be erased. It is also good if you have a POCO class because it won't dirty it with persistent functions. Do not forget to add the **System.Data.Objects.DataClasses** namespace.

How to use EDMFunction

The Entity Model Function is defined inside the CSDL tag; it is also defined in the C# and finally we can call it. As you have seen, this method is only a shell and does not have any code inside. It can only be executed on the server side.

Here is an example:

```
var result = (from p in db.Products
              select new { p.ProductID, DetailTotal = MyStaticClass.Total(p)
          }).ToList();
```

Entity Framework Object Context Life Cycle compared to Linq to SQL Data Context Life Cycle

Release Date: 22-Sep-11
Url: http://patrickdesjardins.com/blog/?post_type=post&p=248

Entity Framework Object Context

The Object Context created from the Entity Model holds all objects during its life cycle. But this one should catch your attention because it can become very large with all the objects state tracking. Remembering hundreds or thousands of object states is not a simple task. Moreover, this object caches values. If you have a medium or a big application the RAM memory can become very high, and not only that but the performance in general will decline.

ObjectContext class inherits from **IDisposable** interface so you can, and should, use USING statement when using Entity Framework. The problem with this approach is that the object tracking is lost the next line after everything is garbaged. So, it solves only the problem concerning the memory. If you are getting information and know that you are going to change it then it is better not to use USING, but still use .Dispose at the end. But, if you get information only, or you update the information right away, it is better to use USING.

States

Entity Framework has five possibles states. The first one is when adding a new object. The state is then *Added*. Once saved the state of this object becomes *Unchanged*. When an object is deleted, its state changes to *Deleted* until the object context saves it to the database. From there, it goes to *Detached*. The *Modified* state is a little bit more tricky. When using Entity

Object (not POCO) when a scalar object is changed, the state automatically changes to *Modified*. For POCO, it requires a call to *DetectChanges* to be able to mark the object as *Modified* or to change it manually. When an object is loaded from the object context, its default state is *unchanged*.

Here is a complete example that uses the *Northwind* database and Entity Framework where the state changes from the creating to the removing phase.

Let's take this code that created a new *Order* for a *Customer* and then remove it.

```
var db = new NorthwindEntities(); //Add a new Order
var firstCustomer = db.Customers.First();
Debug.WriteLine("---Customer loaded---");
Debug.WriteLine("FirstCustomer:" +
db.ObjectStateManager.GetObjectStateEntry(firstCustomer).State);
var newOrder = new Orders(); // db.CreateObject<Orders>(); would do the samething
Debug.WriteLine("---Orders Created---");
Debug.WriteLine("FirstCustomer:" +
db.ObjectStateManager.GetObjectStateEntry(firstCustomer).State);
Debug.WriteLine("newOrder: N/A because not yet inside the ObjectContext so not
state yet. Could attach before adding to get state but not applicable now because
the key is generated by the db and can't attack without key.");
Debug.WriteLine("newOrder:" +
db.ObjectStateManager.GetObjectStateEntry(newOrder).State);
firstCustomer.Orders.Add(newOrder);
Debug.WriteLine("---Orders added---");
Debug.WriteLine("FirstCustomer:" +
db.ObjectStateManager.GetObjectStateEntry(firstCustomer).State);
Debug.WriteLine("newOrder:" +
db.ObjectStateManager.GetObjectStateEntry(newOrder).State);
db.SaveChanges();
Debug.WriteLine("---Object Context save---");
Debug.WriteLine("FirstCustomer:" +
db.ObjectStateManager.GetObjectStateEntry(firstCustomer).State);
Debug.WriteLine("newOrder:" +
db.ObjectStateManager.GetObjectStateEntry(newOrder).State);
Debug.WriteLine("---Remove the created object---");
firstCustomer.Orders.Remove(newOrder);
Debug.WriteLine("FirstCustomer:" +
db.ObjectStateManager.GetObjectStateEntry(firstCustomer).State);
Debug.WriteLine("newOrder:" +
db.ObjectStateManager.GetObjectStateEntry(newOrder).State);
db.SaveChanges();
Debug.WriteLine("---Object Context save---");
Debug.WriteLine("FirstCustomer:" +
db.ObjectStateManager.GetObjectStateEntry(firstCustomer).State);
```

```
Debug.WriteLine("newOrder:" +
db.ObjectStateManager.GetObjectStateEntry(newOrder).State);
}
```

The output of this code is :

```
---Customer loaded
---FirstCustomer:Unchanged
---Orders Created
---FirstCustomer:UnchangednewOrder: N/A because not yet inside the ObjectContext
so not state yet. Could attach before adding to get state
---Orders added
---FirstCustomer:UnchangednewOrder:Added
---Object Context save
---FirstCustomer:UnchangednewOrder:Unchanged
---Remove the created object
---FirstCustomer:UnchangednewOrder:Modified
---Object Context save
---FirstCustomer:UnchangednewOrder:Unchanged
```

We could also explore the state with the event.

```
var db = new NorthwindEntities();
db.ObjectStateManager.ObjectStateManagerChanged
    += new
System.ComponentModel.CollectionChangeEventHandler(ObjectStateManager_ObjectStateM
anagerChanged); //Get existing Customer that has Ordervar
customersWithOrder = db.Customers.Where(customer => customer.Orders.Count>15);
//Add a new Ordervar
firstCustomer = db.Customers.First();
var newOrder = new Orders(); // db.CreateObject<Orders>(); would do the samething
firstCustomer.Orders.Add(newOrder);
db.SaveChanges();
firstCustomer.Orders.Remove(newOrder);
db.DeleteObject(newOrder);db.SaveChanges();
```

This produces:

```
-->LifeCycle.Customers
-->Add-->LifeCycle.Orders
-->Add-->LifeCycle.Orders
-->Add-->LifeCycle.Orders
-->Add-->LifeCycle.Orders
-->Add-->LifeCycle.Orders
-->Add-->LifeCycle.Orders
-->Add-->LifeCycle.Orders
-->Add-->LifeCycle.Orders
-->Add-->LifeCycle.Orders
-->Remove-->LifeCycle.Orders
```

```
-->Remove
```

I prefer the first output because it is clearer.

Thread

The *ObjectContext* class is not thread safe. You must have one object context per thread or create your own thread synchronization process.

Linq to SQL Data Context

As the *ObjectContext*, the *DataContext* class holds the track of each object state. It knows what has been modified, deleted or added. Also, Linq to SQL uses state even if nothing has changed in the object. When loaded, the object will be *Unchanged*, or if you create a new object or deserialize an object it will be *Untracked*.

When an object is attached, by default its state will be *PossiblyModified* and this is until the *SubmitChange*. The next three states are very common: *ToBeInserted*, *ToBeModified*, *ToBeDeleted*. The last possible state is when an object has been *SubmitChange* when it was *ToBeDeleted*. When this happens, the object is still in the DataContext but with the *Deleted* state.

Thread

The Linq to SQL *DataContext* class is not thread safe. It should not be static, either

Where and when should EF or Linq2Sql live

Matt Warren, software achitect at Microsoft on the C# programming language product team and member of the team that created LINQ to SQL, explains this question with a design pattern (http://bit.ly/1jx249o). This ORM should be treated as the Unit of Work pattern.

A **Unit of Work** keeps track of everything you do during a business transaction that can affect the database. When you are done, it figures out everything that needs to be done to alter the database as a result of your work.

That's it. The ORM object should live until the business task is done. For example, you need to edit an employee, you create the object when loading it, it is alive until it is saved or the task is cancelled. It does not remain in the memory until the application closes.

How to use POCO Object with Entity Framework and use lazy, eager, and explicit loading

Release Date: 14-Mar-12
Url: http://patrickdesjardins.com/blog/?post_type=post&p=805

When using a POCO Object you have less stuff automatically done by Entity Framework. This does not mean that you have less power with this framework.

You can still use Entity Framework with a complex object by using many different loadings like lazy loading, eager loading and explicit loading.

Eager Loading with POCO

Eager Loading with Entity Framework and POCO means that the object will be loaded with one query but you need to specify which related objects you want to load. This is pretty much the most efficient way to do it, if you know that you will use most of the data objects.

```
var dbContext = new NDbContext("...");
dbContext.Configuration.LazyLoadingEnabled = false;
var XYZs = dbContext.XYZs.Include("MyPropertyThatLinkToAnObjectInsideXYZObject");
foreach (var x in XYZs)
{
    dbContext.ObjectContext().LoadProperty(x, o => o.XYZInsideObject);
    Console.WriteLine("x contain the subobject : " + x.XYZInsideObject.Id);
}
```

This will produce only one query to the database that will contain a JOIN between the table of XYZ and XYZInsideObject.

Explicit loading with POCO

Explicit means that you want to load on demand the information of a related object. This means that you load the information only if desired and you need to specify explicitly when to load it.

```
var dbContext = new NDbContext("...");
dbContext.Configuration.LazyLoadingEnabled = true;
var XYZs = dbContext.XYZs;
foreach (var x in XYZs)
{
```

```
    dbContext.ObjectContext().LoadProperty(x, o => o.XYZInsideObject);
    Console.WriteLine("x contain the subobject : " + x.XYZInsideObject.Id);
}
```

As you can see, in line 7 it uses *ObjectContext()*; this method is created by the developer if required when using POCO. This needs to be added to your custom *DbContext*. Normally, this is generated by Entity Framework but since we work with POCO, it is inside the *DbContext* created manually.

```
public class NDbContext : DbContext
{
    public ObjectContext ObjectContext()
    {
        return (this as IObjectContextAdapter).ObjectContext;
    }

    //...
    public DbSet<XYZ> XYZs { get; set; }
    //...
}
```

DbContext hides the complexity of the *ObjectContext* but to use **Explicit**, it is required to have access to it.

Lazy loading with POCO object and Entity Framework

POCO entities can have proxy objects that support change tracking or lazy loading (differed loading). That means that for using lazy loading you need to activate to *true* the property *LazyLoadingEnabled* and*ProxyCreationEnabled*. One particularity is that each navigation property must be declared as public and virtual. This will work for a Property to one object or any property that is inherited from ICollection<>.

```
var dbContext = new NDbContext("...");
dbContext.Configuration.LazyLoadingEnabled = true;
dbContext.Configuration.ProxyCreationEnabled = true; /*Default value is true, do
not need to set it here*/
var xyzs = dbContext.XYZs;
foreach (var x in XYZs)
{
    Console.WriteLine("x contain the subobject : " + x.XYZInsideObject.Id);
}
```

If you try the code above with **LazyLoadingEnabled** to false, the code will crash with a NullReferenceException to line 9, where the console tries to access the property, because it is not loaded.

Entity Framework with POCO

Complex objects are well loaded and the way you want with Entity Framework. You can **Lazy load** which will create more queries to the database than **Explicit load** or you can **Eager load** and have less queries to the database but more data in the same time. What is great is that you can have all those types of technical stuff under the same project to use the best one for each task.

Entity Framework using POCO and custom SQL Database Schema

Release Date: 15-Mar-12
Url: http://patrickdesjardins.com/blog/?post_type=post&p=815

First of all, the code in this post is not all mine. I do not remember the source and if anyone knows please let me know and I will acknowledge the creator.

Entity Framework uses the default schema when accessing the database. It uses the "dbo" one usually.

You may need to use Entity Framework with different schema. This can be done by overriding the creation of the model that is done with the method "OnModelCreating." This can be done inside your custom *DbObject* class.

```
public string DefaultSchema { get; set; }

protected override void OnModelCreating(DbModelBuilder modelBuilder)
{
    if (!String.IsNullOrEmpty(DefaultSchema))
    {
        var entityMethod = modelBuilder.GetType().GetMethod("Entity");
        foreach (PropertyInfo dbSet in GetType().GetProperties().Where(t =>
t.PropertyType.IsGenericType &&
t.PropertyType.GetGenericTypeDefinition().Equals(typeof (DbSet<>))))
        {
            var entityType = dbSet.PropertyType.GetGenericArguments();
            var entityMethodGeneric = entityMethod.MakeGenericMethod(entityType);
            var entityConfig = entityMethodGeneric.Invoke(modelBuilder, null);
            var toTableMethod = entityConfig.GetType().GetMethod("ToTable", new[]
{typeof (string), typeof (string)});
            var tableName = GetTableName(entityType.FirstOrDefault());
```

```
        toTableMethod.Invoke(entityConfig, new object[] {tableName,
DefaultSchema});
        }
    }
    base.OnModelCreating(modelBuilder);
}

private string GetTableName(Type type)
{
    var tableAttribute =
type.GetCustomAttributes(false).OfType<System.ComponentModel.DataAnnotations.Table
Attribute>().FirstOrDefault();
    return tableAttribute == null ? type.Name : tableAttribute.Name;
}
```

With the code above, you can set the DefaultSchema and the query will be made with the schema desired.

Entity Framework and the missing class EntityConfiguration

Release Date: 16-Mar-12
Url: http://patrickdesjardins.com/blog/?post_type=post&p=822

Many blogs were written with **EntityConfiguration** class which does not exist in EF4.1 release version and above.

If you need to do the mapping of your properties with table columns, you should not use **EntityTypeConfiguration** or **ComplexTypeConfiguration** class. Those classes are in the namespace "System.Data.Entity.ModelConfiguration".

This will let you in your *DbContext* class override the method "OnModelCreating" and set the configuration desired.

```
protected override void OnModelCreating(DbModelBuilder modelBuilder)
{
    //...
    modelBuilder.Configurations.Add(new MyClassConfiguration());
    base.OnModelCreating(modelBuilder);
}

//In an other class:
public class MyClassConfiguration : EntityTypeConfiguration<MyClass>
{
    public MyClassConfiguration()
    {
```

```
        ToTable("MySuperOtherNameTable");
        Property(c => c.Code).HasColumnName("Code_Col1");
        Property(c => c.Name).HasColumnName("Name_FR_CANADA");
    }
}
```

This allows you to have Entity Framework on a database that has been constructed without having the same name of your model. It uses the fluent interface of Entity Framework to accomplish this task. Entity Framework lets you do it by attribute also (this will be discussed later). Of course, this requires more manual labor but can be great to bypass some objects, one object or even a part of an object. Indeed, this can be used only on a few properties of your object and lets Entity Framework handle the rest of your object automatically.

Entity Framework with POCO object using Data Annotations for database tables columns mapping

Release Date: 17-Mar-12
Url: http://patrickdesjardins.com/blog/?post_type=post&p=827

It is possible when using a POCO object with Entity Framework to use <u>DataAnnotation</u> or to use the Fluent API.

The DataAnnotation requires adding a reference to "<u>System.Component.Model.DataAnnotations</u>"

```
using System.ComponentModel.DataAnnotations;
```

This is pretty easy but has the disadvantage of corrupting your POCO object with a database indicator (column name).

```
public class MyObject
{
    public int ID { get; set; }

    [Column("Code_SuperWeirdTableColumnName")]
    public string Code { get; set; }

    [Column("Name_EN_USA")]
    public string Name { get; set; }
}
```

As you can see in the example above, the property *Code* is linked to

Code_SuperWeirdTableColumnName which lets you have a proper name inside your model object and still use another name in the table. It is the same for the *Name* of the *MyObject* class. It will be linked to Name_EN_USA.

Entity Framework 4.3 with **POCO** and track change

Release Date: 18-Mar-12
Url: http://patrickdesjardins.com/blog/?post_type=post&p=835

Entity Framework has changed between version 4.1 and 4.3 quite a lot concerning track change. Most of the time, you will read on the Internet that you need the **ObjectStateManager** property of the DbContext you create for your POCO. With Entity Framework version 4.3 you won't see that property.

The version 4.3 of EF contains a property Configuration where you can set the *LazyLoading*, the *ProxyCreation*, the *AutoDetectChange* and the *ValidateOnSave*. By default, all these options are set to True.

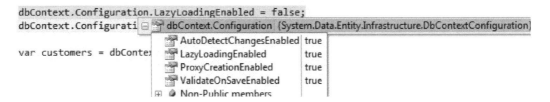

Here is an example where I have disabled the **Lazy Loading** and also disabled the **Proxy Creation**.

```
var dbContext = new MyDbContext(connectionString);
dbContext.Configuration.LazyLoadingEnabled = false;
dbContext.Configuration.ProxyCreationEnabled = false;
dbContext.Configuration.AutoDetectChangesEnabled = true;
dbContext.Configuration.ValidateOnSaveEnabled = false;
var myObjects = dbContext.MyObject.Include("MySubObject");
foreach (var c in myObjects)
{
    c.UpdateDate = DateTime.Now.ToString();
}
dbContext.SaveChanges();
```

This will automatically update the field *UpdateDate* to the database. If *AutoDetectChange* is set to False, the *DbContext* will not be notified that a change has been made.

```
dbContext.Configuration.LazyLoadingEnabled = false;
dbContext.Configuration.ProxyCreationEnabled = false;
dbContext.Configuration.AutoDetectChangesEnabled = true;
dbContext.Configuration.ValidateOnSaveEnabled = false;
```

The code above will not update to the database when executing **dbContext.SaveChanges()**.

If you want to do it manually, you will need to call the **dbContext.ChangeTracker.DetectChanges()**.

```
var dbContext = new MyDbContext(connectionString);
dbContext.Configuration.LazyLoadingEnabled = false;
dbContext.Configuration.ProxyCreationEnabled = false;
dbContext.Configuration.AutoDetectChangesEnabled = false;
dbContext.Configuration.ValidateOnSaveEnabled = false;
var myObjects = dbContext.MyObject.Include("MySubObject");
foreach (var c in myObjects)
{
    c.UpdateDate = DateTime.Now.ToString();
}
dbContext.ChangeTracker.DetectChanges();
dbContext.SaveChanges();
```

As you can see in the code above, the detect changes has been called manually.

You can see the state of each object by looping into the ChangeTracker.Entries().

```
var e = dbContext.ChangeTracker.Entries();
foreach (var dbEntityEntry in e)
{
    Console.WriteLine(dbEntityEntry.State);
}
```

The code above will display the state of all objects modified even if the **AutoDetectChangesEnabled** is set to false. Of course, if this is set to False and you do not call dbContext.ChangeTracker.DetectChanges() before checking the *ChangeTracker* all states will be set to unmodified. One interesting thing to notice is that the Entries property contains all objects and sub-objects modified. If you change one property to one object, all its sub-objects will also be inside Entries().

Entity Framework 4.3 without ObjectStateManager, how to verify if an object changed

Release Date: 19-Mar-12
Url: http://patrickdesjardins.com/blog/?post_type=post&p=849

Previously, a few months ago, it was possible to access the ObjectStateManager and to use the method GetObjectStateEntry with the object desired to get the state.

```
Customer customer = //...
ObjectStateEntry ose = context.ObjectStateManager.GetObjectStateEntry(customer);
Console.WriteLine("Customer object state: {0}", ose.State);
customer.Country = "USA";
Console.WriteLine("Customer object state: {0}", ose.State);
```

Version EF4.3 doesn't have the ObjectStateManager available. It is possible to get the state but with the property ChangeTracker.

To see a specific object state you will need this property, the ChangeTracker, with a Linq query.

```
var e = dbContext.ChangeTracker.Entries<Customer>().Single(p => p.Entity ==
myCustomer);
Console.WriteLine("Customer state: " + e.State);
```

ChangeTracker.Entries can be generic as the example above or not. In both cases, it returns a list of objects that are listed by the tracker. It doesn't mean that all objects inside the tracker have changed. The Linq query, with the Single() method, will search to get a Single correspondence to your object by comparing the Entity inside the Entry list to the customer that is wanting to get the state.

The model backing the context has changed since the database was created, EF4.3/5.0

Release Date: 19-Mar-12
Url: http://patrickdesjardins.com/blog/?post_type=post&p=856

Entity Framework version 5.0 (and since 4.1) can throw the exception that the model and the database cannot be mapped correctly. In fact, EF is saying that the model has changed since the database has been created.

The model backing the "MyContext" context has changed since the database was created. Consider using Code First Migrations to update the database (http://go.microsoft.com/fwlink/?LinkId=238269)

To resolve this problem, you will find on the Web a lot of solutions but most of them work with previous versions of Entity Framework 5.0.

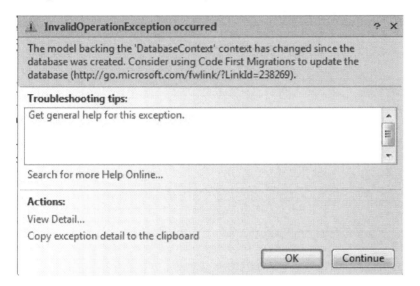

The solution from this version is to use the static method SetInitializer and bind to the context a Null value. If you are working on a Web solution, the best position to write the code is in the Application_Start of your Global.asax.cs file.

```
protected void Application_Start()
{
    AreaRegistration.RegisterAllAreas();
    RegisterRoutes(RouteTable.Routes);
    //...
    Database.SetInitializer<MyContext>(null);
}
```

Using this code removes the error and lets you handle manually the creation of the database.

Entity Framework 4.3 and ProxyCreationEnabled

Release Date: 20-Mar-12
Url: http://patrickdesjardins.com/blog/?post_type=post&p=867

The property ProxyCreationEnabled is by default set to True. This property is required to be able to do LazyLoading and also to keep track of changes to the object.

But in some situations you may need to set it to false. One case is to gain on performance. Entity Framework will generate a proxy class which contains some overhead that will contain the previous state of the object. Furthermore, creating an object with a proxy makes them not serializable. Finally, some controls like Telerik suite (version 2012.1.214.340), cannot bind to proxy classes.

To set the DbContext to false for proxy, you need to set the property Configuration.ProxyCreationEnable = false. This property is available to any DbContext object.

Entity Framework 4.3 POCO object relationship zero to many

Release Date: 21-Mar-12
Url: http://patrickdesjardins.com/blog/?post_type=post&p=872

If you have a relationship of zero to many of your master objects, you won't have in the database any reference to the detail object. It is the detail object that has a foreign key to the master. But, on the C# class side, the master will have a collection of the detail.

To make this work, you need to have a repository that will do the include correctly if you want to use eager loading.

```
MyDbContext.Libraries.Include("Book");
```

You also need to specify the collection as ICollection, or IEnumerator won't work, and if it does, you will end up with an error. This property needs to be also virtual.

```
public virtual ICollection<Book> Books { get; set; }
```

A specified Include path is not valid. The EntityType "DataAccessLayer.Database.Book" does not declare a navigation property with the name "BooksCollection."

Linq to Entity does not load data right after calling the context

Release Date: 22-Mar-12

Url: http://patrickdesjardins.com/blog/?post_type=post&p=876

Linq to Entity does not execute directly the SQL query to the database when the query is done. This is called **Deferred execution**.

The SQL will be executed when the code loops through it with a foreach or if the code uses .ToArray(), .ToList(), .ToDictionary() or .ToLookup().

Here is an example, mostly taken from MSDN, showing when the data is loaded from the SQL server.

```
using (AdventureWorksEntities context = new AdventureWorksEntities())
{
    IQueryable<Product> productsQuery = context
                                .Products; //productsQuery is not loaded yet
    IQueryable<Product> largeProducts = productsQuery
                .Where(p => p.Size == "L"); //largeProducts is not loaded yet
    foreach (var product in largeProducts)         //Execute query
    {
        Console.WriteLine(product.Name);
    }
}
```

Here is a second example where the deferral is not taking long since we are using ToList() which calls the database.

```
using (AdventureWorksEntities context = new AdventureWorksEntities())
{
    var productsQuery = context.Products
                        .Where(p => p.Size == "L")
                        .ToList(); //Executed here
}
```

One advantage is that you can refine the query in a later stage without affecting the performance since it will be executed once. It also lets you have the flexibility to build the query in multiple steps. Finally, it lets you execute the query at the latest stage possible which is good so that you have the latest version of the data.

Handling multiple repositories with Entity Framework

Release Date: 24-Mar-12
Url: http://patrickdesjardins.com/blog/?post_type=post&p=890

If you are using one dbcontext per repository, you may end by having a problem with the reference between each of your objects. Let's say that you have an object A with an object B and A is handled by RepoA and you change the object B which is handled by the context inside repoB, then you won't have any changes done. This is because the dbcontext contains only a reference for RepoA in RepoA and it is not aware of what has been changed in the other dbcontext in RepoB.

The best way to solve this issue is to share the dbcontext among all your repositories. This can be easily done if you are using a repository factory (Abstract Factory pattern). When you create your repository factory you should create the database context and set it to all repositories when they are instantiated.

```
public class RepositoryFactory : IRepositoryFactory
{
    private IClassA a;
    private IClassB b;
    private IClassC c;
    private readonly DatabaseContext dbContext;

    public RepositoryFactory()
    {
        this.dbContext = new DatabaseContext();
    }

    public IClassA RepoA
    {
        get { return a ?? (a = new RepoA(this.dbContext)); }
    }

    public IClassB RepoB
    {
        get { return b ?? (b = new RepoB(this.dbContext)); }
    }

    public IClassC RepoC
    {
        get { return c ?? (c = new RepoC(this.dbContext)); }
    }
}
```

Entity Framework 4.3 delete cascade with code first (POCO)

Release Date: 19-Apr-12
Url: http://patrickdesjardins.com/blog/?post_type=post&p=1023

If you have a parent->child relationship between two of your classes and you delete the parent, you may want to delete all children. To do this, you need to have a "DELETE CASCADE" statement on your foreign key. Here is a simple example:

```
CREATE TABLE [Parent]([ID] [int] IDENTITY(1,1) NOT NULL
,[Description] [nvarchar](100) NULL
,CONSTRAINT [PK_Parent] PRIMARY KEY CLUSTERED)
GO

CREATE TABLE [ParentDetail]([ID] [int] IDENTITY(1,1) NOT NULL
,[Parent_ID] [int] NOT NULL
,CONSTRAINT [PK_ParentDetail] PRIMARY KEY CLUSTERED)
GO

ALTER TABLE [ParentDetail]  WITH CHECK
ADD  CONSTRAINT [FK_ParentDetail_Parent]
FOREIGN KEY([Parent_ID])
REFERENCES [Parent] ([ID])
ON DELETE CASCADE)
GO
```

The problem is that if you are using Entity Framework 4.3 and try to delete a Parent entity, you will end up having this error :

An error occurred while saving entities that do not expose foreign key properties for their relationships. The EntityEntries property will return null because a single entity cannot be identified as the source of the exception. Handling of exceptions while saving can be made easier by exposing foreign key properties in your entity types. See the InnerException for details.

The inner exception message will contain something similar to this:

Cannot insert the value NULL into column 'Parent_ID', table 'ParentDetail'; column does not allow nulls. UPDATE fails. The statement has been terminated.

So, what does it mean? It tries to delete the Parent and to set into each ParentDetail the ID NULL because it has been erased. This is not what we want. In fact, we would like to have all ParentDetail removed as well. This is partly why we have to specify in the SQL to have a cascade.

You can do it manually in your project:

```
var listDetail = parent.ParentDetails.ToList();
```

```
foreach (var ParentDetail in listDetail)
{
    Database.ParentDetails.Remove(ParentDetail);
}
Database.Parents.Remove(Parent);
Database.SaveChanges();
```

This will produce multiple amounts of SQL statements on the SQL Server - one for each detail and one for the Parent itself.

But, if you go to your database context and you specify in the **OnModelCreating** a rule about the cascade, it will work as it is supposed to do.

```
protected override void OnModelCreating(DbModelBuilder modelBuilder)
{
    //...
    modelBuilder.Entity<Parent>()
            .HasMany(e => e.ParentDetails)
            .WithOptional(s => s.Parent)
            .WillCascadeOnDelete(true);
    //...
}
```

Now you can simply delete the Parent without having to delete manually all children.

```
Database.Parents.Remove(Parent);
Database.SaveChanges();
```

On the SQL server side, you can see the database has the same amount of delete statements executed. So, you do not save on the amount of query but save on the amount of logic to handle on the C# side because you do not have to take care to delete every detail.

On a special note, you do not need to have the table having a reference with the On Delete Cascade. You can handle the cascade only on the Entity *DbContext* with *OnModelCreating*. If you specify it on the SQL Server Database side, this will enforce the integrity on the database side but won't be automatically applied on the delete with EF.

Entity Framework 4.3 : How to insert, update, delete master-detail entity

Release Date: 02-Jun-12
Url: http://patrickdesjardins.com/blog/?post_type=post&p=1058

I have already talked about complex objects in a previous post concerning Entity Framework and complex entities (page 85 Entity Framework Update a complex object) with MVC and Entity Framework. This time, I'll explain how to insert, update and delete the detail of a master-detail scenario.

First of all, you need to update the master properties. This is done by getting the entity from the database and updating all its scalar information from the controller (if you are using Asp.Net MVC).

```
[HttpPost]
public ActionResult Update(MyModel formModel)
{
    var fromDatabase = Database.MyModel.Single(formModel.ID); //Scalar
    Database.Entry(fromDatabase).CurrentValues.SetValues(formModel);
    Database.Entry(fromDatabase).State = EntityState.Modified;
}
```

The next step is to update relationships that are easier, which are the 1 to 1 relations or the 0 to 1 relations. These would have in the MyModel an object that references another object. To update the reference it just needs to be set to the object and to be sure that the Database context knows about it. From the primary key of the object, everything will be bound correctly.

```
// Relationship -> 1 to 1
if (formModel.OneOneObject != null)
{
    Database.OneOneObjects.Attach(formModel.OneOneObject);
}
fromDatabase.OneOneObject = formModel.OneOneObject;
```

The last step is to handle a 0 to many relationship. This needs to work in multiple cases like adding a new detail, removing a detail or editing a scalar property of this entity.

The first thing to do if the master doesn't have any children is to remove any trace of them. To do this you need to null the reference and if you do not allow NULL in the database, kill all children referenced to the master.

```
// Relationship -> MyModelDetail
if (formModel.MyModelDetails != null && formModel.MyModelDetails.Any())
{
    //Here Update, individual delete, and insertion
}
else
```

```
{
    fromDatabase.MyModelDetails = null;
    var MyModelDetailsToRemove = Database.MyModelDetails.Where(x => x.MyModel.ID
== formModel.ID);
    foreach (var MyModelDetailToRemove in MyModelDetailsToRemove)
    {
        Database.MyModelDetails.Remove(MyModelDetailToRemove);
    }
}
```

As you can see, we set to NULL the reference to any detail and we remove from all children any reference to the master.

Now, we need to replace line 3 of the previous code, which is the update, insert, delete of the master-detail relationship.

```
foreach (var MyModelDetail in formModel.MyModelDetails)
{
    MyModelDetail.MyModel = fromDatabase;
    if (MyModelDetail.ID == 0)
    {
        Database.MyModelDetails.Add(MyModelDetail);
    }
    else
    {
        if (!Database.Set<MyModelDetail>().Local.Any(e => e.ID ==
MyModelDetail.ID))
        {
            Database.MyModelDetails.Attach(MyModelDetail);
        }
        var fromDatabaseMyModelDetail = Database.MyModelDetails.Single(x => x.ID
== MyModelDetail.ID);

Database.Entry(fromDatabaseMyModelDetail).CurrentValues.SetValues(MyModelDetail);
        Database.Entry(fromDatabaseMyModelDetail).State = EntityState.Modified;
    }
}
```

This code loops all children and assigns the master reference. Then, it checks if the unique identifier has been set. This will indicate if we insert or we need to update. The first case inserts the object at the database context, the second case will attach the object if it is not attached yet and will set the new values. We could have for both cases updated the nonscalar property for all children. This can be done by simply processing the same way we just did for the master but at the child level.

The last thing we need to do, and not forget, is to remove children that are not any more required to be attached to the master. This can be done with Linq to get all children that have not been submitted by the user.

```
if (fromDatabase.MyModelDetails != null)
{
    foreach (var MyModelDetailToRemove in fromDatabase.MyModelDetails
    .Where(x => !formModel.MyModelDetails.Any(u => u.ID == x.ID)).ToList())
    {
        Database.MyModelDetails.Remove(MyModelDetailToRemove);
    }
}
```

This code simply creates a list of children (MyModelDetail) that are not present in the list submitted by the user. It checks with the database. The use of ToList() is required because we remove children which are in the list that we are looping.

How to map 1 table to 2 objects with Entity Framework 4.3 Code-First (POCO)?

Release Date: 19-Jun-12
Url: http://patrickdesjardins.com/blog/?post_type=post&p=1142

In some scenarios, your database table may look different from your classes. You could have a class that contains an object which is a subdivision of some data with high cohesive representation and at the same time you may not want to divide this information in a 1 to1 table. This is often the case if you cannot refactor an existing database or the case where information belongs in a single table but since the data is conceptually better to be together in a second object, you need it to be different from your database. In that case, Entity Framework calls this scenario **"Complex Type"**.

Let say that you have a table with these fields:

```
[Table]
-Field1
-Field2
-Field3
-Field4
```

And let's say that you end up having classes like this:

```
[Class1]
-Field1
-Field2
-Class2 object here

[Class2]
-Field3
-Field4
```

In fact, as you can see, the Class1 can access Class2 data with the property Class2. For example : myClass1.Class2.Field3.

To be able to automatically map data with Entity Framework, you need to set up a complex type.

First of all, you need to ensure that the property doesn't have a null value. This means that you have to initialize this property. The best way is to initialize the inner object (Class2) in the constructor of the main class (Class1).

Second, Entity Framework will do this mapping of the property inside the inner object with the name of this property. That means that Entity Framework will think that the table looks like this:

```
[Table]
-Field1
-Field2
-Class2_Field3
-Class2_Field4
```

If you do not want to alter your table, you will need to configure the Database Context.

```
protected override void OnModelCreating(DbModelBuilder modelBuilder)
{
    modelBuilder.Configuration.Add(new MyTable2Configuration());
    //Add subsequent configuration here...
}

public class MyTable2Configuration : ComplexTypeConfiguration<Class2>
{
    public MyTable2Configuration()
    {
        Property(o => o.Field3).HasColumnName("Field3");
```

```
        Property(o => o.Field4).HasColumnName("Field4");
    }
}
```

You do not have to configure the Table1 class, only the complex type. If you need more information about Complex Type, you can always check this blog (http://bit.ly/1id68jQ) which gives additional information.

How to simplify comprehension of a complex Entity Framework Query

Release Date: 16-Jul-12
Url: http://patrickdesjardins.com/blog/?post_type=post&p=1189

You may run into a case where the Linq to Entity query is long and complex.

If you are using a layer of abstraction to access your database (DAL "Data Access Layer") that returns **IQueryable** you may be surprised that you can divide your query into multiple IQueryable and merge all Linq to Entity back into a single IQueryable.

The first step is to create your method into your DAL.

```
public IQueryable<MyModel> GetMyModel()
{
    //Linq to Entity is returned here
}
```

The second step is to create a query in a logical group. Let's say you desire to have all objects of your MyModel that are over $100 and another condition is that you also want all those over $20 if they have a discount.

You can do it with a single Linq to Entity, but in some situations (more complex than the one exposed here) you may find it easier to cut the problem into a sub query.

This can be done by using multiple IQueryables.

```
public IQueryable<MyModel> GetMyModel()
{
    var query1 = //Linq to Entity with condition for > 100$
    var query2 = //Linq to Entity with condition for > 20$ && Discount > 0$
    //return query1 + query 2
}
```

The last step is to merge query 1 and query 2. You can do it in two differents ways with Linq. The first one is to use the Union keyword and the second is with Concat.

The difference between the two is that Union will merge only when not already present and Concat will merge everything. Here is a small snippet of code that illustrates this theory.

```
public static decimal Total(Product product)
{
    var set1 = new int[] {1, 2, 3};
    var set2 = new int[] {3, 4, 5};
    var result = set1.AsQueryable().Concat(set2.AsQueryable()); // count == 6
    var result2 = set1.AsQueryable().Union(set2.AsQueryable()); // count == 5
}
```

Our example for Union could look like this:

```
public IQueryable<MyModel> GetMyModel()
{
    var query1 = //Linq to Entity with condition for > 100$
    var query2 = //Linq to Entity with condition for > 20$ && Discount > 0$
    return query1.union(query2); //Both condition
}
```

Since we are using IQueryable, none of the queries are executed until their execution. That means that that SQL Server will receive a single query (with multiple sub queries).

How to use DateTime in Select with Linq to Entity (Entity Framework 4.3)

Release Date: 26-Jul-12
Url: http://patrickdesjardins.com/blog/?post_type=post&p=1197

If you want to create in your SELECT a new DateTime within your Linq to Entity query, you will reach an exception telling you that you cannot use a parameterless class.

To solve this problem, you need to use a special function that only Linq to Entity can use. Entity Framework has some methods that will convert C# code into SQL function. In our case, the method is called "***EntityFunctions.CreateDateTime(…)***".

Instead of having something like this:

```
var data = (from i in Database.Users
```

```
                    group i by new {y = i.InvoiceDate.Year
                                    , m = i.InvoiceDate.Month}
                    into g
                    select new UserStatistic {
                        Date = new DateTime(g.Key.y, g.Key.m, 1)
                        , Experience = g.Sum(o => o.Exp));
                    }
            );
```

You need to use the EntityFunctions.CreateDateTime :

```
var data = (from i in Database.Users
            group i by new {y = i.InvoiceDate.Year, m = i.InvoiceDate.Month}
            into g
            select new UserStatistic {
                            Date = EntityFunctions.CreateDateTime(g.Key.y,
g.Key.m, 1, 0, 0, 0)
                            , Experience = g.Sum(o => o.Exp)
});
```

Both codes do the same thing, but the second works with Entity Framework. This is because it uses Linq to Entity that converts the statement into SQL and hence does not know how to create a .Net DateTime object.

You can find the complete exhaustive list of entity functions at Microsoft's MSDN web site (http://bit.ly/1mB64vU).

Linq to Entity with dynamic Where clause

Release Date: 01-Aug-12
Url: http://patrickdesjardins.com/blog/?post_type=post&p=1214

Some scenarios, like searching with criteria, can lead to having a custom *where* clause. You may want to get information from one or more criteria.

You can write many Where clauses and queries depending on the information received, but this will rapidly lead to a n^2 problem.

```
public void DisplayData(int status = -1, DateTime creationDate = DateTime.Min,
decimal price = 0)
{
    var myData = _dataContext.Data;
    if (status != -1 && creationDate == DateTime.Min && price == 0)
    {
```

```
        Display(myData.Where(d => d.Status == status);
    }
    else if (status != -1 && creationDate != DateTime.Min && price == 0)
    {
        Display(myData.Where(d => d.Status == status && d.Date == creationDate);
    }
    else if (...)
    {
        //...    }}
    }
}
```

With three filters, it requires having nine if statements. This isn't a good way to do it. There are many ways to work with predicates (http://bit.ly/1f130XN) but the simplest is by using the LinqKit dll (http://bit.ly/1rgDr70). This dll contains a PredicateBuilder that uses standard Lambda Expression but abstracts the complexity of the syntax.

```
public void DisplayData(int status = -1, DateTime creationDate = DateTime.Min,
decimal price = 0)
{
    var predicate = PredicateBuilder.True<MyObject>();
    if (status != -1)
    {
        predicate = predicate.And(e => e.Status == status);
    }
    else if (creationDate != DateTime.Min)
    {
        predicate = predicate.And(e => e.Date == creationDate);
    }
    else if (price != 0)
    {
        predicate = predicate.And(e => e.Price == price);
    }
    var myData = _dataContext.Data;
    var filter = myData.AsExpandable().Where(predicate);
}
```

As you can see, now it is one *if* statement per filter. We used *AND* but we could have used *OR*. The documentation is simple and the library is free, and open source.

There are a few important details to keep in mind. The first one is that it must be used on an **IQueryable** collection, not IEnumerable. This will give you the possibility to pass in the Where clause an Expression<func> instead of a simple func. This gives the advantage of letting Linq To Entity handle the filter to the database instead of running it as an object predicate with Linq to Object.

The second thing is the **AsExpandable().** It converts the **IQueryable** into an **IExpandable**. It leverages Linq to Entity to execute complex expressions.

With this procedure of using predicate with Linq to Entity, you can define your filter with Expression in an external class that returns an Expression<func> and uses the correct filter depending on the situation. It makes your code cleaner.

Concerning unit testings, you need to compile the expression before using it. This is done with a single line of code.

```
Expression<Func<MyObject, bool>> expression= GetMyFilterBuiltWithPredicate();
var function = expression.Compile();
var responseInBoolean = function(myObject);
```

The first line is where you get your filter. This could have been the predicate builder object. The second line compiles the expression into a function and the last line passes an object to test the predicate and receives the answer as a Boolean. You can then assert the response.

Conflicting changes to the role X of the relationship Y have been detected.

Release Date: 14-Aug-12
Url: http://patrickdesjardins.com/blog/?post_type=post&p=1261

Entity Framework can be hard to debug. I found this error when someone used a reference to an object and also an integer for the ID within the same object and changed both of them. When this happened, Entity Framework raised an error because it cannot know which one is the correct reference.

```
public class MyEntity
{
    public virtual MySecondEntity MySecond { get; set; }
    public int MySecondEntityID { get; set; }
}
```

The code above can trigger the error:

Conflicting changes to the role X of the relationship Y have been detected.

To solve this problem, you only need to change the scalar property (integer) and not touch the complex attribute (the property).

But, let's say that you have this error without having this kind of structure. Let's say you only use a reference to the object (like I do).

```
public class MyEntity
{
    public virtual MySecondEntity MySecond { get; set; }
}
```

How can I have this error? Well, I had this problem when MyEntity was brand new (ID = 0) and when MySecond was also a reference to MyEntity. This is because MySecondEntity has a reference to MyEntity which is ID = 0. Those two MyEntity will be treated as two different entities by Entity Framework. The trick to solve this issue is to set to NULL the reference inside MySecondEntity and let Entity Framework set in the database the reference. This can be done because the new MyEntity does have a reference to the MySecondEntity property.

To conclude, if you have a conflicting change and you are using code first with property reference, be sure when you insert a new entity that both do not reference to an entity with a new ID. Just one part of the navigation needs to be defined.

Understand basic navigation with Entity Framework Code First (4.3) with 1 to 0..1 relationship

Release Date: 16-Aug-12
Url: http://patrickdesjardins.com/blog/?post_type=post&p=1245

Most of the work is done in your **DbContext** when we talk about configuration of your entities. This is also true for navigation properties that can be set via the fluent interface of Entity Framework.

The first step is to override the method **OnModelCreating**.

```
protected override void OnModelCreating(DbModelBuilder modelBuilder)
{
    //...
}
```

From there you can work in two different ways. The first is to create a class for each entity's configuration. The second is to work directly in the **OnModelCreation** method. I prefer the first one because it is cleaner with a bigger project.

```
protected override void OnModelCreating(DbModelBuilder modelBuilder)
{
    modelBuilder.Configurations.Add(new MyEntityConfiguration());
}

//...
public class MyEntityConfiguration : EntityTypeConfiguration<MyEntity>
{
    public MyEntityConfiguration()
    {
        //Configurations here
    }
}
```

As you can see, the type inherited by the configuration class is *EntityTypeConfiguration* but could be *ComplexTypeConfiguration* for a complex type instead of an entity type.

To make it shorter, for the purpose of this blog post, I will not use the classes approach, but in real life I would suggest you use it.

HasRequired and HasOptional

These two keywords work in conjunction with the use of a virtual object inside your classes. They will specify the type of relationship between entities.

HasRequired is implicit if you declare a virtual property for your class. For example, the code below displays two classes and both of them refer to each of them. This is a 1 to 1 implicit relationship.

```
public class User
{
    public int Id { get; set; }
    public string Username { get; set; }
    public virtual Profile Profile { get; set; }
}

public class Profile
{
    public int Id { get; set; }
    public string PostalCode { get; set; }
    public virtual User User { get; set; }
}
```

No configuration is required; nevertheless, you could have written in the **DbContext** some code that explicitly defines the navigation type.

```
protected override void OnModelCreating(DbModelBuilder modelBuilder)
{
    modelBuilder.Entity<User>()
                .HasRequired(t => t.Profile);
}
```

This scenario is good for the case where a *User* requires a *Profile* but *Profile* class can be created without being linked to a *User*. If you want to specify whether it is the class *Profile* or user *User* that will contain the relationship then you need to use the clause **WithRequiredPrincipal** or **WithOptionalPrincipal**.

```
protected override void OnModelCreating(DbModelBuilder modelBuilder)
{
    modelBuilder.Entity<User>()
                .HasRequired(t => t.Profile)
                .WithRequiredPrincipal(t => t.User);
}
```

The first code that was using HasRequired only was in fact using implicitly "WithOptional(t=>t.User)." The User would have the relation inside the table and not the profile. The second code also specified with **WithRequiredPrincipal** that the User will hold the foreign key.

Has or With

You have HasRequired, HasOptional, HasMany and HasForeignKey. At the same time you have WithRequired, WithOptional, WithMany. What is the main difference among those methods with *Has* and*With*? The first one, the *Has*, represents the navigation property. The second one, the *With*, represents the reverse property configuration. Let's say you have class A and class B. If you configure the entity A, every call with the keyword *Has* will be on the class A property.You can see this within the lambda expression that will be of type A with the return of type B. However, if you use a property with *With* in the prefix, you will configure a B to A relationship. For example :

```
modelBuilder.Entity<A>().HasRequired(a => a.B).WithOptional(b => b.A);
```

To clarify even more the Has and With, here is a more complex scenario that involves many classes.

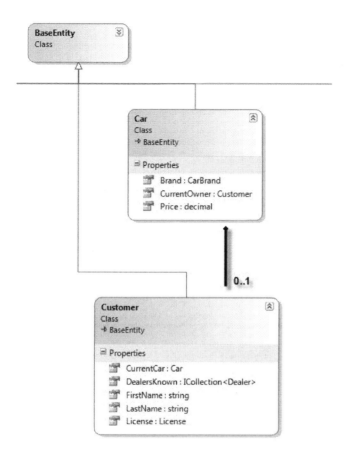

Let's focus on the *Car* class and the *Customer* class. In this scenario, a car can have or not have an owner (Customer). The customer can have or not have a current car (*Car*). This is a circular reference because the current car and the current owner are always the same. There are three ways to do it with Entity Framework Code First using Fluent API. The first one is to define the **Entity Type Configuration** on the *Car*. The second is to define the relationship on the *Customer* Entity Type Configuration. The third possibility is to define both sides. Of course, the last one will require you to have something cohesive between both configurations but has the advantage of being very explicit.

```
public class CarConfiguration : EntityTypeConfiguration<Car>
{
    public CarConfiguration()
    {
        HasOptional(x => x.CurrentOwner)
                .WithOptionalPrincipal(t => t.CurrentCar); //User contain the
Customer FK
```

```
        }
}

public class CustomerConfiguration : EntityTypeConfiguration<Customer>
{
    public CustomerConfiguration()
    {
        HasKey(x => x.Id);
        HasOptional(x => x.CurrentCar)
                .WithOptionalDependent(t => t.CurrentOwner); //Defined inside the
CarConfiguration (up-side-down), may not be required
    }
}
```

In the first scenario, we would have only the **HasOptional** statement on the *CarConfiguration* class without having anything in the *CustomerConfiguration*. It is the reverse for the second scenario. The last one is exactly the whole code you see above, with both navigations defined.

In case you think you can only set up the HasOptional on both without seting up the WithOptionalPrincipal or WithOptionalDependent, you are wrong.

This will lead to an error:

Unable to determine the principal end of an association between the types 'EFCodeFirst.Models.Car' and 'EFCodeFirst.Models.Customer'. The principal end of this association must be explicitly configured using either the relationship fluent API or data annotations.

How come? Because it is impossible for Entity Framework to know which, between the *Customer* or the *Car*, contains the reference to the object. This is because if one of the objects requires the reference and the other one does not, Entity Framework will create the table with the reference in the table with the FK required. This is why having the code below will not work and will raise the error described.

```
public class CarConfiguration : EntityTypeConfiguration<Car>
{
    public CarConfiguration()
    {
        HasKey(x => x.Id);
        HasOptional(x => x.CurrentOwner); //Error!!!
    }
}

public class CustomerConfiguration : EntityTypeConfiguration<Customer>
```

```
{
    public CustomerConfiguration()
    {
        HasKey(x => x.Id);
        HasOptional(x => x.CurrentCar); // Error!!!
    }
}
```

The only time you can write **HasOptional** or **HasRequired** without defining the other side of the navigation is when you have the class having the reference to the other object and the other one does not. If we want to do it with our class *Car* and *Customer* we just need to remove from *Customer* the *Car* property like the following code.

```
public class Car : BaseEntity
{
    public Customer CurrentOwner { get; set; } //Relationship : One to (zero or
one)
}

public class Customer : BaseEntity
{
    //public Car CurrentCar { get; set; }
    //Relationship: One to (zero or one)
    public License License { get; set; }
    //Relationship: One to (zero or one)
}

public class CarConfiguration : EntityTypeConfiguration<Car>
{
    public CarConfiguration()
    {
        HasKey(x => x.Id);
        HasOptional(x => x.CurrentOwner);
    }
}

public class CustomerConfiguration : EntityTypeConfiguration<Customer>
{
    public CustomerConfiguration()
    {
        //Nothing
    }
}
```

DropCreateDatabaseIfModelChanges will create your database every time you start your application

Release Date: 18-Aug-12
Url: http://patrickdesjardins.com/blog/?post_type=post&p=1272

DropCreateDatabaseIfModelChanges is an implementation of *IDatabaseInitializer* that will delete, recreate, and optionally re-seed the database with data only if the model has changed since the database was created.

That means that if you are developing something and want to have the database updated to your model changes, you need to create a class that inherits **DropCreateDatabaseIfModelChanges** . This implementation requires you to use the type Database Context because it is a generic class. The class that you will create will inherit from *DropCreateDatabaseIfModelChanges*.

```
public class DatabaseContextInitializer :
DropCreateDatabaseIfModelChanges<DatabaseContext>
{
    protected override void Seed(DatabaseContext dbContext)
    {
        // seed data
        base.Seed(dbContext);
    }
}
```

Once created, you need to set the DbContext to know about this Initializer. This is done by setting it inside the OnModelCreating of your DbContext.

```
protected override void OnModelCreating(DbModelBuilder modelBuilder)
{
    Database.SetInitializer(new DatabaseContextInitializer());
    base.OnModelCreating(modelBuilder);
}
```

You can set inside Seed some altered table statements or anything you want to be loaded into the database.

The **DropCreateDatabaseIfModelChanges** should only be used on the development machine because in production it will cause the suppression of all your real data when the model changes.

There is also the implementation called **DropCreateDatabaseAlways** which will drop every time the context is initialized. This is also only good for development purposes.

What is the goal of using database context initializer?

The goal is to create all your models inside the code and let Entity Framework create for you the database. This is why it is called the **Code First** approach because you work on the classes and let Entity Framework handle the database. Once it is created, you can remove the statement and deploy.

What is the implication of migrating Entity Framework 4 to Entity Framework 5

Release Date: 30-Aug-12
Url: http://patrickdesjardins.com/blog/?post_type=post&p=1337

I had to take care when updating Entity Framework from version 4.3 to version 5. Even if the Framework has been released about two weeks ago and this might look rapid, it is not because it has been in RC for a few months and in beta for even more time. Sometimes, instead of fighting against features like adding classes to support enumeration or doing some gymnastics with C# to turn around bugs, it is just a better idea to upgrade.

First of all, we use **NutGet** to get the package but we do not use the default mechanism. Once downloaded, we take the DLLs and we move them into a specify DLL directory. You may not have to do this, but sometimes politics forces you to do it so the first step is to copy the DLLs.

However, unlike Entity Framework version 4.0 to 4.1 or to 4.3, Entity Framework version 5 contains two DLLs. One was compiled with the version of Microsoft .Net Framework 4.0 and one with version 4.5. Since we had not switched to 4.5 yet, I had to copy version 4.0.

Once the DLL changed, and there was validation that the project was well referenced to this new DLL, I hit the compile button and saw many errors that had been fixed rapidly.

Namespace changes

The first thing you have to know is if you use data annotation, the namespace has changed.

```
using System.ComponentModel.DataAnnotations;
```

became:

```
using System.ComponentModel.DataAnnotations.Schema;
```

You have to change some of your classes to use the new Schema. This was required for us because we use data annotation (not a lot but still in over a hundred places).

NotMappedAttribute is not NotMapped

I do not know why but the application I am working on sometime uses *NotMapped* and sometime *NotMappedAttribute*. Well, with Entity Framework 5.0, *NotMappedAttribute* does not work. It is now only **NotMapped**.

And that was it. Not a big deal. We are using Code First, so no EDMX file is present and so then nothing to update. The DbContext hasn't changed and everything compiled correctly. The migration of EF4 to EF5 took 10 minutes, and this is what I like!

Entity Framework increasing performance with AutoDetectChangesEnabled

Release Date: 04-Sep-12
Url: http://patrickdesjardins.com/blog/?post_type=post&p=1354

If you need to insert a lot of data into the framework with Microsoft Entity Framework, you may want to set the **AutoDetectChangesEnabled** to false. This will improve performance because the *DetectChanges* will not execute the detection of changes in the object.

```
public virtual void DetectChanges(bool force = false)
{
    if (this.AutoDetectChangesEnabled || force)
    {
        this.ObjectContext.DetectChanges();
    }
}
```

To disable the auto detect changes you need to set the context to false. The *AutoDetectChanges* is inside the Configuration property.

```
context.Configuration.AutoDetectChangesEnabled = false;
```

This method *DetectChanges* will be called when you use the Add, Attach, Find, Local, or Remove members on *DbSet*. Also, it will be called if you use **GetValidationErrors**, **Entry**, or **SaveChanges** members on *DbContext*. This is the reason that batch Adding objects with Entity Framework can be slow, because *DetectChanges* makes a copy every time entities are added to the database context. It verifies if a change has been made when everything is commited to the database (saved). Every time that *DetectChange* is called, it has to go through all of your tracked entities, so the more stuff you have in your context the longer it takes to manipulate Entity Framework.

It is possible to disable the detect change and call it manually to increase performance. But, in most cases you can keep the detection automatically without a big loss of performance.

```
YourDbContext.ChangeTracker.DetectChanges(); //Manually detect changes
```

From my experience, the performance is not affected if you play with less than 100 objects. It is easier to let the framework handle changes in this case. But, if you need to add or modify over 100 objects, I recommend that you manually remove the automatic changes detection and manually call the *DetectChanges*.

Entity Framework boosts select performance with AsNoTracking() method

Release Date: 12-Sep-12
Url: http://patrickdesjardins.com/blog/?post_type=post&p=1358

Entity Framework provides a method that removes the tracking ability of objects and that will increase the performance. Of course, the drawback is that the **DbContext** will not be able to know if an entity has changed.

Let's start with a simple example. First, the model which contains an ID (in BaseEntity) and a FirstName and LastName.

```
public class Customer : BaseEntity
{
    public string FirstName { get; set; }
    public string LastName { get; set; }
```

}

We will add 5000 rows to the database to be able to get some time information about loading these 5000 customers into the view.

```
DECLARE @count INTDECLARE @firstname varchar(100)
DECLARE @lastname varchar(100)
SET @count = 0
WHILE (@count < 5000)
BEGIN
SET @firstname = 'FirstName' + cast(@count as varchar)SET @lastname = 'LastName' +
cast(@count as varchar)
INSERT INTO [Autoshop].[dbo].[Customers] ( [FirstName],[LastName])
VALUES (   @firstname , @lastname     )
SET @count = (@count + 1)
END
```

Finally, we will time how long it takes Entity Framework to generate the loading of the object into the view.

```
public ViewResult Index()
{
    var watch = new Stopwatch();
    watch.Start();
    var customers = db.Customers.Include(c => c.License).ToList();
    watch.Stop();
    ViewBag.TimeElapsed = watch.ElapsedMilliseconds;
    return View(customers);
}
```

The result from several tests gave me (on my machine) **237 ms**. Now, let's do the same test with AsNoTracking().

```
public ViewResult Index()
{
    var watch = new Stopwatch();
    watch.Start();
    var customers = db.Customers.Include(c => c.License)
                                .AsNoTracking().ToList();
    watch.Stop();
    ViewBag.TimeElapsed = watch.ElapsedMilliseconds;
    return View(customers);
}
```

Now I have an average of **108 ms**. **It is about 2 times faster** with 5000 rows of a simple

Entity.

The Entity Framework keyword **AsNoTracking()** gives a big boost of speed if you need to display data without having them tracked by Entity Framework. Most reports, lists or data that are displayed to the user as information should use **AsNoTracking()** since it removes overhead that is not used.

What AsNoTracking() does behind the scenes is a good question. First, AsNoTracking came from the **DbExtensions.cs** file. It is an extension method (static method) that will call the dbQuery.AsNoTracking() if the dbQuery is defined, and if yes will call AsNoTracking of this one which will simply return a new DbQuery with a parameter of **IInternalQuery** with the specialty of being AsNoTracking. This leads us to some implementations. The one that concerns us is the *InternalQuery* that looks like this:

```
public virtual IInternalQuery<TElement> AsNoTracking()
{
    return (IInternalQuery<TElement>) new
InternalQuery<TElement>(this._internalContext
                        , (ObjectQuery)
DbHelpers.CreateNoTrackingQuery((ObjectQuery) this._objectQuery));
}
```

As you can see, it creates a new *InternalQuery* with the second parameter that uses **DbHelpers.CreateNoTrackingQuery(…)**. The second parameter should be *ObjectQuery*. This raises the question, what does the DbHelpers.CreateNoTrackingQuery do to remove the overhead?

```
public static IQueryable CreateNoTrackingQuery(ObjectQuery query)
{
    IQueryable queryable = (IQueryable) query;
    ObjectQuery objectQuery = (ObjectQuery)
queryable.Provider.CreateQuery(queryable.Expression);
    objectQuery.MergeOption = MergeOption.NoTracking;
    return (IQueryable) objectQuery;
}
```

It does the same thing as if you had set the **ObjectContext** property *MergeOption* to *NoTracking*. The only advantage is that it does not affect every **DbContext** but only specific queries. In **Code First**, you no longer have access to *MergeOption* since you are no longer using the *ObjectContext* but the *DbContext*. **DbContext** is a lightweight version of *ObjectContext*. This is why you should now use the extension *AsNoTracking* instead of configuring the *ObjectContext* (that even if you use *DbContext* could be accessed).

For the curious, you could access the *ObjectContext* from the *DbContext* by casting the dbContext with *IObjectContextAdapter*.

```
ObjectContext objectContext = ((IObjectContextAdapter)dbContext).ObjectContext;
```

Automatic migration was not applied because it would result in data loss

Release Date: 12-Oct-12
Url: http://patrickdesjardins.com/blog/?post_type=post&p=1544

When you are using Entity Framework and try to use the **migration** tool you may have this message:

Automatic migration was not applied because it would result in data loss

I had this error while doing this exact command inside the **Package Manager Console**.

```
Update-Database -Verbose
```

This happens because you have some data inside the table and the migration tool wants to drop the table. This creates a conflict for the migration tool and instead of making the decision to delete the data it shows this error. If you are using the migration tool because you want to create the whole database and seed data with the seed method then you can force the table drop.

You simply need to use *force*.

```
Update-Database -Verbose -Force
```

Entity Framework 5.0 and Timespan type

Release Date: 22-Oct-12
Url: http://patrickdesjardins.com/blog/?post_type=post&p=1539

Entity Framework version 5, like its previous version, does not map **timespan**. The following error will raise when you try to:

There is no store type corresponding to the conceptual side type 'Edm.Time(Nullable=True,DefaultValue=,Precision=)' of primitive type 'Time'.

I thought that Entity Framework 5 was able with SQL Server 2008 R2 to map Timespan to Time. I was wrong. However, there is a workaround.

```
public Int64 TimeBetweenExercicesTicks { get; set; }

[NotMapped]
public TimeSpan TimeBetweenExercices
{
    get { return TimeSpan.FromTicks(TimeBetweenExercicesTicks); }
    set { TimeBetweenExercicesTicks = value.Ticks; }
}
```

First, you should want to still use in your code the TimeSpan type because it is convenient to manipulate time. But, on the other hand, Entity Framework does not map the type. Fortunately, we can map the ticks and simply ignore the property with the TimeSpan type.

The example above shows you this scenario where an entity is required to have the time between two exercises. In fact, the *TimeBetweenExercises* is not mapped to the database but the underlying property *TimeBetweenExercisesTicks*. Since an **Int64** can be mapped we do not lose any precision by converting ticks to/from timespan so we can use this time.

Entity Framework Schema specified is not valid error

Release Date: 12-Dec-12
Url: http://patrickdesjardins.com/blog/?post_type=post&p=1740

"Schema specified is not valid. Errors: \r\nThe mapping of CLR type to EDM type is ambiguous because multiple CLR types match the EDM type 'MyClassName'. Previously found CLR type 'MyNameSpaceContext.Context.MyClassName', newly found CLR type 'MyNameSpaceModel.Domain.MyClassName'."

This error occurs only if you have two classes with the same name in a different namespace. It can be quite easy to reproduce without having the goal to do it. How it is done? It is done because Linq to Entity uses model classes instead of context classes. Entity Framework can only manipulate classes that are registered to it, context classes, and not other classes even if those are very similar.

For example, if you want to return a list of MyClassName (context) classes which are inside a collection of MyClassName (domain model), you could have this problem.

```
var fromDatabase = _dataContext.Set<MyClassName>()
            .Where(p => listMyClass
                    .Select(d => d.ID)
                        .Contains(p.ID));
```

This will not work because *listMyClass* contains a list of *MyClassName*, but from the domain model, not the context. It is easy to get wrong because usually the service layer and the repository layer receive as a parameter domain object and not directly the context. To solve this issue, you need to proceed in two steps. The select to get the list of IDs must be done outside Linq To Entity. This way, the code will be executed as Linq to Object and won't affect Entity Framework.

```
var arrayId = listMyClass.Select(d => d.ID)
        .ToArray();
var fromDatabase = _dataContext.Set<MyClassName>()
        .Where(p => arrayId.Contains(p.ID));
```

That's it! Now it works because *listMyClass* is transformed into an array of IDs that Entity Framework understands.

Microsoft Entity Framework in theory

Release Date: 06-Sep-11
Url: http://patrickdesjardins.com/blog/?post_type=post&p=71

Microsoft Entity Framework (EF) has been available with the Microsoft .Net Framework 3.5 since the first service pack. This is pretty interesting for WPF (Windows Presentation Foundation) forms, Console, or traditional Windows form applications that do not need to add an additional assembly into their setup package.

What is Entity Framework in short?

In short, the Entity Framework is an ORM. An ORM is an Object Relational Mapping. The ORM goal is to map Business Logic (also know as Model classes) to the persistent storage. It lets the developer concentrate on model objects without caring about how to load/save them from the database. But, Entity Framework also can generate model objects from an existing database or can generate the database tables. This is very powerful and a time saver.

How does Entity Framework work?

Entity Framework works under the hood with XML files. In fact, Visual Studio will hide all the complexity of those XML files.

Communication

Entity Framework communicates to the database using multiple communication channels. This gives some flexibility to the developer about how to access the persistent data. One way is directly to the EntityClient Provider using **Entity SQL Query**. While it is very powerful, the two other ways are simpler and are used most often. The second way is by using Entity SQL Query. This is like SQL statement but for the Entity Framework. It is also called **ESQL**. The third and last way to communicate is by using the Linq channel. **Linq to Entities** is very similar to Linq to SQL or Linq to Object but with some restrictions. So the last two, HSQL and LinqToEntities, pass through an additional layer called **Object Service**. This Object Service will be instanced in your code and queries will be made with it. The Object Service role is to translate the easy syntax into a Command Tree to be able to execute query via the ADO.NET Data provider. As you may already know, the Entity Framework uses ADO.NET technologies. So we went through the call from the code to the database. But, what happens once the database has executed the query? The data is sent back to the Object Service inside an EntityDataReader and the developer will receive all rows inside an IEnumerable. The T is the type of the entity requested from the Object Service.

How to install Entity Framework 4.1 RC

Release Date: 23-Sep-11
Url: http://patrickdesjardins.com/blog/?post_type=post&p=283

You need to open the solution where you want to have the latest version of EF. If you are running under .Net 3.5, there is a big chance that you are running version 1. If you are running on .Net 4.0 you should be on the EF version 4. The 4.1 requires some manual changes.

First, be sure you have the NuGet extension.

NuGet package installed

Second, open the console of NuGet and type: install-package EntityFramework. To open the console you need to go to View > Other Windows > Package Manager Console.

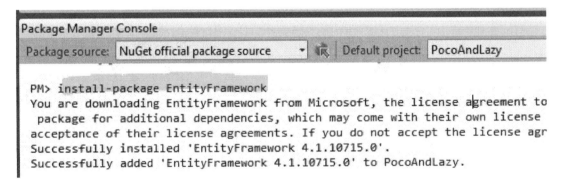

Installation of Entity Framework 4.1 RC

EntityFramework 4.1 will be installed on the solution that is active.

You can also use the NuGet Package Manager which gives you a visual interface to download Entity Framework. This is located in Project > Manage NuGet Package.

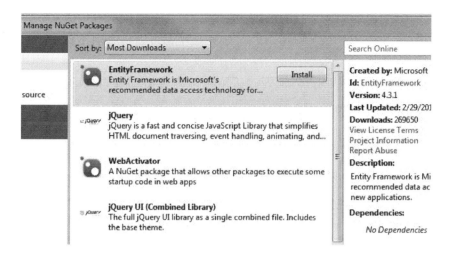

Once done, your project will have a reference to the DLL of Entity Framework.

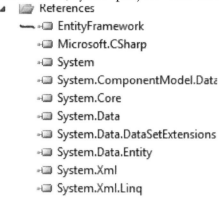

- ▲ 📁 References
  - ↳ ◦⬚ EntityFramework
  - ◦⬚ Microsoft.CSharp
  - ◦⬚ System
  - ◦⬚ System.ComponentModel.Data
  - ◦⬚ System.Core
  - ◦⬚ System.Data
  - ◦⬚ System.Data.DataSetExtensions
  - ◦⬚ System.Data.Entity
  - ◦⬚ System.Xml
  - ◦⬚ System.Xml.Linq

Model validation and Entity Framework 4.3

Release Date: 15-Apr-12
Url: http://patrickdesjardins.com/blog/?post_type=post&p=987

In a previous post concerning the IValidatableObject with Asp.Net MV3 (page 16, how to validate model object) we have discussed the power of the **IValidatableObject** interface with MVC framework which is a fast solution to handle errors in the model, errors in the model binding and errors in the controller.

What is great about using the Microsoft ecosystem is that most of the framework works well together. If you are using the ORM Entity Framework and you are validating your business logic with the**IValidatableObject** interface you can benefit from that before executing

SaveChanges() on your database context so that Entity Framework will call all model validations. This means that you cannot forget to call it, or it means that you do not need to explicitly check for the validation. If something is wrong with the model validation, when the SaveChanges() is called, Entity Framework will throw an exception.

Here is an example in which we try to save an entity which failed because a business logic added into the Validate method of the inherited class IValidateObject failed. Without having to check if the ModelState.IsValid, Entity Framework calls the Validate method of all changed entities and raises an exception of **DbEntityValidationException**. This is an awesome protection that ensures that nothing goes beyond the controller if something is wrong with the model; the database is clean.

I am pretty sure that at this point, someone will say that the exception defeats the purpose in many scenarios where you would like to handle particularly all errors from all model objects and display something to the user (or log them). Well, you can skip the exception and go directly to the model error.

```
var fromDatabase = dContext.Cars.Single(p => p.Id == car.Id);
dContext.Entry(fromDatabase).CurrentValues.SetValues(car);
if (!dContext.GetValidationErrors().Any())
{
    dContext.SaveChanges();
}
else
{
    //Display the error in the list dContext.GetValidationErrors()
}
```

As you can see, this way you check if there are any problems and then you save if none. On the other hand, if errors occur you can display them. This is very powerful because you have the entity which is problematic, all its properties that are in error, and all its error messages. This is possible because the **GetValidationErrors** function returns a *DbEntityValidationResult* which contains the Entry itself, the state if it is valid or not and a collection of errors in the *DbValidationError* format which means that you know what property is in error with the message.

```
string errors = string.Empty;
foreach (var dbEntityValidationResult in dContext.GetValidationErrors())
{
    errors += dbEntityValidationResult.|
}


ModelState.IsValid)

//Update code to be placed here

return RedirectToAction("CarList");
```

▣	Entry
◈	Equals
◈	GetHashCode
◈	GetType
▣	IsValid
◈	ToString
▣	ValidationErrors

Property ICollection<DbValidation
Gets validation errors. Never null.

At this point, you know that Entity Framework works in a team with MVC's **ModelState**. You do not need to add custom code in a generic model class that will contain the validation method. It is already built in. Also, if you are using Entity Framework as ORM, you can benefit from the extra security that your database won't be altered by wrong data because Entity Framework takes care to call the Validate method of all your objects before using them.

Entity Framework 4.3: An object with the same key already exists in the ObjectStateManager

Release Date: 16-Apr-12
Url: http://patrickdesjardins.com/blog/?post_type=post&p=997

This situation occurs if you already have the object inside the DbContext and you try to Attach your instance. Most of the time you can manage it by just removing the Attach method but in some cases you might not know if the instance is inside the DbContext and you may like to check it before attaching.

This can be done with the help of **DbSet** and its **Local** property, which is a collection of Locally attached entities.

```
if (!Database.Set<MyObject>().Local.Any(e => e.ID == myObject.ID))
{
    Database.MyObjects.Attach(myObject);
}
else
```

```
{
    myObject = Database.Set<MyObject>().Local.Single(e => e.ID == myObject.ID);
}
```

The first line verifies if the Local repository contains your object or not. This line uses the primary identifier (ID). If it doesn't contain anything, the object is attached. Otherwise, your object will take the reference of the one of the Local repositories. This way, it won't create a new instance of your object. Without the fourth line, you could end up with a new entry into the database even if the primary key is the same as an existing one (Entity Framework will do an Insert and the ID will auto-increment).

I am still curious to know why, in some simple projects, I can simply attach and never have the possibility of having the same object twice in the Local property.

Understand basic navigation with Entity Framework Code First (4.3) with 1 to many relationship

Release Date: 07-Sep-12
Url: http://patrickdesjardins.com/blog/?post_type=post&p=1277

Like configuring Entity Framework Code First for 1 to 1 or 1 to 0 (page 188, Understand basic navigation with Entity Framework) relation, you need to go in your DbContext and configure your entities.

For 1 to many, the syntax is quite the same but is changed to satisfy the needs of one to many. First, of all, unlike 0 to 1 or 1 to 1 the choice of the relation is simpler. The foreign key is always at the "1" side. That means that if you have a Dealer that sells many cars, every car will have a reference in the database of its seller.

Let's use the same objects that we did previously with the 1 to 1 relation.

```
public class Dealer : BaseEntity
{
    public string Name { get; set; }
    public ICollection<Car> CarToSale { get; set; } //Relationship: Many to one
(one side)
    public ICollection<Customer> Customers { get; set; } //Relationship: Many to
many  (two side)
}
```

and the car is like:

```
public class Car : BaseEntity
{
    public decimal Price { get; set; }
    public CarBrand Brand { get; set; } //Relationship : One to one
    public Customer CurrentOwner { get; set; } //Relationship : One to (zero or
one)
}
```

As you can see, I only used the CarToSale property, which is the one that will link to the Car. This is a little bit the reverse of what I just said about having the Car table having the reference to the Dealer, right? Well, in fact, the way we will configure the DbContext will still put the Foreign Key of the table the way we previously stated.

First, let's configure the dealer by stating that we have many cars associated with it.

```
    public class DealerConfiguration : EntityTypeConfiguration<Dealer>
    {
        public DealerConfiguration()
        {
            HasMany(x => x.CarToSale); //One to many
        }
    }
```

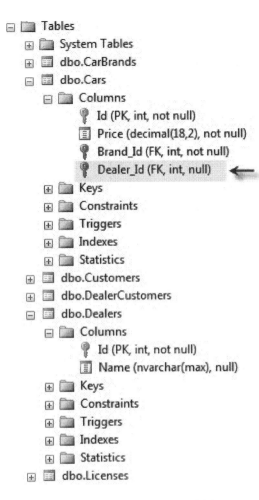

But, let's say that we want to add in our model the property *Dealer* inside the car. For the car, the relation is **1 to 0..1**.

So, it is now possible to join to the car the dealer by setting the car to the dealer or setting the dealer to the car.

```
//Add to the database from the car
using (var db = new DatabaseContext())
{
    var dealer = new Dealer() {Name = "Patrick"};
    var car = new Car {Brand = new CarBrand(), Seller = dealer};
    db.Dealers.Add(dealer);
    db.Cars.Add(car);
    db.SaveChanges();
}
```

or

```
//Add to the database from the Dealer
using (var db = new DatabaseContext())
{
    var car = new Car {Brand = new CarBrand()};
    var dealer = new Dealer()
                {Name = "Melodie", CarToSale = new Collection<Car> {car}};
    db.Dealers.Add(dealer);
    db.Cars.Add(car);
    db.SaveChanges();
}
```

In both cases, the table still has the foreign key inside the car and the dealer is not aware (from the table Dealer alone) of the car he has sold. From the Entity Framework Entities, both know. Both can read the value and both can save the value as we just saw.

Required relation of one to many.

For the moment, if we take a look at the database, the generated table contains a NULL at the dealer_id foreign key.

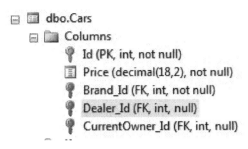

Let's say that we want to have this field as a required field. We want **"Not NULL"** to be generated into the table column property.

```
public CarConfiguration()
{
    HasRequired(x => x.Seller); //One to many is now a required field. It's really
1 to * and not 0 to *
}
```

This produces:

dbo.Cars
  Columns
    Id (PK, int, not null)
    Price (decimal(18,2), not null)
    Brand_Id (FK, int, not null)
    CurrentOwner_Id (FK, int, null)
    Seller_Id (FK, int, not null)

Not bad! Now we have what we want, a required field for the *Dealer* (called seller from the car perspective). Could we have configured this from the *Dealer's* entity instead of using the *Car* configuration? Of course!

```
public class DealerConfiguration : EntityTypeConfiguration<Dealer>
{
    public DealerConfiguration()
    {
        HasMany(x => x.CarToSale).WithRequired(e => e.Seller); //One to many (1 to
*)
    }
}
```

So, now you are able to create **0..*** and **1..*** relationships with Entity Framework.

Linq GroupJoin and Join differences

Release Date: 29-Aug-11
Url: http://patrickdesjardins.com/blog/?post_type=post&p=37

Linq lets you query a collection and one of its possible actions is the **GroupJoin**.

A GroupJoin is in SQL what we call a "Left Outer JOIN" while a Join in SQL refers to "Inner Join." In short, a GroupJoin will make a link between two entities even if the right side of the link has nothing to link to. In contrast, the Join will link two entities only if both entities contain a link between them.

To demonstrate the GroupJoin and the Join, a small example with Northwind Database will be used. This database schema and data are free at Microsoft. Once downloaded, this will create an SQL file that needs to be executed. Once executed, you will see multiple tables. For our example, only the tables Customers and Orders will be used.

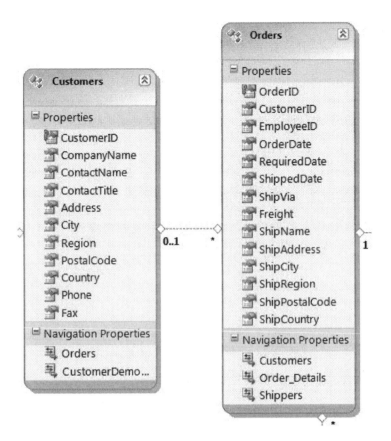

Northwind's Customers and Orders schema

The Customers can contain multiple Orders. The Order contains a link to the Customer.

We could have used any type of project, but to be short I have used an ASP.NET Webform and have created an ASPX page containing HTML:

Group EntityFramework

On the code-behind the code is executed:

```
NorthwindEntities db = new NorthwindEntities();
var source = db.Customers.Where(c => c.CustomerID.StartsWith("A"))
    .GroupJoin(db.Orders, c => c.CustomerID, o => o.CustomerID, (c, o) => new
{Customer = c, Order = o});
string html = string.Empty;
foreach (var cust in source)
{
```

```
    html += "</pre><h2>" + cust.Customer.CompanyName + "</h2>";
    html += "";
    foreach (var order in cust.Order)
    {
        html += "";
    }
    html += "<table><tbody><tr><th>Order id</th><th>Order date</th></tr><tr><td>"
+ order.OrderID + "</td><td>" + order.OrderDate +
"</td></tr></tbody></table><pre>";
}
this.groupEF.Controls.Add(new LiteralControl(html));
sqlGroupef.Text = (source as ObjectQuery).ToTraceString();
```

All right, so the LINQ query selected all clients that start with the letter A to filter a little bit the amount of returning data and then join to this result all orders. The second parameter of the GroupJoin is the "On" statement that we used to see in SQL. It tells how to join the two entities. Once it is done, the code within the foreach statement loops all customers and the inner foreach loop and order.

The output looks like this:

GROUP ENTITYFRAMEWORK

ANA TRUJILLO EMPAREDADOS Y HELADOS
Order id	Order date
10308	1996-09-18 00:00:00

AROUND THE HORN
Order id	Order date
10355	1996-11-15 00:00:00

ANTONIO MORENO TAQUERÍA
Order id	Order date
10365	1996-11-27 00:00:00

AROUND THE HORN
Order id	Order date
10383	1996-12-16 00:00:00

AROUND THE HORN
Order id	Order date
10453	1997-02-21 00:00:00

ANTONIO MORENO TAQUERÍA
Order id	Order date
10507	1997-04-15 00:00:00

ANTONIO MORENO TAQUERÍA
Order id	Order date
10535	1997-05-13 00:00:00

AROUND THE HORN
Order id	Order date
10558	1997-06-04 00:00:00

ANTONIO MORENO TAQUERÍA
Order id	Order date
10573	1997-06-19 00:00:00

This is generated with almost the same code as before but instead of using GroupJoin only the Join is used. Also, since no grouping is done, the second foreach is not needed.

```
NorthwindEntities db = new NorthwindEntities();
var source = db.Customers.Where(c => c.CustomerID.StartsWith("A"))
          .Join(db.Orders, c => c.CustomerID, o => o.CustomerID, (c, o) => new
{Customer = c, Order = o});
string html = string.Empty;
foreach (var cust in source)
```

```
{
    html += "</pre><h2>" + cust.Customer.CompanyName + "</h2>";
    html += "";
    html += "";
    html += "<table><tbody><tr><th>Order id</th><th>Order date</th></tr><tr><td>"
        + cust.Order.OrderID + "</td><td>" + cust.Order.OrderDate +
"</td></tr></tbody></table><pre>";
}
this.groupEF.Controls.Add(new LiteralControl(html));
sqlGroupef.Text = (source as ObjectQuery).ToTraceString();
```

The output produces a cross join without any grouping. This is why we can see the Customer repeated in the output. If we want to group the results of the join without using GroupJoin it is possible. In fact, it is possible to create the same output with Join if using the On statement and Equal together. Here is the change required :

```
NorthwindEntities db = new NorthwindEntities();
var source = from c in db.Customers
                where c.CustomerID.StartsWith("A")
                join o in db.Orders on c.CustomerID equals o.CustomerID into g
                select new {Customer = c, Order = g};
string html = string.Empty;
foreach (var cust in source)
{
    html += "</pre><h2>" + cust.Customer.CompanyName + "</h2>";
    html += "";
    foreach (var order in cust.Order)
    {
        html += "";
    }
    html += "<table><tbody><tr><th>Order id</th><th>Order date</th></tr><tr><td>"
        + order.OrderID + "</td><td>"
        + order.OrderDate + "</td></tr></tbody></table><pre>";
}
this.groupEF.Controls.Add(new LiteralControl(html));
sqlGroupef.Text = (source as ObjectQuery).ToTraceString();
```

To be sure that what we state is real, let's compare the generated MSIL for the two Linq examples. The first one is the GroupJoin and the second one is the Join with an On and Into.

```
var source = db.Customers
    .Where(c => c.CustomerID.StartsWith("A"))
    .GroupJoin(db.Orders, c => c.CustomerID, o => o.CustomerID, (c, o) => new {
Customer = c, Order = o });
var source2 = from c in db.Customers
                where c.CustomerID.StartsWith("A")
```

```
join o in db.Orders on c.CustomerID equals o.CustomerID
into g
select new { Customer = c, Order = g };
```

Both generate the exact same MSIL:

```
IQueryable arg_244_0 = db.Customers;
ParameterExpression parameterExpression = Expression.Parameter(typeof (Customers),
"c");
IQueryable arg_381_0 = arg_244_0.Where(Expression.Lambda >
(Expression.Call(Expression.Property(parameterExpression, (MethodInfo)
MethodBase.GetMethodFromHandle(ldtoken(get_CustomerID()))), (MethodInfo)
MethodBase.GetMethodFromHandle(ldtoken(StartsWith())), new Expression[]
{Expression.Constant("A", typeof (string))}), new ParameterExpression[]
{parameterExpression}));
IEnumerable arg_381_1 = db.Orders;
parameterExpression = Expression.Parameter(typeof (Customers), "c");
Expression > arg_381_2 = Expression.Lambda >
(Expression.Property(parameterExpression, (MethodInfo)
MethodBase.GetMethodFromHandle(ldtoken(get_CustomerID()))),
new ParameterExpression[] {parameterExpression});
parameterExpression = Expression.Parameter(typeof (Orders), "o");
Expression > arg_381_3 = Expression.Lambda >
(Expression.Property(parameterExpression, (MethodInfo)
MethodBase.GetMethodFromHandle(ldtoken(get_CustomerID()))),
new ParameterExpression[] {parameterExpression});
parameterExpression = Expression.Parameter(typeof (Customers), "c");
ParameterExpression parameterExpression2 = Expression.Parameter(typeof
(IEnumerable), "o");
var source = arg_381_0.GroupJoin(arg_381_1, arg_381_2, arg_381_3,
Expression.Lambda(Expression.New((ConstructorInfo)
MethodBase.GetMethodFromHandle(ldtoken(.ctor())), typeof (<>
f__AnonymousType0 >).
TypeHandle),
new Expression[] {parameterExpression, parameterExpression2},
new MethodInfo[] {(MethodInfo)
MethodBase.GetMethodFromHandle(ldtoken(get_Customer())), typeof
(<>f__AnonymousType0>).TypeHandle), (MethodInfo)
MethodBase.GetMethodFromHandle(ldtoken(get_Order())), typeof
(<>f__AnonymousType0>).TypeHandle)}),
new ParameterExpression[] {parameterExpression, parameterExpression2}));
```

The file compare results show the exact same code:

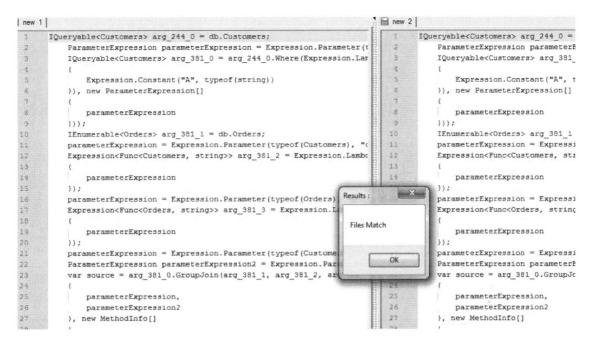

MSIL is exactly the same for GroupJoin or Join

To conclude, the GroupJoin is a short lambda version of the Join statement with the On and Into. It is possible to do a simple Join with only a Join statement. Linq lets you do other types of Join like Cross Join.

How to use Linq to query a property that is not in your database but in your class model

Release Date: 29-Mar-12
Url: http://patrickdesjardins.com/blog/?post_type=post&p=903

One of my teammates would like to query some data with Linq but always gets an error message saying that the Linq to Entity could not find the property desired. In fact, the exception was relevant because the property was made up in the model and was using two other properties available from the database.

To figure out more about the problem let's say that in the database you have the fields: ID, Name_Fr, Name_En. Let's say that in your model you have: ID, Name_Fr, Name_En and also Name. You would like to sort data by name. If you use directly your Entity Framework data context to query with Linq To Entity you will get an error because database context will try to do an SQL query with the field Name which does not exist. The solution is to use Linq to Entity to query everything and to sort with Linq to Object.

So, instead of doing :

```
MyDatabaseContext.MyPeople.OrderBy(c => c.Name);
```

You would have to do :

```
MyDatabaseContext.MyPeople.AsEnumerable().OrderBy(c => c.Name);
```

The **AsEnumerable()** will execute the query which will return a collection of *IEnumerable* instead of *IQueryable*. The difference is that *MyPeople* is **IQueryable** which does not execute the query until the collection is enumerated (with ForEach for example) or until the query is transformed into a list (for example with ToList()).

The difference between **AsEnumerable()** and **ToList()** concerns performance. The **AsEnumerable()** is faster than **ToList()** if you do a subsequent filtering (where, for example) operation. The reason is that it will filter the query before looping instead of looping the whole collection and then looping to filter.

Linq to SQL and Entity Framework cache

Release Date: 24-Sep-11
Url: http://patrickdesjardins.com/blog/?post_type=post&p=300

Linq to SQL has a caching system that relies on the primary key of each object. Inside the data context, an identity map keeps the value of the retrieved data. Everything is handled by the data context and you have to worry about nothing. Keep in mind that if someone else changes the value the cache will not be refreshed.

If you change the data on your side, the cache will also not be updated. This can be problematic in some situations. If this behavior is not what you want, you can disable the caching feature of Linq to SQL with a property of the data context.

```
myDataContext.ObjectTrackingEnabled = false;
```

Or, you can refresh the specific object.

```
myDataContext.Refresh(RefreshMode.OverwriteCurrentValues, myObjectToRefresh);
```

The reason behind this technical choice is that initially it was developed for performance of consecutive calls of the same object. The goal is not to have a real caching system.

To conclude, the title mentions Entity Framework and I have not said anything about it yet. The reason is that Entity Framework reacts the same way as Linq to SQL for the cache.

Entity Framework explicit loading, lazy loading and eager loading

Release Date: 04-Sep-11
Url: http://patrickdesjardins.com/blog/?post_type=post&p=140

Entityframework sets lazy loading to *false* as a default mechanism for loading its entity data. In other words, this means that the default value is set to **eager loading** or **explicit loading**. This behavior can be modified by the developer if needed by changing the *Lazy Loading Enable* of the conceptual model's property, or with code by changing the *OptionContext* property *LazyLoadingEnabled*.

To understand correctly how lazy loading works, let's get an example from the *NorthWind* database. The model generated from this database gives us a Customer entity that contains orders (of type Order).

```
var db = new NorthWindContainer(); //Instantiate the Object Context
db.ContextOptions.LazyLoadingEnabled = false; //Default value
var collectionData = db.Customers.First().Orders;
Console.WriteLine("All orders from the first customer using lazy loaded to "
            + db.ContextOptions.LazyLoadingEnabled);
foreach (var order in collectionData)
{
    Console.WriteLine(order.OrderID);
}
Console.WriteLine(collectionData.Count + " shown");
```

In the example above, line 3 gets all orders from the first customer. The lazy loading of the Object Context is set to false (the default value). The console will show nothing from the loop and a count of 0. This is because lazy loading is not enabled.

```
SELECT TOP (1) 1.[CustomerID] AS [CustomerID]
```

```
, 1.[CompanyName] AS [CompanyName]
, 1.[ContactName] AS [ContactName]
, 1.[ContactTitle] AS [ContactTitle]
, 1.[Address] AS [Address]
, 1.[City] AS [City]
, 1.[Region] AS [Region]
, 1.[PostalCode] AS [PostalCode]
, 1.[Country] AS [Country]
, 1.[Phone] AS [Phone]
, 1.[Fax] AS [Fax]
FROM [dbo].[Customers] AS 1
```

As you can see, the SQL reflects the results that we have - nothing to take the orders.

In fact, in this mode, to be able to get all the data, a new line must have been written between the request to get all orders and the display. The following code contains the Load() method that will go to the database to load orders.

```
var db = new NorthWindContainer();
db.ContextOptions.LazyLoadingEnabled = false; //Default value
var collectionData = db.Customers.First().Orders;
collectionData.Load(); //Explicit loading
Console.WriteLine("All orders from the first customer using lazy loaded to "
    + db.ContextOptions.LazyLoadingEnabled);
foreach (var order in collectionData)
{
    Console.WriteLine(order.OrderID);
}
Console.WriteLine(collectionData.Count + " shown");
```

This means that when using the default value (eager loading/explicit loading) the value loaded is only the value of the object and not the object of the class. To load the object of the class, the developer needs to use *Load()* on the desired object. This can be interesting if the object is big and you do not need to load the whole object.

The *Load* method is called. This means that it is an explicit loading. Eager loading does not require the call to *Load* method. Further examples will show you. For the moment, let's check the SQL statement generated to see how it reflects the change.

```
SELECT TOP (1) 1.[CustomerID] AS [CustomerID]
, 1.[CompanyName] AS [CompanyName]
, 1.[ContactName] AS [ContactName]
, 1.[ContactTitle] AS [ContactTitle]
```

```
,  1.[Address] AS [Address]
,  1.[City] AS [City]
,  1.[Region] AS [Region]
,  1.[PostalCode] AS [PostalCode]
,  1.[Country] AS [Country]
,  1.[Phone] AS [Phone]
,  1.[Fax] AS [Fax]
FROM [dbo].[Customers] AS 1

exec sp_executesql N'SELECT [Extent1].[OrderID] AS [OrderID],
[Extent1].[CustomerID] AS [CustomerID], [Extent1].[EmployeeID] AS [EmployeeID],
[Extent1].[OrderDate] AS [OrderDate], [Extent1].[RequiredDate] AS [RequiredDate],
[Extent1].[ShippedDate] AS [ShippedDate], [Extent1].[ShipVia] AS [ShipVia],
[Extent1].[Freight] AS [Freight], [Extent1].[ShipName] AS [ShipName],
[Extent1].[ShipAddress] AS [ShipAddress], [Extent1].[ShipCity] AS [ShipCity],
[Extent1].[ShipRegion] AS [ShipRegion], [Extent1].[ShipPostalCode] AS
[ShipPostalCode], [Extent1].[ShipCountry] AS [ShipCountry]FROM [dbo].[Orders] AS
[Extent1]WHERE [Extent1].[CustomerID] = @EntityKeyValue1',N'@EntityKeyValue1
nchar(5)',@EntityKeyValue1=N'ALFKI'
```

Using Lazy Loading

This is a pretty manual task and if you want to use lazy loading instead of explicit loading it is possible. This will give the control of loading objects of the class to the system.

The C# code will be like this:

```
var db = new NorthWindContainer(); //Instantiate the Object Context
db.ContextOptions.LazyLoadingEnabled = true; //Default value
var collectionData = db.Customers.First().Orders;
Console.WriteLine("All orders from the first customer using lazy loaded to " +
db.ContextOptions.LazyLoadingEnabled);
foreach (var order in collectionData)
{
    Console.WriteLine(order.OrderID);
}
Console.WriteLine(collectionData.Count + " shown");
```

This produces exactly the same output for the SQL.

```
SELECT TOP (1) 1.[CustomerID] AS [CustomerID]
,  1.[CompanyName] AS [CompanyName]
,  1.[ContactName] AS [ContactName]
,  1.[ContactTitle] AS [ContactTitle]
,  1.[Address] AS [Address]
,  1.[City] AS [City]
,  1.[Region] AS [Region]
```

```
,  1.[PostalCode] AS [PostalCode]
,  1.[Country] AS [Country]
,  1.[Phone] AS [Phone]
,  1.[Fax] AS [Fax]
FROM [dbo].[Customers] AS 1
```

```
exec sp_executesql N'SELECT [Extent1].[OrderID] AS [OrderID],
[Extent1].[CustomerID] AS [CustomerID], [Extent1].[EmployeeID] AS [EmployeeID],
[Extent1].[OrderDate] AS [OrderDate], [Extent1].[RequiredDate] AS [RequiredDate],
[Extent1].[ShippedDate] AS [ShippedDate], [Extent1].[ShipVia] AS [ShipVia],
[Extent1].[Freight] AS [Freight], [Extent1].[ShipName] AS [ShipName],
[Extent1].[ShipAddress] AS [ShipAddress], [Extent1].[ShipCity] AS [ShipCity],
[Extent1].[ShipRegion] AS [ShipRegion], [Extent1].[ShipPostalCode] AS
[ShipPostalCode], [Extent1].[ShipCountry] AS [ShipCountry]FROM [dbo].[Orders] AS
[Extent1]WHERE [Extent1].[CustomerID] = @EntityKeyValue1',N'@EntityKeyValue1
nchar(5)',@EntityKeyValue1=N'ALFKI'
```

Caching

Also, if we run all the examples with the same method we will realize that even if the collectionData is accessed twice the database will be called once because the object context has cached the collection. Here is a snippet of three calls: One with the lazy loading to false with a load call, another with the lazy loading to true, and one to false without the load. Interestingly, the last one will display value because the collection was already loaded.

```
var db = new NorthWindContainer();
db.ContextOptions.LazyLoadingEnabled = false; //Default value
var collectionData = db.Customers.First().Orders;
collectionData.Load();
Console.WriteLine("All orders from the first customer using lazy loaded to " +
db.ContextOptions.LazyLoadingEnabled);
foreach (var order in collectionData)
{
    Console.WriteLine(order.OrderID);
}
Console.WriteLine(collectionData.Count + " shown");

db.ContextOptions.LazyLoadingEnabled = true;
collectionData = db.Customers.First().Orders;
Console.WriteLine("All orders from the first customer using lazy loaded to " +
db.ContextOptions.LazyLoadingEnabled);
foreach (var order in collectionData)
{
    Console.WriteLine(order.OrderID);
}
Console.WriteLine(collectionData.Count + " shown");

db.ContextOptions.LazyLoadingEnabled = false; //Default value
```

```
collectionData = db.Customers.First().Orders;
Console.WriteLine("All orders from the first customer using lazy loaded to " +
db.ContextOptions.LazyLoadingEnabled + " back to False");
foreach (var order in collectionData)
{
    Console.WriteLine(order.OrderID);
}
Console.WriteLine(collectionData.Count + " shown");
Console.ReadLine();
```

Advanced example and eager loading

The previous example does not show the real power of **eager loading**. Let's go back quickly to the lazy loading code.

```
var db = new NorthwindEntities();
db.ContextOptions.LazyLoadingEnabled = true; //Default value
foreach (var customer in db.Customers)
{
    Debug.WriteLine("Customer " + customer.CustomerID);
    foreach (var order in customer.Orders)
    {
        Debug.WriteLine("|-->Order " + order.OrderID);
    }
}
```

This will produce one SQL to retrieve all *Customers* and then one SQL for each order. This is a problem called "N+1". You will have one initial SQL hit and an additional hit for each customer. This leads to a huge performance problem. The magic of lazy loading suddenly disappears. Of course, lazy loading is useful in some moments like accessing only one object and its objects, as in all previous examples. The same thing occurs with explicit loading. To make it work, the *Load* should have been called between the two foreachs.

```
var db = new NorthwindEntities();
db.ContextOptions.LazyLoadingEnabled = false;
foreach (var customer in db.Customers)
{
    Debug.WriteLine("Customer " + customer.CustomerID);
    customer.Orders.Load(); //Explicit loading
    foreach (var order in customer.Orders)
    {
        Debug.WriteLine("|-->Order " + order.OrderID);
    }
}
```

The N+1 problem is still there. With eager loading, this would result with a single query. To notify which object to load inside the class, the use of *Include* is required. Here is an example:

```
var db = new NorthwindEntities();
db.ContextOptions.LazyLoadingEnabled = true;
var customers = db.Customers.Include("Orders");
foreach (var customer in customers)
{
    Debug.WriteLine("Customer " + customer.CustomerID);
    foreach (var order in customer.Orders)
    {
        Debug.WriteLine("|-->Order " + order.OrderID);
    }
}
```

Line 2 and line 3 have changed. Line 2 says to use eager loading while line 3 indicates that it needs to load to object Orders inside the Customers. This produces a single SQL.

```
SELECT [Project1].[C1] AS [C1]
, [Project1].[CustomerID] AS [CustomerID]
, [Project1].[CompanyName] AS [CompanyName]
, ...
FROM ( SELECT [Extent1].[CustomerID] AS [CustomerID]
, [Extent1].[CompanyName] AS [CompanyName]
, [Extent1].[ContactName] AS [ContactName]
, ...1 AS [C1]
, [Extent2].[OrderID] AS [OrderID]
, [Extent2].[CustomerID] AS [CustomerID1]
, [Extent2].[EmployeeID] AS [EmployeeID]
, ...
FROM  [dbo].[Customers] AS [Extent1]
LEFT OUTER JOIN [dbo].[Orders] AS [Extent2]
    ON [Extent1].[CustomerID] = [Extent2].[CustomerID]) AS [Project1]
ORDER BY [Project1].[CustomerID] ASC
, [Project1].[C2] ASC
```

This LEFT OUTER JOIN (also known as LEFT JOIN) does what you would have been doing in SQL to get additional information if available.

Entity Framework mapping to stored procedure

Release Date: 12-Sep-11
Url: http://patrickdesjardins.com/blog/?post_type=post&p=160

Sometimes logic is stored in a stored procedure and it is still required to call it instead of using the normal entity framework way to update, delete or save. Fortunately, the entity framework lets you change the basic behavior of the auto-generated SQL for those operations by SQL Stored Procedure call.

Another scenario is that you may want to simply call a stored procedure without having to map it to a specific entity. This can call function import. This can return almost anything from the scalar, to a collection, or a complex type. Even a call to a void stored procedure is possible.

Mapping Insert, Update, Delete

Let's start with the mapping of the three basic SQL functions. The first thing to do is to go to the visual designer and right click on the entity you want to map the SQL queries.

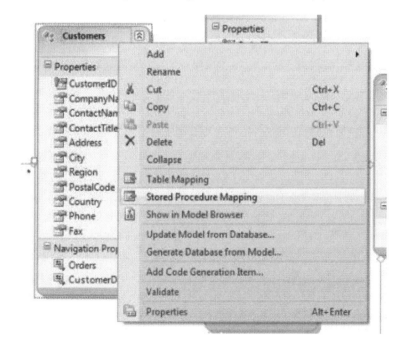

This will pop up the "Mapping Details." From there, it will be possible to select a function for each function. If nothing is present in the dropdown, you'll need to add the stored procedure to the entity model. To do this, right click on the model, select to generate the model from the database and select under Stored Procedure the desired one. Afterward, go back to the mapping details.

To test this, let's use the Microsoft Northwind database and add inside the SQL server manager this new stored procedure:

```
CREATE PROCEDURE UpdateRegion(@id INT,@txt VARCHAR(50))
AS
BEGIN
    UPDATE region  SET RegionDescription = @txt
    WHERE RegionID = @id
END
```

After that, let's add it into the entity model and map the stored procedure to the update function of the region table.

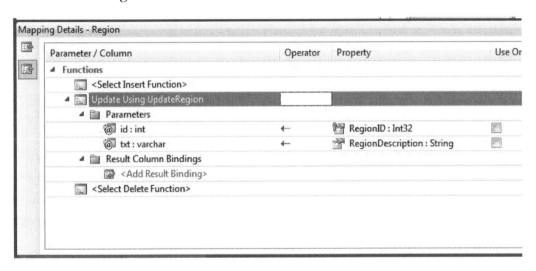

Also, you do not need to modify all of the three functions, only the one you want.

To see the difference, let's try to change the region without the stored procedure mapped and with it mapped to see how the generated SQL changes.

```
var db = new NorthWindContainer();
var region = db.Region.First();
Console.WriteLine("The first region description is : " +
region.RegionDescription);
region.RegionDescription = "Est";
db.SaveChanges();
region = db.Region.First();
Console.WriteLine("The first region description is : " +
region.RegionDescription);
Console.ReadLine();
```

This produces without the stored procedure mapped:

```
exec sp_executesql N'update [dbo].[Region]set [RegionDescription] = @0where
([RegionID] = @1)'
    ,N'@0 nchar(50),@1 int',@0=N'Est',@1=1
```

And with:

```
exec [dbo].[UpdateRegion] @id=1,@txt='Est'
```

Before going to the next part of this post, in the mapping details there are two columns that we have not yet talked about. The first one is *Use Original Value* and the second one is *Rows Affected Parameter.* The original value is a Boolean that is set to false by default. If you change it to true, this will pass to the database the original loaded value of the entity. This can be used in situations where multiple concurrences could have changed the value and you want the original one. The second column is the "Rows Affected Parameter." This can be used if you have an integer parameter with an output specification in the stored procedure that will return the number of rows that have been changed. In the example above, that would be the value 1 that would have been passed if we had changed the stored procedure to have an additional parameter of type Int (@paramReturnValue integer OUTPUT).

Executing a function in SQL Server with Entity Framework

The second way to use a stored procedure is to call the stored procedure from the object context. To create the mapping this time, it needs to go in the **Model Browser** and open the **Stored Procedure** folder. From there, the context menu of the right click lets you select the desired stored procedure.

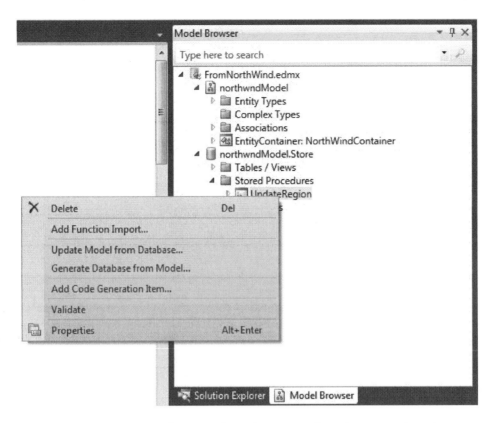

Once added, the stored procedure is set under the Function Imports of the Entity Framework Model.

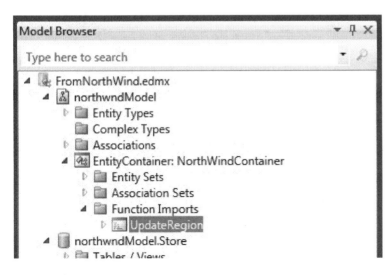

When it is added, you can do the call by using directly the object context followed by the name of the function. At any time you can change the name of it by going into the Model Browser and going to the property of the function.

```
db.UpdateRegion(1, "Estern!");
```

If the stored procedure returns a complex entity, the wizard will let you create the complex entity and you will be able to use it from the code. If it is a scalar, the wizard will let you select the good one and you will be able to use it.

Entity Framework and the Connection String

Release Date: 04-Oct-11
Url: http://patrickdesjardins.com/blog/?post_type=post&p=228

A connection string is a string with a key value pair in it that indicate where to get the connection to the server for persistence. In Entity Framework something changed from the standard and it is the location of the CSDL, SSDL and MSL file.

Here is an example of a connection string that connects to a file database named "qwe."

```
<add name="AdventureWorks_DataEntities"

connectionString="metadata=res://*/MyEFModel.csdl|res://*/MyEFModel.ssdl|res://*/MyEFModel.msl;
    provider=System.Data.SqlClient;
    provider connection string=&quot;
    Data Source=.\SQLEXPRESS;  AttachDbFilename=|DataDirectory|\qwe.mdf;
    Integrated Security=True;  C
    onnect Timeout=30;
    User Instance=True;
    MultipleActiveResultSets=True &quot;" providerName="System.Data.EntityClient"
/>
```

Here is an example of a connection string for Entity Framework 4 to an SQL Server:

```
<add name="NorthwindEntities"

connectionString="metadata=res://*/NorthWindEntityDataModel.csdl|res://*/NorthWindEntityDataModel.ssdl|res://*/NorthWindEntityDataModel.msl;
    provider=System.Data.SqlClient; provider connection string=&quot;
    Data Source=.\SQLEXPRESS;
    Initial Catalog=Northwind;
    Integrated Security=True;  MultipleActiveResultSets=True&quot;"
    providerName="System.Data.EntityClient" />
```

You can see one major difference and that is the **AttachDbFilename** for one when the other has an **Initial Catalog**. Also, the file-based database lets you use the **User Instance** when the SQL server won't. But it is not a big deal because User Install just makes the database use the current user as the runner of the database instance instead of the "NT AUTHORITY\NETWORK SERVICE. Also you can see the use of the |DataDirectory| keyword in the path of the database file. This keyword is read by the System.Data.Common.DbConnectionOptions and will translate this string with AppDomain.CurrentDomain.BaseDirectory. The base directory is the assembly directory.

How Entity Framework Manages Connection String

Entity Framework generates the *Object Context* with multiple constructors. One of the constructors takes the name of the connection string where it should read it. This is the case in the first line of the code below. This name is an entry in the connectionString element inside the configuration element of the app.config (or web.config for web application).

```
public AdventureWorks_DataEntities() : base("name=AdventureWorks_DataEntities",
"AdventureWorks_DataEntities")

public AdventureWorks_DataEntities(string connectionString) :
base(connectionString, "AdventureWorks_DataEntities")

public AdventureWorks_DataEntities(EntityConnection connection) : base(connection,
"AdventureWorks_DataEntities")
```

The second constructor lets you put in a string format directly the connection string. You could also get the connection string from the .config file and load it with this second constructor.

```
string connectionString = ConfigurationManager.ConnectionStrings["qwe"];
```

The third constructor lets you use an EntityConnection object. This object contains not only the traditional connection string but also the conceptual model data (CSDL, MSL, SSDL files). This lets you create dynamically a connection string with object. To use EntityConnection class, the help of EntityConnectionStringBuilder and SqlConnectionStringBuilder may be wise. You can get an MSDN Tutorial about creating EntityConnection at Microsoft (http://bit.ly/1fmUPzx).

Entity Framework 5.0 requires you to use .Net 4.5 with Enum support

Release Date: 31-Aug-12
Url: http://patrickdesjardins.com/blog/?post_type=post&p=1342

You can migrate your EF4.5 to EF5.0 without the need of Microsoft .Net but if you use some features like the support of **enumeration** that provides EF5.0 you will need to have the .Net Framework 4.5.

What does it mean? It means that you need to have Visual Studio 2012. So a simple migration of Entity Framework 5.0 became an endeavour of a few hours but at the end worked well.

I think it was worth it, if the business you are working on accepts changing their tool (VS2010 to VS2012).

How to use Linq to query a property that is not in your database but in your class model

Release Date: 29-Mar-12
Url: http://patrickdesjardins.com/blog/?post_type=post&p=903

One of my teammates would like to query some data with Linq but always gets an error message saying that the Linq to Entity could not find the property desired. In fact, the exception was relevant because the property was made up in the model and was using two others properties available from the database.

To figure out more about the problem let's say that in the database you have the field: Id, Name_Fr, Name_En. Let's say that in your model you have: Id, Name_Fr, Name_En and also Name. You would like to sort data by name. If you use directly your Entity Framework's data context to query with Linq To Entity you will get an error because database context will try to do an SQL query with the field Name which doesn't exist. The solution is to use Linq to Entity to query everything and to sort with Linq to Object.

So, instead of doing :

```
MyDatabaseContext.MyPeople.OrderBy(c => c.Name);
```

You would have to do:

```
MyDatabaseContext.MyPeople.AsEnumerable().OrderBy(c => c.Name);
```

The **AsEnumerable()** will execute the query which will return a collection of *IEnumerable* instead of *IQueryable*. The difference is that MyPeople is IQueryable which doesn't execute the query until the collection is enumerated (with ForEach for example) or until the query is transformed into a list (for example with ToList()).

The difference between **AsEnumerable()** and **ToList()** is concerning performance. The **AsEnumerable()** is faster if you do a subsequent filtering (.Where for example) operation. The reason is that it will filter the query before looping instead of looping the whole collection and then looping to filter.

Creating an HTML Extension with the possibility to add an HTML Attribute with HTMLHelperAnonymousObjectToHTMLAttributes

Release Date: 03-Jul-12
Url: http://patrickdesjardins.com/blog/?post_type=post&p=1169

When you are building an **HTML Extension**, it is always a good idea to provide an overload of your extension that can have an additional HTML attribute. This leads to the possibility to insert class, style or any other HTML attribute to the control that you are rendering.

First of all, you need to create the overload of your extension. You can also add at the last parameter the default value to null because the type of this parameter should be object.

```
public static MvcHtmlString MyExtensionXZY<TModel, TProperty>(this
HtmlHelper<TModel> htmlHelper, string anyThing)
{
    //...
}

public static MvcHtmlString MyExtensionXZY<TModel, TProperty>(this
HtmlHelper<TModel> htmlHelper, string anyThing, object htmlAttributes)
{
    //...
```

```
}
```

Or this can be with a default value:

```
public static MvcHtmlString MyExtensionXZY<TModel, TProperty>(this
HtmlHelper<TModel> htmlHelper, string anyThing, object htmlAttributes = null)
{
    //...
}
```

In both cases, the next step is to transform the object into a Dictionary. Why do we accept an object just to transform it into a Dictionary a few lines after? The reason is to let an anonymous object be used. This way, it is possible to call the HTML helper without having to declare the dictionary every time we want to use it.

```
@Html.MyExtensionXZY("Test", new {class= "MyClass"});
```

The last step is to assign the attributes' values to the HTML control that we are building. This can be done with a single line of code if you use an **HtmlHelper** method that is available in its static class.

```
myControl.MergeAttributes(
        System.Web.Mvc.HtmlHelper.AnonymousObjectToHtmlAttributes(htmlAttributes)
        , true);
```

What it does is take the object's HTML Attribute and convert it into a dictionary. The method AnonymousObjectToHtmlAttributes is available in System.Web.Mvc.HtmlHelper:

```
public static RouteValueDictionary AnonymousObjectToHtmlAttributes(object
htmlAttributes)
{
    RouteValueDictionary result = new RouteValueDictionary();
    if (htmlAttributes != null)
    {
        foreach (PropertyDescriptor property in
TypeDescriptor.GetProperties(htmlAttributes))
        {
                result.Add(property.Name.Replace('_', '-'),
                        property.GetValue(htmlAttributes));
        }
    }
    return result;
}
```

Once this is converted, it will be used with the MergeAttributes method of your new control. This method is available if you are using the System.Web.Nvc.TagBuilder class which lets you create an HTML tag. Once done with the TagBuilder, you only need to call the .ToString() of the object and you will get the generated HTML. As you may have noticed, the MergeAttributes has "True" as its second parameter. This informs the builder that if an attribute was already available, override it with the new one. This lets you have the final control of the rendering of your control.

Differences between Join, Inner Join, Left Join, Left Outer Join, Right Join, etc

Release Date: 27-Aug-11
Url: http://patrickdesjardins.com/blog/?post_type=post&p=60

For a few months, I have noticed that some people near me still do their **join** between tables in the **Where** clause. It works even if it has its limitations but the biggest problem comes in maintenance. Later, a big query becomes hard to modify because the criteria to refine the upcoming data are mixed up with joining where clauses.

To solve this problem, it is simpler to use Join keyword between each of them for joining tables. The Where clause is still important to refine the data. In this post, I will describe the differences among all possible Joins from an SQL perspective and write a little bit about their homologous Linq syntax. After all, we are a .Net blog!

In SQL, some statements are the same. The only difference is how it is written.

Join and Inner Join

To begin with, a query with **Join** is the same thing as **Inner Join**. What is a Join or an Inner Join? It is what people are doing with the Where clause; it compares two keys and joins them only if a relationship exists. Here is a simple example with the Join done inside the Where clause:

```
SELECT EmployeeTerritories.EmployeeID AS 'ET.EMPID'
     , EmployeeTerritories.TerritoryID AS 'ET.TID'
     , Territories.TerritoryID AS 'T.TID'
FROM EmployeeTerritories, Territories
WHERE EmployeeTerritories.TerritoryID = Territories.TerritoryID
AND EmployeeTerritories.EmployeeID
```

These tables can be found in the Microsoft NorthWind database (http://bit.ly/1tzBswo). Line 3 does the join when line 4 refines the query. The database's table schema below illustrate for you the relationship between the table EmployeeTerritories and Territories.

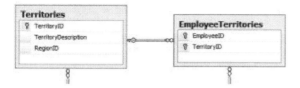

This produces:

```
ET.EMPID|ET.TID|T.TID
---------------------
1          06897    06897
1          19713    19713
2          01581    01581
2          01730    01730
2          01833    01833
2          02116    02116
2          02139    02139
2          02184    02184
2          40222    40222
3          30346    30346
3          31406    31406
3          32859    32859
3          33607    33607
```

The same result is output using the **Join** keyword or the **Inner Join**.

```sql
SELECT EmployeeTerritories.EmployeeID AS 'ET.EMPID'
    ,  EmployeeTerritories.TerritoryID AS 'ET.TID'
    ,  Territories.TerritoryID AS 'T.TID'
FROM EmployeeTerritories
JOIN Territories
   ON Territories.TerritoryID = EmployeeTerritories.TerritoryID
WHERE EmployeeTerritories.EmployeeID <= 3
```

Or

```
SELECT EmployeeTerritories.EmployeeID AS 'ET.EMPID'
    , EmployeeTerritories.TerritoryID AS 'ET.TID'
    , Territories.TerritoryID AS 'T.TID'
FROM EmployeeTerritories
INNER JOIN Territories
    ON Territories.TerritoryID = EmployeeTerritories.TerritoryID
WHERE EmployeeTerritories.EmployeeID <= 3
```

Left Join and Left Outer Join

These two are also the same. In fact, the **Outer** keyword is implicit every time in an SQL query.

The following query returns exactly the same as the Join but there is a reason why.

```
SELECT EmployeeTerritories.EmployeeID AS 'ET.EMPID'
    , EmployeeTerritories.TerritoryID AS 'ET.TID'
    , Territories.TerritoryID AS 'T.TID'
FROM EmployeeTerritories
LEFT JOIN Territories
    ON Territories.TerritoryID = EmployeeTerritories.TerritoryID
WHERE EmployeeTerritories.EmployeeID <= 3
```

The reason is that all *EmployeeTerritories* have their territories defined in the Territories table. Let's say that in the future a territory is deleted. The territory 19713 is deleted but not in the EmployeeTerritories table. The result will be:

```
ET.EMPID|ET.TID|T.TID
---------------------
1         06897    06897
1         19713    NULL
2         01581    01581
2         01730    01730
2         01833    01833
2         02116    02116
2         02139    02139
2         02184    02184
2         40222    40222
3         30346    30346
3         31406    31406
3         32859    32859
3         33607    33607
```

You can see that the T.TID returned NULL. Left Join or Left Inner Join lets you return all data from the Where criterion and try to Join. If data is found, it will output them, otherwise it will return NULL. This is different from Inner Join or Join that would have simply not returned this row.

Right Join or Right Outer Join

The Right Join statement, also known as Right Outer Join, is the mirror of the Left Outer Join. That mean that all results are from the Joined table and then the join is tried. If no data is found, NULL is returned.

Cross Join

Cross Join is a Cartesian product. That means that all data from the left side are joined to the right. The previous example with the Where statement that is a query to '<=3' has three EmployeeTerritories. The Join *Territories* table contains 53 territories. If we execute a Group Statement to know how many *Territories* the *EmployeeTerritories* have per EmployeeID this will give you the number to multiply by 53 to know the amount or row returned.

```
SELECT EmployeeID
     , count(TerritoryID)
FROM EmployeeTerritories
```

```
WHERE EmployeeTerritories.EmployeeID <= 3
GROUP BY EmployeeID
```

```
EmployeeID|count(TerritoryID)
--------------------------------
1                2
2                7
3                4
```

This gives a total of 13 Employees/Territories that will be Cross Joined to 53 territories, for a total of 689 rows. Here is the Cross Join query:

```
SELECT distinct(EmployeeTerritories.EmployeeID) AS 'ET.EMPID'
       , EmployeeTerritories.TerritoryID AS 'ET.TID'
       , Territories.TerritoryID AS 'T.TID'
FROM EmployeeTerritories
CROSS JOIN Territories
WHERE EmployeeTerritories.EmployeeID <=3
```

As you can see, the CROSS JOIN does not need to have the ON keyword because all rows are joined.

Full Join and Full Outer Join

This join is combining the Left Join and Right Join. In fact, even some databases do not support Full Join (like SqlLite), but Microsoft SQL Server does.

The same query modified for Full Join returns 13 rows also.

```
SELECT EmployeeTerritories.EmployeeID AS 'ET.EMPID'
     , EmployeeTerritories.TerritoryID AS 'ET.TID'
     , Territories.TerritoryID AS 'T.TID'
FROM EmployeeTerritories
FULL JOIN Territories
   ON Territories.TerritoryID = EmployeeTerritories.TerritoryID
WHERE EmployeeTerritories.EmployeeID <= 3
```

This returns the same thing because, as in the Left and Right example, it always had a joined value on the other table. But with a Full Join, it can be possible to see a returned value with NULL in the left or in the right column. The result could be like this:

```
1       - 2
NULL  - 3
4       - NULL
```

Conclusion

All those Joins can be executed in Linq. Most of them have a similar syntax except the Full Join, which is more tricky. In another post, a default will be provided for all those joins.

Patrick Desjardins

3. C#

This chapter groups every post written during 2011 and 2012 about C# and .Net Framework general articles. Most of them are still coherent and effective two years later as the framework only evolved.

Getting resource value with explicit localization

Release Date: 19-Jun-12
Url: http://patrickdesjardins.com/blog/?post_type=post&p=1147

Sometimes, it is interesting to get a string value from a resource file without getting the one from the current **Thread.CurrentThread.CurrentUICulture**. Some scenarios may be that you are logged in a specific language and you need to send something to someone who is in a different language.

To be able to do this, you need to change the line of code that uses the static property and call the ResourceManager instead.

Let's say that your resource file name is "MyResource.resx". If you have set the visibility to public, the file MyResource.Designer.resx will contain a static property for all your entries. If you have a key value of "Res1" inside your file you will have a static property called "Res1" which will return a string.

```
public class MyResource
{
    public static string Res1
    {
        get { return ResourceManager.GetString("Res1", resourceCulture); }
    }
}
```

If you want to have access to a specific language without using the current resource culture, you need to instead call the resource by this static property to call the resource manager directly.

```
//Instead of :
string myString = MyResource.Res1;
//You have to call :
```

```
string     myString     =     MyResource.ResourceManager.GetString("Res1",     new
CultureInfo("FR"));
```

That's it. Of course, you have to make sure that you have the culture requested. Otherwise, an exception will be thrown.

Getting resource value with explicit localization

Release Date: 19-Jun-12
Url: http://patrickdesjardins.com/blog/?post_type=post&p=1147

Microsoft has been working on the garbage collector since version 1 of the .Net framework. Nevertheless, since Framework 4 they have increased their efforts to make this more efficient. The version 4.5 (still in RC version at this moment) goes a step further with a garbage collector that runs concurrently from the user thread. This results in a shorter time to recycle memory for large applications. The new garbage collector is called "<u>background server garbage collection</u>".

Heap balancing

Another improvement is that now the garbage collector heap is balanced (small and large object). That means that if a thread is using a lot of resources while other threads are not, the charge will be distributed evenly on all thread's heaps. This will reduce the time before cleaning memory.

Scheduler

A third improvement concerns the time when the garbage collector can recycle its memory. It is possible to activate a mode "SustainedLowLatency" which will let you set a schedule for when it is more appropriate to recycle memory. This lets you have a monster memory computer that will recycle only in a time frame or with an exception if the server runs low in memory.

Large memory allocation

Also, it is now possible with Microsoft Framework 4.5 to have large memory allocated without having the "OutOfMemoryException." Before, any allocation over 2 GB would raise an out of memory exception. Now, if the physical machine has more than 2 GB, then you can have more than 2 GB of memory allocation.

How to handle multiple global constants in an application

Release Date: 22-Oct-12
Url: http://patrickdesjardins.com/blog/?post_type=post&p=1706

The best way to have something organized and have constants in a single place is to have a class that will have an inner class. This way, you can organize by theme your constants.

```
public static class GlobalConstants
{
    public static class Division1
    {
        public const string Const1 = "123";
        public const string Const2 = "qwe";
        public const string Const3 = "asdfgh";
    }

    public static class Division2
    {
        public const string Const1 = "123";
    }
}
```

Of course, it is always better to have your constant in the class where they are more related. For example, the default value for a specific property of a class should be directly inside this class. But, for global constants that are used across the application, having a global constants class can do the job.

How to handle a null property with Automapper

Release Date: 28-Nov-12
Url: http://patrickdesjardins.com/blog/?post_type=post&p=1696

AutoMapper is a library that you can find now at GitHub (https://github.com/AutoMapper/AutoMapper). It is the same one that has been hosted on CodePlex previously. The purpose of the AutoMapper library is to allow you to transfer value from one object to another. This is useful when you are working with a DTO object or when you need to map properties between your model and the view model.

In this article, I show how to handle a null property. This case occurs if you have a source object that has a null property and you want to have in the destination a value. A simple example would be that you have a *User* class that can have a class *Address*. If this one is null, you may want to have in the destination an empty string or a default string value.

```
public class UserSource
{
    public Address Address { get; set; }
}

public class UserDestination
{
    public string Address { get; set; }
}
```

First, the mapping needs to have the indication of your action.

```
AutoMapper.Mapper.CreateMap<UserSource, UserDestination>()
        .ForMember(dest => dest.Address, opt => opt.NullSubstitute("Address not
found"));
```

This indicates to map *Address* to *Address* (default behavior) but has the optional **NullSubstitute** which lets you specify an object to be used for the mapping if the source object is null. In the previous example, a string has been used but a default object could have been used without problem.

Here is how to call the mapper. The mapping is done without any other option than normal mapping.

```
var model = AutoMapper.Mapper.Map<UserSource, UserDestination>(user);
var models = AutoMapper.Mapper.Map<IEnumerable<UserSource>,
                            IEnumerable<UserDestination>>(users);
```

How to create a mapping to a primitive type with AutoMapper.

Release Date: 30-Nov-12
Url: http://patrickdesjardins.com/blog/?post_type=post&p=1714

If you want to map one of your complex objects to a primitive you cannot use the ForMember method of Automapper to do it. Instead, you have to use the ConvertUsing.

Here is a case of ComplexType which represents a Boolean value.

```
Mapper.CreateMap<ComplexType, bool>().ConvertUsing(f => f.ID);
Mapper.CreateMap<bool, ComplexType>().ConvertUsing(f => new ComplexType(f));
```

This is useful if you have view models that represent primitive data and you want them to be represented into a view model object.

C# System.Transactions namespace

Release Date: 01-Oct-11
Url: http://patrickdesjardins.com/blog/?post_type=post&p=359

You can use your *DbConnection* to get your transaction but the System.Transactions namespace gives you another option for handling the transaction.

This namespace works with SQL Server 2005 and later and offers support for **distributed transactions**. At first, this transactions namespace will handle the transaction as a **local lightweight transaction** but if it detects that multiple connections are open the transaction switch is **distributed transactions**. This behavior is also known as "implicit transaction" because the developer does not explicitly show how to handle it.

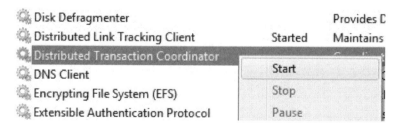

DTC's service needs to be started

For example, here is the example we previously did with the SqlDbConnection with the use of the System.Transactions instead of the one provided by the connection.

```
public int SaveCustomers(IEnumerable<Customer> customers)
{
    ConnectionStringSettings connectionStringSettings =
ConfigurationManager.ConnectionStrings["ApplicationServices"];
    int rowsAffected = 0;
    using (var connection = new
SqlConnection(connectionStringSettings.ConnectionString))
```

```
    {
        connection.Open();
        using (System.Transactions.TransactionScope ts = new
System.Transactions.TransactionScope())
        {
            using (var command = new SqlCommand())
            {
                command.Connection = connection;
                foreach (var customer in customers)
                {
                    if (customer.IsNew)
                    {
                        command.CommandText = "INSERT INTO customers (CustomerID,
CompanyName) VALUES (@id, @name)";
                    }
                    else
                    {
                        command.CommandText = "UPDATE customers SET CompanyName =
@name WHERE CustomerID = @id";
                    }
                    command.CommandType = System.Data.CommandType.Text;
                    command.Parameters.Clear(); //Remove
                    command.Parameters.Add(new SqlParameter("id", customer.Id));
                    command.Parameters.Add(new SqlParameter("name",
customer.Name));
                    rowsAffected += command.ExecuteNonQuery();
                }
                ts.Complete();
            }
        }
        connection.Close();
    }
    return rowsAffected;
}
```

As you can see, a few lines have been removed and some changed. You will notice that now we do not have any try-catch. That's right, USING handles any problem and if the *Transaction.Complete()* is not called, it is automatically a RollBack. If multiple connections are inside the transaction, all of them will be under the scope of the transaction distributed transactions coordinator.

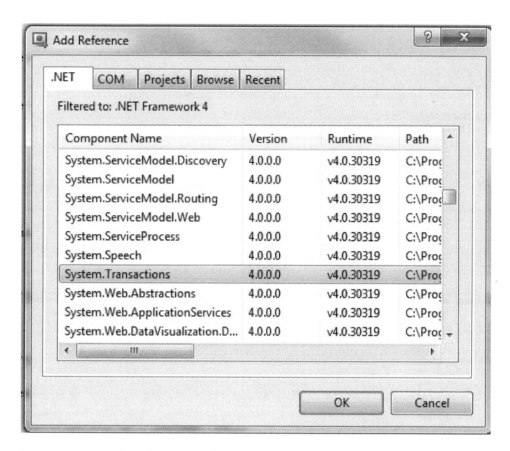

Ssytem.Transactions Reference DLL

Unfortunately, this namespace is only pertinent if you use SQL Server 2005 and higher. In fact, you should always use this if you are in a Microsoft SQL server 2005, 2008 or higher. The only time that it's not possible to use it is with another type of database. The reason to use this one instead of the ADO.NET transactions is the automatic handling of lightweight transactions and distributed transactions.

Transaction Scope Options

System.Transactions let's you set a type for your transaction via the enumeration TransactionScopeOption.

```
= new System.Transactions.TransactionScope(TransactionScopeOption.|))
```

opeOption TransactionScopeOption.Required		Required
is required by the scope. It uses an ambient transaction if one already exists. Otherwise, it		RequiresNew
transaction before entering the scope. This is the default value.		Suppress

Transaction Scope Option

Required

If a transaction exists, a new declaration of the transaction will simply join the first one. If none is defined, a new transaction will be initiated. This can be useful in the scenario where you have one method that calls two methods. You create the transaction and inside you add the two methods. Inside those methods you can have some database calls with or without transaction scope. At the end, all will be under the same transaction. This is very powerful and lets you have an automatic transaction over multiple methods.

RequiresNew

This will create a new independent transaction. This can be useful if you want to execute something whatever the state of the existing transaction. For example, you have a logging system that logs data into the database. You may want to log even if they are a problem.

Suppress

This removes the transaction behavior for all calls inside the transaction. This gives you the leverage to do stuff outside the transaction while being inside an existing transaction.

The use of System.Transactions to handle DTC is very useful. First, it lets you use Lightweight Transaction Manager(LTM) instead of DTC when possible. This gives you a big performance boost. Second, you do not need to inherit from ServicedComponent, so you can have a cleaner object with the possibility to inherit from what you desire. The last thing is that it does not use any COM+ object. So nothing is loaded in the Component Services.

Decimal literal and Float literal

Release Date: 06-Oct-11
Url: http://patrickdesjardins.com/blog/?post_type=post&p=424

Some maybe don't know, but if you want to write a double value in code you cannot write:

```
double myVariable = 100;
```

This will not work because the value will be treated as an integer. To resolve this issue, the simplest way to do it is to mark it as a decimal to the compiler with the suffix 'd' or 'D'.

```
double myVariable = 100d;
//or
double myVariable = 100D;
```

The same thing is good for float type. Instead of using the literal 'd' or 'D' you need to use the character 'F' or 'f'.

This is so basic that sometimes you may wonder why Visual Studio marks it as an error. To help yourself remember what is the character to mark a number into a specific type like double or float, remember it's the first letter of the type.

How to load application resource into a stream

Release Date: 17-Oct-11
Url: http://patrickdesjardins.com/blog/?post_type=post&p=480

Sometimes it can be useful to get a file that is a resource into the application. For example, using an XML file as a resource for testing purposes instead of having it outside the application.

File Property

The first step is to get the file into the project and click on Build Action to resource in the properties of the file.

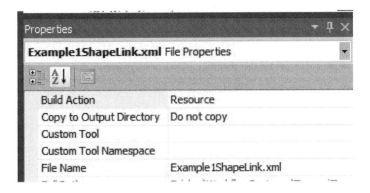

File Property

Application.GetResourceStream Methods

After that, the only code required will be to read this resource from your C# code. To extract the content of this resource you need to use the *GetResourceStream* method of the *System.Windows.Application*. Don't worry if you are a Silverlight user, you still have access to this namespace. This method takes a URI as parameter. This is where it can be tricky. First, you need to use a syntax that will define the namespace and then a relative path to the file.

Let's say that my project name is Project1 and the file is in Folder1/Folder2. The file name is Test.xml. You have a URI that would look like this.

```
... = new Uri("Project1;component/Folder1/Folder2/Test.xml", UriKind.Relative)
```

As you can see, the path needs to have the "component" before all directories.

Example of using XML with file resource

So, if you want to load a text file you will need to write:

```
//...
StreamResourceInfo sr1 = MediaTypeNames.Application.GetResourceStream(
    new Uri("Project1;component/Folder1/Folder2/Test.xml", UriKind.Relative));
var file = new StreamReader(sr1.Stream);
return file.ReadToEnd();
```

How to overload the square bracket operator in C#

Release Date: 03-Nov-12

Url: http://patrickdesjardins.com/blog/?post_type=post&p=515

This is pretty simple. In fact, I am writing this because most examples show you this:

```
public object this[int index]
{
    get { return collection[index]; }
    set { collection[index] = value; }
}
```

In fact, you should return the type of your collection. So, if your object contains a collection of *Person* then you should write :

```
public Person this[int index]
{
    get { return collection[index]; }
    set { collection[index] = value; }
}
```

This way, the value returned doesn't need to be casted.

Unit testing System.UnauthorizedAccessException: [InvalidCrossThreadAccess]

Release Date: 21-Dec-11
Url: http://patrickdesjardins.com/blog/?post_type=post&p=656

When unit testing you can get this kind of error if you try to use a class that uses a different thread from the main one.

At first, I didn't realize that I was using another thread because I was testing my Shape class. After some minutes, I realized that I was using the System.Windows.Shape and not mine. Once the reference set correctly I was able to remove this error and have my test work.

Test method UT.ShapeTest.CreateNewShape threw exception: System.UnauthorizedAccessException: [InvalidCrossThreadAccess] Arguments: ...

MSTest and the error Method should be marked static

Release Date: 26-Dec-11

Url: http://patrickdesjardins.com/blog/?post_type=post&p=661

If you came from the world of NUnit you may have gotten the error "Method should be marked static" without any indication of which method it is referring to.

With **NUnit**, you were using *TestFixtureSetUp* as an attribute to a class's method to get it executed before all tests, and only once. With MSTest you have to use the attribute *ClassInitialize*.

So, if you are used to writing:

```
[TestFixtureSetUp]
public void Init()
{
    //Some code executed once
}
```

You cannot simply use:

```
[ClassInitialize]
public void Init()
{
    //Some code executed once
}
```

In fact, the **Microsoft Unit Testing** framework requires this method to be public with a parameter of *TestContext*.

```
[ClassInitialize]
public static void Init(TestContext ctx)
{
    //Some code executed once
}
```

Once this is set as it should be, with the static method and the TestContext attribute, the error "Method should be marked static" will be removed and you will be fine.

Insert data into Excel with C#

Release Date: 15-Feb-12
Url: http://patrickdesjardins.com/blog/?post_type=post&p=710

It is possible with .Net to write data into Excel's cells. This can be done by using the library of **Microsoft.Office**.

The first step is to add a reference into your project by right clicking on the References folder and add the COM of Microsoft Office Excel.

Here is a small example that shows you how to open an Excel worksheet and add a value to two cells. It will save the content back the to the same file. The first approach does not use the Dynamic keyword, which would be more verbose. The second example does the same thing in less code by using Dynamic.

```
_Application docExcel = new Microsoft.Office.Interop.Excel.Application();
docExcel.Visible = false;
docExcel.DisplayAlerts = false;
_Workbook workbooksExcel = docExcel.Workbooks.Open(@"C:\test.xlsx"
    , Type.Missing
    , Type.Missing
    , Type.Missing
    , Type.Missing
    , Type.Missing
    , Type.Missing
    , Type.Missing
    , Type.Missing
    , Type.Missing
    , Type.Missing
    , Type.Missing
    , Type.Missing
    , Type.Missing
    , Type.Missing);
_Worksheet worksheetExcel = (_Worksheet) workbooksExcel.ActiveSheet;
((Range) worksheetExcel.Cells["1", "A"]).Value2 = "aa";
((Range) worksheetExcel.Cells["1", "B"]).Value2 = "bb";
workbooksExcel.Save();
workbooksExcel.Close(false, Type.Missing, Type.Missing);
docExcel.Application.DisplayAlerts = true;
docExcel.Application.Quit();
```

Second example with Dynamic:

```
_Application docExcel = new Application {Visible = false};
dynamic workbooksExcel = docExcel.Workbooks.Open(@"C:\test.xlsx");
var worksheetExcel = (_Worksheet) workbooksExcel.ActiveSheet;
((Range) worksheetExcel.Cells["1", "A"]).Value2 = "test1";
((Range) worksheetExcel.Cells["1", "B"]).Value2 = "test2";
workbooksExcel.Save();
workbooksExcel.Close(false);
```

```
docExcel.Application.Quit();
```

As you can see, it is a lot easier to maintain with dynamic.

How to pass method to a parameter to use its name later

Release Date: 01-Mar-12
Url: http://patrickdesjardins.com/blog/?post_type=post&p=753

The interface **INotifyPropertyChanged** requires an event called event *PropertyChanged* that takes a String as a parameter. This String represents the name of the property changed.

This kind of behavior exists in many other systems. Recently, I had to use a small project called Peta POCO, which is a tiny-tiny-tiny ORM for .Net. This also required marking properties as modified.

In both cases, the problem is that when setting the property you need to add automatically the name of the property between quotes. When refactoring the name of the property, there is a chance that you would miss the name change of this String. Most refactoring tools won't change String value, and that's a good thing.

But, you can simply create a method that uses the Lambda Tree Expression to be able to pass the method itself. This way, refactoring the name won't be a problem later.

How to do it is pretty straightforward.

```
protected void Modified(Expression<Func<string>> prop)
{
    if (prop == null)
    {
        throw new ArgumentNullException("prop", @"You must have selected a
method");
    }
    var body = prop.Body as MemberExpression;
    if (body == null)
    {
        throw new ArgumentException("The body must be a member expression");
        //USE : body.Member.Name
    }
}
```

I put a comment in the above code that indicates how to get the property name. This way, you can add it to your own list or call the *PropertyChanged* of **INotifyPropertyChanged** .

The use of this method is pretty easy also:

```
Modified(()=>this.MyProperty)
```

Another option is to use System.Reflection.MethodBase. This option lets you get the current Method name. This is also a good option but with the disadvantage that you can only have the current Property/Method and not be able to notify other fields. Sometimes, you may need to notify multiple Properties of a change. This won't give you this flexibility.

```
System.Reflection.MethodBase.GetCurrentMethod().Name.Replace("set_",
string.Empty);
```

The code above gives the string of the Property/Method that this line has executed. If it is inside a Property you will need to remove "set_" if you use it inside the setter, or "get_" if you use it inside the getter.

```
 public string CustomerEmail
{
    get { return _customerEmail; }
    set
    {
        _customerEmail = value;

Modified(System.Reflection.MethodBase.GetCurrentMethod().Name.Replace("set_",
string.Empty));
    }
}
```

Another method that is relatively similar to the previous one is to use the **Stacktrace** to get the method called. This gives you the advantage of not having to set any name or property reference to the method/property and of just having a method in the inherit class that handles the name of the previous stack method called. This has the disadvantage that you cannot have multiple fields to be notified. This is a good default approach but the one with Lambda Expression should also be implemented to give the developer the leverage to be able to call multiple property changes.

```
private string GetPropertyName()
{
    var callStackTrace = new StackTrace();
    var propertyFrame = callStackTrace.GetFrame(1);
    var properyAccessorName = propertyFrame.GetMethod().Name;
```

```
        return properyAccessorName.Replace("get_", "").Replace("set_", "");
}
```

The code above could be in the top model class that all your model classes inherit. This way, you just need to call another method like, for example, "Update()" which will refer to this GetPropertyName(). Do not forget that if you call GetPropertyName() from a class in the model class to change GetFrame(1) by GetFrame(2) the Stack will have YouProperty>Update()>GetPropertyName.

How to use an anonymous object to extend an object property for the instance of one method call.

Release Date: 09-Mar-12
Url: http://patrickdesjardins.com/blog/?post_type=post&p=780

I had to use a method that with reflection would take the property's name and value to create an SQL query. The problem is that the library was limited to methods directly inside the object passed and not the value of an inner object. For example, if class A contains an object B, we were not able to access B properties.

We could have done something much nicer like looping through all objects to get the desired sub-properties but to make it short, and because we wanted just to have the unique identifier of those objects, we decided to overload the method of the library to extend the properties for the time of this method call.

```
MyMethod(myObject, new {MyNewPersonalMethodName1 = myObject.SubObject.Id1,
MyNewPersonalMethodName2 = myObject.SubObject.Id2});

//or

MyMethod(myObject, myOtherObjectToUseProperties);
```

This is a representation of how it was done. The MyMethod was overloaded to accept a second parameter. This one will be used to receive an anonymous object. This way, it is easy to have a name <-> value relationship and it gives us the possibility to pass a complete real object if desired or simply pass an anonymous object as a parameter.

```
public void MyMethod(object myObject, object extendedProperties)
```

```
{
    //You can do something with all properties of myObject and its value here
    //Here you can do something with the extended properties
    if (extendedProperties != null)
    {
        var typeInfo = extendedProperties.GetType();
        var propertyInfo = typeInfo.GetProperties();
        foreach (PropertyInfo p in propertyInfo)
        {
            var nameToUpdate = p.Name;
            var valueToUpdate = (object) p.GetValue(extendedProperties, null);
            //Do somethind with nameToUpdate and valueToUpdate
        }
    }
}
```

The next step is to use reflection to be able to get all properties' names and values. After that, it's easy to be able to get the name to build an SQL query or a JSON object from object.

Instead of using your collection .Count() > 0, use .Any()

Release Date: 23-Mar-12
Url: http://patrickdesjardins.com/blog/?post_type=post&p=881

If you are using a **collection**: ICollection, IList, List, which does not use an enumerator to navigate, the fastest way to check if the collection contains anything is to use .Length or .Count.

But, if you are using IEnumerator<> which contains GetEnumerator() and MoveNext() the fastest way is to use .Any(). The reason is that Any() will do one loop and find that it has information so stop looping. If the collection is 10 in size or 9000 in size, both will do one loop so the speed is O(1).

LINQ-to-Objects implementation of Count() will call the .Count property for optimization but if you have used LINQ with a WHERE statement or any other Linq filter function, you will have an iterator-block-based sequence and this Count() optimization won't be applied. In fact, it will loop all the collections to get the count. That means that the performance is O(n).

To keep it simple, for performance and maintainability, .Any is the best to use to know if something is inside a list.

Parsing integer to enumerator with value out of the enumerator range

Release Date: 31-May-12
Url: http://patrickdesjardins.com/blog/?post_type=post&p=1108

If you want to convert an integer value into the enumerator that contains this value you can explicit cast the value.

```
public enum MyEnumType
{
    KeyA = 1,
    KeyB = 2
}

private class Program
{
    private static void Main(string[] args)
    {
        int myIntegerValue = 1;
        MyEnumType enu = (MyEnumType) myIntegerValue;
        Console.Read();
    }
```

}

This will work if the value, in our example 1, is in the MyEnumType. It will also work if we use an integer over 2.

```
namespace EnumParsing {
    public enum MyEnumType {
        KeyA = 1,
        KeyB = 2
    }

    class Program {
        static void Main(string[] args) {
            int myIntegerValue = 3;
            MyEnumType enu = (MyEnumType)myIntegerValue;
            Console.Read()    enu 3
        }
    }
}
```

Since the **.Net Framework 4**, we can use *Parse* and *TryParse* on the enumerator. The *TryParse* lets you parse the name of the enumerator or the value. This means you can parse "KeyA" and it will retrieve the enum for the value 1 or you can parse 1 and it will retrieve the enum for the value 1.

```
public enum MyEnumType {
    KeyA = 1,
    KeyB = 2
}

class Program {
    static void Main(string[] args) {
        int myIntegerValue = 1;
        string myStringNamedValue = "KeyA";         enu KeyA
        MyEnumType enu = (MyEnumType)Enum.Parse(typeof(MyEnumType),myIntegerValue.ToString());
        MyEnumType enu2 = (MyEnumType)Enum.Parse(typeof(MyEnumType), myStringNamedValue);
        Console.Read();
    }                           enu2 KeyA
}
```

In real application, if the data is from outside (user input) then it is always better to use *TryParse* because this will indicate if it can parse without throwing an exception. Here is an example with *Parse* with the wrong value followed by one with *TryParse*.

```
public enum MyEnumType {
    KeyA = 1,
    KeyB = 2
}

class Program {
    static void Main(string[] args) {
        int myIntegerValue = 4;                    ● enu 4
        string myStringNamedValue = "KeyC";
        MyEnumType enu = (MyEnumType)Enum.Parse(typeof(MyEnumType),myIntegerValue.ToString());
        MyEnumType enu2 = (MyEnumType)Enum.Parse(typeof(MyEnumType), myStringNamedValue);
        Console.Read();
    }                           ● enu2 0
}
```

> ⓘ **ArgumentException was unhandled**   ✕
> Requested value 'KeyC' was not found.

As you can see *Parse* works with an integer that is out of range but not for the named enumerator parsing, just for the value conversion.

What about *TryParse*? Same thing! It will return TRUE even if the value is out of range.

```
public enum MyEnumType {
    KeyA = 1,
    KeyB = 2
}

class Program {
    static void Main(string[] args) {
        int myIntegerValue = 4;
        string myStringNamedValue = "KeyC    ● success1 true     ● enu 4
        MyEnumType enu;
        bool success1 = Enum.TryParse(myIntegerValue.ToString(), out enu);
        MyEnumType enu2;
        bool success2 = Enum.TryParse(myStringNamedValue, out enu2);
        Console.Read();
    }                              ● success2 false    ● enu2 0
}
```

This can be problematic if you don't have control over the value. For example, the value is passed from Ajax call from the client side to your server as an Integer. You want to convert this into an enumerator to proceed as usual on the server. The way to ensure that the value is legitimate is to use **Enum.IsDefined**.

```
public enum MyEnumType {
    KeyA = 1,
    KeyB = 2
}

class Program {
    static void Main(string[] args) {
        int myIntegerValue = 4;
        string myStringNamedValue = "KeyC";
        MyEnumType enu;
        bool defined1 = Enum.IsDefined(typeof(MyEnumType), myIntegerValue);
        bool success1 = Enum.TryParse(myIntegerValue.ToString(), out enu);
        MyEnumType enu2;
        bool defined2 = Enum.IsDefined(typeof(MyEnumType), myIntegerValue);
        bool success2 = Enum.TryParse(myStringNamedValue, out enu2);
        Console.Read();
    }
}
}
```

| success1 | true |
| defined1 | false |

| enu | 4 |

| success2 | false |
| defined2 | false |

| enu2 | 0 |

So, every time you want to Parse an enumerator from the external (as an integer from an Ajax request) you should check if the value is defined correctly because only using the parsing tool won't tell you if you are out of range.

Memorystream: Invalid Operation Exception

Release Date: 12-Jun-12
Url: http://patrickdesjardins.com/blog/?post_type=post&p=1129

Memorystream that is initialized with the constructor that takes another stream can raise the exception "Invalid Operation Exception".

The proper way is to use the **Write** property after using the empty constructor.

```
var encoding = new UnicodeEncoding();
Byte[] bytesToCompress = encoding.GetBytes("Test123");
var streamToCompress = new MemoryStream();
streamToCompress.Write(bytesToCompress, 0, bytesToCompress.Length);
```

You can use Unicode encoding but also UTF8 or any other file encoding available.

How to remove trailing slash in C#

Release Date: 26-Jun-12
Url: http://patrickdesjardins.com/blog/?post_type=post&p=1154

I often see people using a substring to remove the last character if the character is a slash in a path or url. This can, if misused, lead to an error because maybe the string is empty and doesn't have count()-1 over 0.

Also, this requires a conditional statement to verify if the string contains at its latest position a slash.

A cleaner way to proceed with this kind of string cleanup it is to use the TRIM function of the string. The method *TrimEnd* lets you specify an array of characters that you want to remove at the end of the specified string.

Here is an example:

```
string fileName = "Test/";
fileName= fileName.TrimEnd(new[] { '/' });
```

With this method you can also specify multiple characters so you may want to remove all slashes or backslashes using the array.

```
string fileName = "Test\\";
fileName= fileName.TrimEnd(new[] { '/', '\\' });
```

Do not forget that this method will trim more than just the last character, but all ending characters. This means that a string ending with two slashes will see both slashes removed. I think it is even better!

When to use cast with AS and with explicit cast

Release Date: 03-Aug-12
Url: http://patrickdesjardins.com/blog/?post_type=post&p=1221

You can cast objects into another object in many way in C#.

Even if both technically do the same thing if successful, they shouldn't be used without thinking.

I often see people using **AS** to cast and never check if the cast is successfully executed.

```
var myObject = myOtherObject as MyObject;
myObject.Property1 = 1;
```

This is wrong. First, the cast can fail which will return null. In that case, a *NullReference* is triggered when the value 1 is set to the property. Second, why use casting with AS? The goal of AS is to cast and if something is wrong return the value NULL. This is good when NULL is an accepted state of the object, which it is not in the current example.

What we want is if the cast goes wrong to be notified, because it should never go wrong.

```
var myObject = (MyObject)myOtherObject;
myObject.Property1 = 1;
```

In case an error occurs, an exception will be thrown with the exception message: InvalidCast.

Nevertheless, you can cast with AS and check if the value is NULL. This is a good way to cast if a NULL value can happen and you need to act differently in that situation.

For example, if you know that, when casting, the value returns Null then you should use:

```
var myObject = myOtherObject as MyObject;
if(myObject != null)
    myObject.Property1 = 1;
else
    //...
```

So, next time you need to cast, ask yourself if you expect to have NULL (you expect that it will not cast because of the design, not because of a bug). If yes, you can use AS. Otherwise, use the explicit cast with the parentheses, which will trigger an exception.

How to add dynamic property to your class with ExpandoObject

Release Date: 05-Dec-12
Url: http://patrickdesjardins.com/blog/?post_type=post&p=1720

In some scenarios, you may want to add dynamic information to your object without having to define a specific type or interface. This type of scenario has been developed by Asp.Net MVC with the ViewBag which lets you add any type of information dynamically. In a project, you may want to have this kind of behavior and be able to add information of a different type and to access it later.

To do that, you need to use the ExpandoObject.

```csharp
public class YourClass
{
    public int Id { get; set; }
    public dynamic Attributes { get; set; }

    public MatriceRow()
    {
        Attributes = new ExpandoObject();
    }
}
```

This is a working example. From there you can use the YourClass class and set attributes.

```csharp
 var myClass = new YourClass();
myClass.Id = 1;
myClass.Attributes.IsBoolean = true;
myClass.Attributes.MyName = "Patrick Desjardins";
```

You cannot define the Attributes property directly to the type of ExpandoObject. If you do, you will get an exception.

'IsBoolean' and no extension method 'IsBoolean' accepting a first argument of type 'System.Dynamic.ExpandoObject' could be found. (Are you missing a using directive or an assembly reference?)

This functionality should be used rarely. It is always better to be strongly typed and not use dynamic because this is only checked when the code is executed rather than when it is compiled.

How to extend (or add) a conditional clause to Expression<T>

Release Date: 27-Sep-12

Author: Patrick Desjardins

If you need to concatenate two expressions (with OR or AND) this can be done easily with the help of the **LinqKit library** (http://www.albahari.com/nutshell/linqkit.aspx).

The idea is to Invoke both expressions with the same model object.

```
Expression<Func<Customer, bool>> filter1
                    = customer => customer.FirstName == "Test";
Expression<Func<Customer, bool>> filter2
                    = customer => customer.LastName == "Test";
Expression<Func<Customer, bool>> filter3
                =       customer       =>       filter1.Invoke(customer)       ||
filter2.Invoke(customer);
```

The last step is to use AsExpendable() and to Expand to the last filter (filter3).

```
IEnumerable<Customer> customers = CustomerRepository.GetAll()
                        .AsExpandable()
                        .Where(filter3.Expand())
                        .OrderBy(c => c.Id);
```

The AsExpendable() method simple creates a wrapper around the IQueryable to create an ExpendableQuery. From here, the provider will change with the concrete provider ExpendableQueryProvider which inherits from IQueryProvider. This will call the .Expand() of the expression.

If you go check the source code of the method ExpendableQuery we can see the wrapping.

```
public static IQueryable<T> AsExpandable<T>(this IQueryable<T> query)
{
    if (query is ExpandableQuery<T>)
    return query;
    else
    return(IQueryable<T>) new ExpandableQuery<T>(query);
}
```

The expand looks like this:

```
public static Expression<TDelegate> Expand<TDelegate>(this Expression<TDelegate>
expr)
{
    return (Expression<TDelegate>) new ExpressionExpander().Visit((Expression)
expr);
```

}

It calls the Visit method of the ExpressionExpander from the Expression.

In short, what you have to remember is that the use of LinqKit.dll makes your life really easier when you manipulate dynamic expressions.

So you have appended two Linq To Entity expressions.

Method with too many parameters

Release Date: 06-Aug-12
Url: http://patrickdesjardins.com/blog/?post_type=post&p=1226

I often see this kind of problem in development. It is not about C# or any other language but often people add parameters on the fly without getting the situation a little bit more in perspective. This is often the case when someone starts working in someone else's code; which happens all the time in development.

Let's start with this example:

```
public void MyUserReport(List<User> users)
{
}
```

This method's goal is to display the list of the users that we have. Later, a modification will be made to highlight a specific user. This is why the method signature will change to

```
public void MyUserReport(IEnumerable<User> users, int userToHighlightId)
{
}
```

The problem is that we also want to be able to display the rating of this highlighted user but not the other one.

```
public void MyUserReport(IEnumerable<User> users, int userToHighlightId, int
ratingScore)
{
}
```

And so on. Every new request for a feature adds new parameters to the method. This shouldn't happen because it will drive the code to have a monstrous method with a huge parameter count. Also, every parameter will require its validation rule. For example, can we put a ratingScore under 0? This is why, instead of passing primitive, we should pass business logic object. Instead of using userToHighlightId for the method and its score, we should pass a User object.

```
public void MyUserReport(IEnumerable<User> users, User userToHighlightId)
{
}
```

Not only does it make the method shorter, but it gives us the leverage to reuse the validation that is already done by the User model class. The rating, if located in the User class, will already have been validated by itself, and inside the Report method we won't have to do any validation. Not only is it better because we do not have to have external validation logic, but it is also the place to validate: inside the model. Cohesion is kept for User and the report class and the maintainability is increased. Furthermore, unit testing the user logic is only at one place and the report can mock the User for its own test (if required).

This situation occurs often, and should not. This happens also at the client side with JavaScript. The same refactoring is possible by simply encapsulating the data into a class and using the class instead of the primitive.

Regex Tool For .Net Developers

Release Date: 13-Oct-11
Url: http://patrickdesjardins.com/blog/?post_type=post&p=458

I am far from being an expert in Regex but with good tools writing a Regex becomes easier.

First, I suggest you download RegexBuilder (http://renschler.net/RegexBuilder) from Renschler. This Regex tool is ideal once the Regex is created to check a few sentences and to quickly see if something is wrong or not.

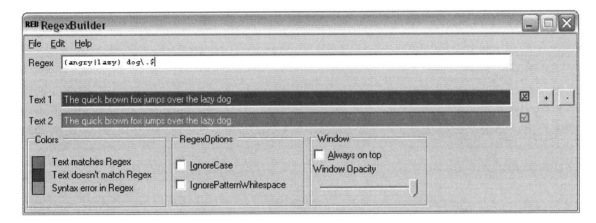

The second tool is something for helping you to create the Regex. This Regex tool is also free by RadSoftware. You can download it here (http://www.radsoftware.com.au/?from=RegexDesigner).

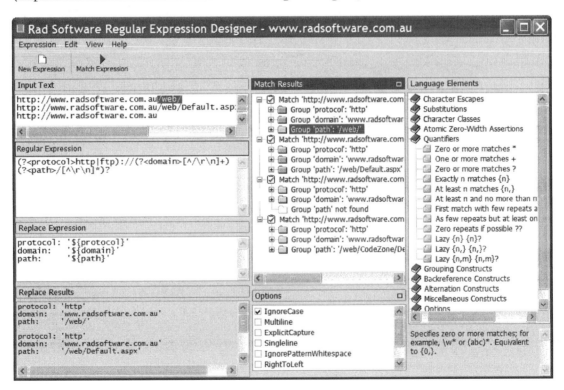

This tool is great to see what will be in your group and it also contains a library of all Regex syntax.

With these two tools you should enjoy a little bit more the creation of Regex.

How to compare elements from the same collection with Linq

Release Date: 10-Dec-11
Url: http://patrickdesjardins.com/blog/?post_type=post&p=624

Let's imagine that you have a collection with a class containing Images. All images are identified by a unique key and a caption that the user enters. You want to verify that the caption entered by the user is unique to the collection. How to do it?

This can be done with **Linq to Object** pretty easily by using two from statements.

```
var hasDouble = (from s1 in this.Images
                 from s2 in this.Images
                 where s1.Key != s2.Key && s1.Caption == s2.Caption
                 select new {Image1 = s1, Image2 = s2}).Any();
```

This will loop through all the images and will compare the caption of all shapes but not compare a node with itself.

I have created an anonymous object because I may want to get those two elements to have the same caption. In that case I just need to call the same code and remove the .Any().

This can be translated to a Lambda expression.

```
var x = this.Shapes.SelectMany(s1 => this.Images, (s1, s2) => new {s1, s2})
                .Where(tt => tt.s1.Key != tt.s2.Key
                          && tt.s1.Caption == tt.s2.Caption)
                .Select(tt => new {Image1 = tt.s1, Image2 = tt.s2});
```

But for this kind of task, Lambda is more confusing, from my point of view.

Linq and grouping with a custom object

Release Date: 03-Dec-12
Url: http://patrickdesjardins.com/blog/?post_type=post&p=1717

Depending on what you want to do, you may want to group by ID or by values. A common case is to group by a unique identifier but also get some connected information like let's say the name. For example, if we want to group every job that everybody had in their life, we would like to group by userid. But we may want to have their full name.

```
var groupedList = nonGroupedList
    .GroupBy(g=> new MyCustomGroupingClass(g.UserId, g.UserFullName));
```

This will not work because every MyCustomGroupingClass will be different from the C# perspective. This is because Linq will compare every object and figure out that every MyCustomGroupingClass has a different object.

```
var groupedList = nonGroupedList
                .GroupBy(g=> g.UserId);
```

This would work, because an integer is comparable, but it does not solve the need to have the user name.

The solution is hidden in the problem: comparing classes. We need to provide a way to compare. This can be done by providing an override to the Equals method of your grouping class.

```
public class MyCustomGroupingClass
{
    public int ID { get; set; }
    public string FullName { get; set; }

    public override bool Equals(object obj)
    {
        if (ReferenceEquals(null, obj))
        {
            return false;
        }
        if (ReferenceEquals(this, obj))
        {
            return true;
        }
        if (obj.GetType() != this.GetType())
        {
            return false;
        }
        return Equals((MyCustomGroupingClass) obj);
    }

    protected bool Equals(MyCustomGroupingClass other)
    {
        return ID.Equals(other.ID) && string.Equals(FullName, other.FullName);
    }
}
```

From here, you will be able to group without problem with Linq and your custom grouping class.

Implementing Performance Counter in your application

Release Date: 11-Oct-11
Url: http://patrickdesjardins.com/blog/?post_type=post&p=445

Microsoft Windows has a Performance Counter application that is located in the Administrator Folder.

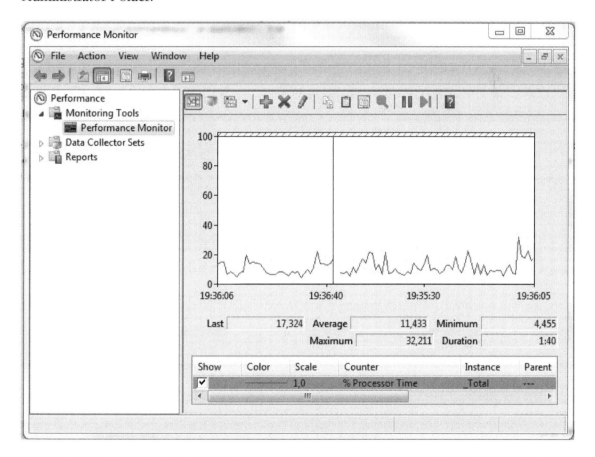

Go to Control Panel\All Control Panel Items\Administrative Tools\ and select *Performance Monitor*. This will open a window with by default the processor performance. What is interesting is that you can see a lot of already coded performance counters by right clicking the list of counters and select *Add Counters…* or press the button with the "+" icon.

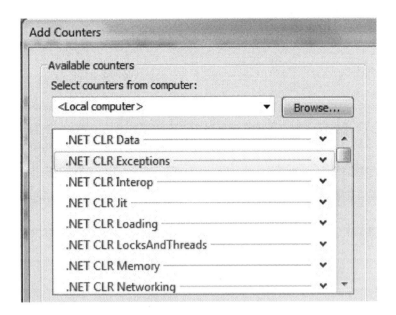

What is interesting is that you can create your own counter inside your application and be able to visualize the result within this Performance Counter.

What you need is the *System.Diagnostics* namespace. From there you can verify if the counter you want to create exists with the static method 'PerformanceCounterCategory.Exists'.

To create your counter, you need 'PerformanceCounterCategory.Create'.

```
PerformanceCounterCategory.Create("CategoryName"
                    , "CategoryHelpText"
                    , PerformanceCounterCategoryType.SingleInstance
                    , "CounterNameInsideTheCategory"
                    , "CounterHelpText.");
```

This code must only be executed when a verification is made with the Exists method of PerformanceCounterCategory or an exception will be thrown.

When you are ready to use the counter you need to use the method Increment or IncrementBy. The first will increment by one and the other with the value passed in a parameter. If it needs to decrease, you will need to pass a negative value.

```
var pc = new PerformanceCounter("CategoryName", "CounterNameInsideTheCategory",
false);
pc.IncrementBy(10);
```

Grouping resource files with its designer

Release Date: 24-Aug-12
Url: http://patrickdesjardins.com/blog/?post_type=post&p=1299

You may come into a project that has resource files that are not linked with their designer file.

The cause is simply that the custom tool has been removed. You only need to set it back and the resource and designer will be linked.

Properties	
Strings.Designer.cs File Properties	
Build Action	Compile
Copy to Output Directory	Do not copy
Custom Tool	PublicResXFileCodeGenerator
Custom Tool Namespace	
File Name	Strings.Designer.cs

This creates the designer file under the resource. You can then delete the old designer files.

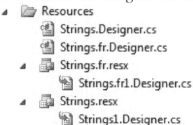

C# Sealed Method

Release Date: 19-Sep-11

Url: http://patrickdesjardins.com/blog/?post_type=post&p=293

The keyword *sealed* is used in the class definition to prevent being derived from. When it is applied to methods, it means that the method cannot be overridden.

Methods can only be overridden when the virtual keyword is used so why is *sealed* required? It is required when a class derives from a class that had a virtual method. This will override and an overridden method can also be overridden. To prevent that, the override method can use the *sealed* keyword.

```csharp
internal class A
{
    public virtual void F()
    {
        Console.WriteLine("A.F");
    }

    public virtual void G()
    {
        Console.WriteLine("A.G");
    }
}

internal class B : A
{
    public override sealed void F()
    {
        Console.WriteLine("B.F");
    }

    public override void G()
    {
        Console.WriteLine("B.G");
    }
}

internal class C : B
{
    public override void G()
    {
        Console.WriteLine("C.G");
    }
}
```

Linq to Object with Cross Join

Release Date: 31-Aug-11
Url: http://patrickdesjardins.com/blog/?post_type=post&p=48

It is possible to perform a **Cross Join** with Linq. A Cross Join is a Cartesian product. It means that if between two sets of values all values will join at one time the other set.

For example:

If we have one set with the letter A and B, and a set with C, D, E than the result should be: A-C, A-D, A-E, B-C, B-D, B-E. Let's do it in code.

```
var x = new string[] {"A", "B"};
var y = new string[] {"C", "D", "E"};
var cross = from x1 in x
            from y1 in y
            select new {x1, y1};
foreach (var output in cross)
{
    Console.WriteLine("{0} - {1}", output.x1, output.y1);
}
Console.Read();
```

This is the console application output:

CrossJoin's Result

To conclude, cross join is pretty straightforward with Linq. This example was done with Linq to Object but can be also be done with Linq to SQL query.

Lambda Expression

Release Date: 28-Sep-11
Url: http://patrickdesjardins.com/blog/?post_type=post&p=328

Lambda Expressions can be of two types:

- Code Delegate (compiled)

- Expression Tree Object (runtime)

The **Code Delegate** is used a lot with Linq. Almost all extensions like Where are a delegate function that is compiled into IL code. It is very fast because it is compiled. On the other hand, some situations when the data is not evaluated against direct memory, or requires some reflection against what is passed, requires Expression Tree Object Lambda.

In the code, you can know if it is a Code Delegate or Expression Tree with the declaration of the parameter. If the method you call uses

```
Func<T,bool> predicate //bool can be something else
```

it is because it is a delegate. In fact, the **Func** method is a predefined delegate that takes one or more parameters with a return value. This can be compiled. Conversely, Expression Tree Object uses

```
Expression<Fun<T,bool>> predicate //bool can be something else
```

Instead of compiling into IL, this generates code to let the framework analyze the expression. It lets the developer know the type, the name of the object and the value of it. This is why Linq To SQL requires using an expression instead of compiling because it needs to read the delegate information and translate it into an SQL statement.

Real-Life Example

I think a simple example could be the one of INotifiedPropertyChanged. This interface gives a method that has for a parameter a string that must be the name of the property that has changed. When going straight from this implementation, some problems may arise like not entering the name of the property correctly or, when refactoring, the tool may not check the string value to change it. To solve this issue, you can use Expression Tree Object to get all methods of the current object and to select one of them.

```
protected virtual void OnPropertyChanged(string propertyName)
{
    PropertyChangedEventHandler handler = this.PropertyChanged;
    if (handler != null)
    {
        var e = new PropertyChangedEventArgs(propertyName);
        handler(this, e);
```

```
        }
}
```

Line 11 contains the Expression Tree Object that contains the delegate Func. This means that it doesn't take any parameter and return a value of type .

```
private MyObject myObject;

public MyObject MyObject
{
    get { return myObject; }
    set
    {
        myObject = value;
        base.OnPropertyChanged(() => MyObject);
        // This was before used like this : base.OnPropertyChanged("MyObject");
    }
}
```

Line 7 contains the Lambda method and in the same line, in comment, you can see the original.

Access to modified closure when having a Linq inside a loop

Release Date: 19-Dec-11
Url: http://patrickdesjardins.com/blog/?post_type=post&p=651

If you have Resharper, you can see sometimes a warning saying that you have "Access to modified closure." If you do not have it, you can still have odd behavior of some kind with the values. In both cases, this means that Linq is accessing a value that might (or not) be modified.

Linq executes delegate functions. If you try:

```
var listInteger = new List<int>() {1, 2, 3, 4, 5}; //Values
var funcs = new List<Func<int>>(); //Delegate function that take a Integer as
parameter
foreach (var v in listInteger) // Add in the list of delegate's functions a
function that return the integer value
{
    funcs.Add(() => v);
}
foreach (var f in funcs) //Execute functions which should just return the value.
{
    Console.WriteLine(f()); // We expect here to have 1,2,3,4,5}
```

```
}
```

you will not see 1,2,3,4,5 but 5,5,5,5,5. The reason is that it accesses a modified variable. The function is not adding the value of v but the pointer to it. This is why it remains on the last value of the loop. But, by using a variable inside the loop, the pointer is to this variable and directly to the good value.

```
var listInteger = new List<int>() {1, 2, 3, 4, 5}; //Values
var funcs = new List<Func<int>>(); //Delegate function that take a Integer as
parameter
foreach (var v in listInteger) // Add in the list of delegate's functions a
function that return the integer value
{
    var vv = v;
    funcs.Add(() => vv);
}
foreach (var f in funcs) //Execute functions which should just return the value.
{
    Console.WriteLine(f()); // We expect here to have 1,2,3,4,5
}
```

Most of the time, no one will have this problem because most of the time the Linq won't execute delegate functions defined somewhere else, but an anonymous function that calls directly the value of the variable. But, as a good practice, it is always better when accessing variables that may be changed to create a temporary variable to remove the undesired effect.

4. JAVASCRIPT AND CSS

This chapter groups every post written during 2011 and 2012 about client side technologies like JavaScript and CSS. Most of them are still coherent and effective two years later, at the time I published this book. If some information is outdated, I still believe it may provide some positive insight to you by showing the evolution of the front end of web development.

How to make three little dots when text is too big for a cell in a table

Release Date: 06-Mar-12
Url: http://patrickdesjardins.com/blog/?post_type=post&p=766

If you are using a grid (third-party) or a simple HTML table you may need to have a fixed column width but not have the text overlap to the next cell if it's bigger than the cell width.

To fix this kind of issue, you may want to add three dots after a certain number of characters. This can be done automatically with CSS3 and it is called an ellipsis.

```
.yourGridClassName td {
    white-space: nowrap;
    overflow: hidden;
    text-overflow: ellipsis
}
```

The *white-space:nowrap* is used to make sure that even if spaces are present nothing will be wrapped underneath. The *overflow:hidden* makes the text not overlap to the next cell or outside the table. Finally, the *text-overflow: ellipsis* adds three little dots to indicate that the text continues but doesn't have enough space to show.

Alternative to clear:both when you need to have a container to expand to your floating content

Release Date: 14-Jun-12
Url: http://patrickdesjardins.com/blog/?post_type=post&p=1127

Instead of adding an HTML tag after floating division, it is better to add a class that will do this. It is better because you do not have to alter the HTML for visual stuff that the CSS is designed to handle. The solution is known as "Clear fix." It is possible with CSS 2.0 to add :after, which will add an element after the one that will carry this class.

```css
.clear-fix:after {
    visibility: hidden;
    display: block;
    font-size: 0;
    line-height: 0;
    content: " ";
    clear: both;
    height: 0;
    width: 0;
}
```

In fact, this will create an invisible division after any DOM element that has the clear-fix class. It will act the same as in the old way,with an empty division with the clear:both style. But it is cleaner.

CSS and the selector nth-child

Release Date: 27-Jul-12
Url: http://patrickdesjardins.com/blog/?post_type=post&p=1204

You may want to have a special style for a specific position. Maybe you want to have the first division different or have every three rows something different.

This can be done with nth-child selector of CSS.

Let's start with a small example:

```css
ul > li:nth-child(3)
{
    color: red;
}
```

This example takes the third "li" element that is directly under a "ul" element and changes the font color to red.

The parameter, when specified with an integer, represents the position of the occurrence of the element. In the example above, 3 is specified, so the third element will be red.

nth-child is powerful because you can use the variable "n" to specify the index of the element.

```
ul>li:nth-child(2n+1)
{
    background-color: red;
}
```

This second example of nth-child has 2n+1 as a parameter. That means that it will start at the position 1 (every sequence starts at 1 not 0). 2n means 2 multiplied by the index. So if we have the following code:

```
<ul>
    <li>n=0</li>
    <li>n=1</li>
    <li>n=2</li>
    <li>n=3</li>
    <li>n=4</li>
    <li>n=5</li>
</ul>
```

2n+1 will be for the first line: 2×0+1 = 1. So the first li will have the style, and the first one will be 1. Then we have 2×1+1 = 3. The second row won't have any style, the third one will, and so on.

To conclude, you have to remember that n starts at 0 but the first element is 1. As we have seen with the ul/li example, the n=0 was colored because n=0+1 = 1, which is the first li of the ul collection.

Using an HTML Label element with a fixed width

Release Date: 29-Jul-12
Url: http://patrickdesjardins.com/blog/?post_type=post&p=1211

You may want to use Label juxtaposed with an input element and want those labels to be a fixed width. This can be the case if you have some columns done with division and you want to have all labels aligned on the left and have all their input control aligned left but at the same distance and not depending on the text's size. For that, you want a fixed width for all labels. This can be done by setting the width but also setting the display to block instead of inline. Also, you will need to make it float.

```
label {
    display: block;
    float: left;
    width: 200px;
}
```

CSS block, inline and inline-block comparison

Release Date: 27-Aug-12
Url: http://patrickdesjardins.com/blog/?post_type=post&p=1307

What is the difference between an element with display block, display inline and display inline-block? It is all about the element's way to take the space within HTML.

Display Block

The display block lets you specify a width and a height, and it acts as a block of space. If you want to have something to its right, the element will need to float because, by default, the block won't let anything be around it. It also lets you use a margin attribute. By default, header tags like H1 use block and you won't be able to add anything to its right; it will go automatically to underneath it. The same thing happens if you use the paragraph tag "p".

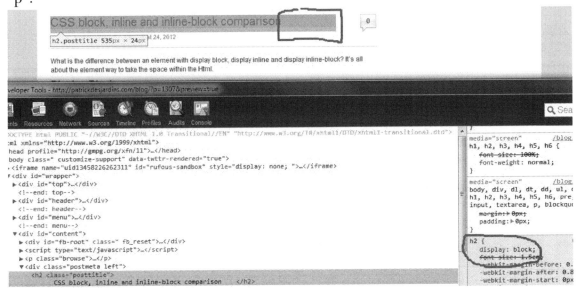

Display Inline

This is the opposite. It will take only the space required, and won't let you set width or height. This is perfect if you want to have add tag within an element. This is the default value for "span" tag. But this won't let you use the margin and sizing feature.

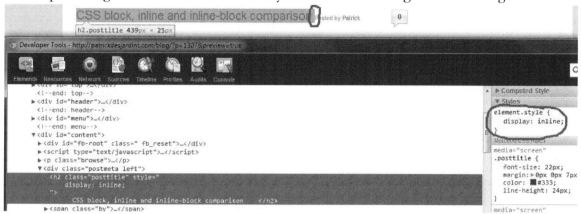

Display Inline-Block

The main goal of inline block is to preserve its block capabilities such as width and height, top and bottom margins, and paddings.

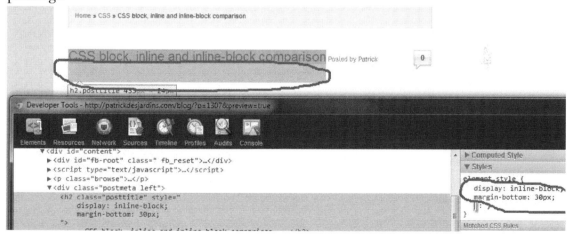

So that's it for display value. Of course you can set display:none if you want to remove the element and its space (inverse of visible which will remove the visual aspect while preserving the space). You can also use display:list-item if you want it to act like list "li" which will add a bullet to every row. This is acting like display:block with a bullet.

Dynamic caching level

Release Date: 03-Sep-12
Url: http://patrickdesjardins.com/blog/?post_type=post&p=1332

I have read an interesting article that talks about the different levels of caching that Dynamic keywords use.

The dynamic lookup is performed at runtime in three different ways. First, it checks if the last dynamic methods and arguments type corresponds to the last call. If yes, it will reuse the compiled code. This is very fast, as fast as using something not dynamic minus the little extra step of validation.

The second way is to check into the complete list of dynamic code that has been called to find a method signature corresponding. This is also very fast. If it found something, it will update the last called method to be faster next time. Otherwise, it goes into the last step.

The last step is to build the method call and to update the list of methods. The pseudo code of the logic is like this:

```
if (lastMethod = currentOneInvoked)
{
    Invoke(currentOneInvoked);
}
else if (listMethod.Find(currentOneInvoked))
{
    Invoke(currentOneInvoked);
}
else
{
    UpdateAndInvoke(currentOneInvoked, arg0, /*...*/);
}
```

So, the dynamic method is slower but is optimized to be as fast as possible.

Selectivizr example: how to use CSS selector with older browser

Release Date: 07-Dec-12
Url: http://patrickdesjardins.com/blog/?post_type=post&p=1725

Selectivizr is a small JavaScript library (under 20k when not compressed and under 5k when compressed) that has the goal to make your CSS work with older browsers like IE8, IE7, IE6. Selectivizr requires you to have a JavaScript library in your HTML file. This is not a problem usually because most websites use JQuery. So, to make it work, first download Selectivizr.

Second, go just under the line where you add JQuery and add the following code.

```
<script src="@Url.Content("~/Scripts/Libs/jquery-1.8.2.js")"
type="text/javascript">
</script>
<!--[if (gte IE 6)&(lte IE 8)]>
    <script type="text/javascript"
src=@Url.Content("~/Scripts/Libs/selectivizr.js")>
    </script>
<![endif]-->
```

Of course, the code above uses Url.Content that comes from the Asp.Net framework but you could simply add both JavaScript with a relative or absolute path manually. So, it works with any web framework like PHP.

From here, all code that was using a more specific selector like :hover, :focus, :first-child, :last-child, :nth-child, :not… will work!

What happens is that it will simulate with JavaScript instead of using CSS for IE 6-8 and will remain with CSS for all other browsers.

JavaScript variables grouping with object acting like namespace

Release Date: 16-Nov-11

Url: http://patrickdesjardins.com/blog/?post_type=post&p=575

In JavaScript , if you need to have multiple global variables in a script you could finish with something like a chunk of `var`.

```
var v1;
var v2;
var v3;
var v4;
var v5;
```

This can cause problems because maybe someone will need to define a variable with the same name (locally or globally). To reduce this problem, you can use a JavaScript object notation (JSON). By using JSON syntax you can create a "virtual" namespace with an object. I say "virtual namespace" because it is not a namespace. In fact, it is an object, but it is created just to group variables instead of letting them be random at the top of a JavaScript file. This is pretty important because if a web page includes many JavaScript files it could end up having two files using the same variable name which would cause one to override the value of the other.

```
var mynamespace = { "v1": "value1"
                  , "v2": "value2"
                  , "v3": "value3"
                  , "v4": "value4"
                  , "v5": "value5"
                  , "v6": "value6" };
```

This way, instead of using in your code v1 directly you use the object v1.

```
mynamespace.v1 = "Patrick";
//...
if(mynamespace.v1 == "Unknown")
{
    //...
}
```

This post covers only the basics. You can have multiple levels of depth as JSON lets you have an inner array or "object." I will cover this later.

Accessing input control of a parent inside a child frame

Release Date: 18-Nov-11
Url: http://patrickdesjardins.com/blog/?post_type=post&p=583

Not long ago, I had to modify a code that was using a **Frameset** with **Frame**.

I had an issue because the code was written for Internet Explorer only and it was accessing the hidden field by using "parent.window.document.myhiddenfield.value".

My first reflex was to remove the window and use getElementById. Like this:

```
parent.document.getElementById('myhiddenfield').value
```

This does not work with Firefox either. After some search, I found that we can use "self.ownerDocument". Like this:

```
elf.ownerDocument.getElementById('bar');
```

Unfortunately, this does not work with Internet Explorer, just Firefox.

My last try was to use JQuery, and that solved most of the compatibility problem.

This is the current implementation that works to get hidden input control (or any other input) from a child frame to a parent that holds the frameset.

```
parent.$("#myhiddenfield").val()
```

How to call anonymous function in JavaScript

Release Date: 18-May-12
Author : Patrick Desjardins

You may have anonymous functions that you want to call later in the same caller method, or pass this method into a parameter of another method by parameter to call this one later. To be able to have a reference to this anonymous function (known as delegate), you need to use a variable that will keep a reference to this anonymous function. Later, when you want to use it, you simply need to call it by writing the variable name with parentheses.

```
var anonymous = function ()
{
    alert("Test123");
```

```
};
anonymous();
```

From there, you can have a more complex prototype (JavaScript class mechanism).

```
function MyClass(val1, val2) {
    this.val1 = val1;
    this.val2 = val2;
    this.function1 = function() { alert(this.val1); }
} //...
var x = new MyClass('Test', 'Hello');
x.function1();
```

This example shows you that you can have an anonymous function that can be called later like the previous example.

Dynamic function in JavaScript

Release Date: 23-May-12
Url: http://patrickdesjardins.com/blog/?post_type=post&p=1103

On some occasions, calling a dynamic function in JavaScript can be useful. This is the case when you have a string that represents the name of the function that you want to execute. One way to do it it to use the **EVAL** keyword in JavaScript. It is not the best way to do it, but it is the way more known by developers. It lets you evaluate JavaScript in a string format. That means that anything given to that function is executed on the client browser. This opens a door to malicious code that could be executed. This is why I will show you a second approach that will not use the EVAL key to execute a dynamic method in JavaScript.

First of all, here is an example of code that executes a dynamic function with the EVAL keyword.

```
function myFunction() { alert('Test'); }
var functionName = "myFunction"; //Dynamic builded
var functionParameter = "firstParameter, secondParameter";//Dynamic parameters
var functionToCall = functionName + "('" + functionParameter + "');";
var ret = eval(functionToCall);
```

As you can see, we could have had some kind of logic to choose the functionName. This could have been generated by the server side or could have been loaded from the database or a Web Service. The dangerous part is that someone could change the functionName to direct JavaScript statements that could harm the user.

Here is a better approach that consists of using the window object to call the method. This, at least, ensures that we are calling a function and not any JavaScript statement. However, it is still possible for it to be hacked and to execute harmful code.

```
function myFunction() { alert('Test'); }
var functionName = "myFunction"; //Dynamic builded
var functionParameter = "firstParameter, secondParameter"; //Dynamic parameters
var functionToCall = window[functionName];
var ret = functionToCall(functionParameter);
```

In both cases, the important thing is not to EVAL data that has been input by the user. The executed dynamic code in JavaScript must be generated only by the developer that has built the system.

JQuery .on() function

Release Date: 16-Jun-12
Url: http://patrickdesjardins.com/blog/?post_type=post&p=1092

JQuery provides good examples concerning adding events to an HTML DOM object dynamically. This means that even if the DOM does not exist, when the event is attached the event will be hooked with the HTML DOM object. The methodology of this thinking has changed since Jquery version 1.3. At first, we had to use the live method.

```
$("a.offsite").live("click", function () { alert("Goodbye!"); }); // jQuery 1.3+
```

In version 1.4.3, we could have used the delegate function.

```
$(document).delegate("a.offsite", "click", function () { alert("Goodbye!"); });
// jQuery 1.4.3+
```

But now, to reduce the confusion between all the functions to attach events (bind(), live(), delegate()) to an HTML DOM object, we simply use the ON function.

```
$(document).on("click", "a.offsite", function () { alert("Goodbye!"); }); //
jQuery 1.7+
```

In this example, since the .on() function is called from the $(document) this will list every

HTML that changed to hook the function if the selector matches.

The syntax of the on function in Jquery is:

```
.on( events [, selector] [, data], handler(eventObject) )or.on( events-
map [, selector] [, data] )
```

This means that you first select the event you want to add, then the selector in the Jquery syntax, and finallywhat you want to hook to.

But you are not limited to listing everything on the web page. This is useful if you load content from Ajax but if you want to add an event only on a specific part of the page you can specify it instead of the document and add the event.

```
$("#myTable tr").on("click", function (event) { alert($(this).text()); });
```

This will add to every line of the myTable the possibility to click. If you want to have a new line (JavaScript added tr) of this grid automatically bound to the click event, you need to change the above code to set up the onclick in the table.

```
$("#myTable").on("click", "tr", function (event) { alert($(this).text()); });
```

This way, it bubbles up to the myTable, which is always available, and the click will occur.

Watch out with attaching from the document. Attaching many delegated event handlers near the top of the document tree can degrade performance rapidly. This is even more true with events like mousemouve that are called a lot of times sequentially.

How to have a JQuery function using callback with parameter

Release Date: 21-Dec-12
Url: http://patrickdesjardins.com/blog/?post_type=post&p=1761

Let's say that you want to use a JQuery function and do something when it ends. This is possible with callback that most JQuery functions do have. Unfortunately, you might want to pass data to the callback function when this one may not let you. How to handle this situation? This is what we will see in this short article concerning JQuery and the callback function.

First of all, why would we want to pass information to callback? Couldn't we simply use the anonymous function and access data from the outer scope? True, but this may lead to a big chunk of code and also cause repeat code. Let's take the following example where an Ajax call is done. We want to hide a division, set the value from the Ajax call and then display the division again. But, we may not want the division already visible; in this case we just want to set the data and display the division.

```
$.ajax({
    type: 'POST'
    , contentType: 'application/json; charset=utf-8'
    , data: /*...*/
    , dataType: 'json'
    , url: /*...*/
    ,success: function(result) {
        var resultJson = $.parseJSON(result);
        if ($("#myDivisionWhereTheDataBelong").is(":visible"))
        {
            $("#myDivisionWhereTheDataBelong").slideUp(150, /*Set data from Ajax
call here + Show Division Again*/);
        }
        else
        {
            /*Set data from Ajax call here + Show Division Again*/
        }
    }
});
```

This illustrates the goal of this article. How can you "set the data from Ajax and show the division" without having the same code twice. The first reflex may be to create a function but let's first write the code repeated in both places to illustrate a functional code that is simply not optimized.

```
$.ajax({
    type: 'POST'
    , contentType: 'application/json; charset=utf-8'
    , data: /*...*/
    , dataType: 'json'
    , url: /*...*/
    , success: function(result) {
        var resultJson = $.parseJSON(result);
        if ($("#myDivisionWhereTheDataBelong").is(":visible")) {
            $("#myDivisionWhereTheDataBelong").slideUp(150, function() {
                $('#FormInput1').val(resultJson.Val1);
                $('#FormInput2').val(resultJson.Val2);
                $("myDivisionWhereTheDataBelong").slideDown(150);
            });
```

```
    } else {
        $('#FormInput1').val(resultJson.Val1);
        $('#FormInput2').val(resultJson.Val2);
        $("myDivisionWhereTheDataBelong").slideDown(150);
    }
  }
});
```

As you can see, it is not pretty because we duplicate code, but it works.

The second step is to create a function but the main problem is that slideUp takes only a callback function that doesn't have any parameter.

```
var showResult = function(resultJson) {
    $('#FormInput1').val(resultJson.Val1);
    $('#FormInput2').val(resultJson.Val2);
    $("myDivisionWhereTheDataBelong").slideDown(150);
}
$.ajax({
    type: 'POST'
    , contentType: 'application/json; charset=utf-8'
    , data: /*...*/
    , dataType: 'json'
    , url: /*...*/
    ,success: function(result) {
        var resultJson = $.parseJSON(result);
        if ($("#myDivisionWhereTheDataBelong").is(":visible")) {
            $("#myDivisionWhereTheDataBelong").slideUp(150, showResult);
        } else {
            showResult(resultJson);
        }
    }
});
```

This will not work because we do not pass the showResult method any parameter, and even by writing "showResult(resultJson)" it will not do much more. In fact, we need to pass a pointer to a function without a parameter.

```
var showResult = function(resultJson) {
    return function() {
        $('#FormInput1').val(resultJson.Val1);
        $('#FormInput2').val(resultJson.Val2);
        $("myDivisionWhereTheDataBelong").slideDown(150);
    };
};
$.ajax({
    type: 'POST'
```

```
    , contentType: 'application/json; charset=utf-8'
    , data: /*...*/
    , dataType: 'json'
    , url: /*...*/
    ,success: function(result) {
        var resultJson = $.parseJSON(result);
        if ($("#myDivisionWhereTheDataBelong").is(":visible")) {
            $("#myDivisionWhereTheDataBelong").slideUp(150,
showResult(resultJson));
        } else {
            showResult(resultJson)();
        }
    }
});
```

Here you can see multiple modifications. First, the function returns another function. This is because we need a parameterless function for the callback. The first method lets you send additional information and return a pointer to a method that has access (because of the closure principle of JavaScript) to the parameter of the outer function. The second modification is in the else. You now call the method which takes a single parameter but it requires you to call again the return anonymous function. This is why you have "showResult(resultJson)()";

HTMLInputElement defaultValue

Release Date: 17-Apr-12
Url: http://patrickdesjardins.com/blog/htmlinputelements-defaultvalue

Did you know that you can find the original value written by the server to the client by calling:

```
var originalName = document.getElementById("txtUserName").defaultValue;
```

Yes, the DOM contains for every HTML element of type **HTMLInputElement** and **HTMLTextAreaElement** the possibility to access the original value. This is interesting to know in case a form has dirty inputs. It's also interesting because it removes the need to hide values in hidden fields or to hide in a JavaScript object all original values.

From the ECMAScript's specification we can see that it is a property that returns a string. It's also possible to know if the value was originally checked in a checkbox with **defaultChecked**.

From here it is easy to know if an HTML form is dirty (has something changed). We just need to loop through all inputs and compare.

```
function TestDirty() {
    var formDirty = false;
    $('#frm :input').each(function() {
        if ($(this).is("input")) {
            var type = $(this).attr('type');
            if (type == "checkbox" || type == "radio") {
                if ($(this).is(':checked') != $(this)[0].defaultChecked) {
                    formDirty = true;
                }
            } else if (type == "hidden" || type == "password" || type == "text") {
                if ($(this).val() != $(this)[0].defaultValue) {
                    formDirty = true;
                }
            }
        }
        else {
            var type = $(this).get(0).tagName;
            if (type == "TEXTAREA") {
                if ($(this).val() != $(this)[0].defaultValue) {
                    return formDirty;
                }
            } else(type == "SELECT")
            {
                if ($(this).val() != $(this)[0].defaultSelected) {
                    return formDirty;
                }
            }
        }
    });
    return formDirty;
}
```

You can have the above code functional: http://jsfiddle.net/r8PH4/20/. The only case that does not seem to work is the select box in which the value is undefined. If someone has the code to fix it, feel free to post it.

Using onclick for JavaScript function instead of href

Release Date: 16-May-12
Url: http://patrickdesjardins.com/blog/?post_type=post&p=1087

Many people use JavaScript functions directly into the **href** attribute of the link tag when they want to execute JavaScript. This lets them execute JavaScript without having to have the fallback of having the browser scrolling to the top. The problem with this method, other than having client script in an attribute which has been created for an anchor link and external link is that it displays the JavaScript code in the status bar of the browser.

```
<a href='javascript:MyFunction(1,2,3)'>Click me</a>
```

To avoid this kind of behavior, that is not very clean, simply use the *onclick* attribute which is dedicated to receive JavaScript calls.

```
<a href='#' onclick="MyFunction(1,2,3);return false;">Click me</a>
```

As you can see, the onclick contains also a second JavaScript statement that indicates to the browser to not execute the link in the href attribute (the hash tag). This will prevent the browser from scrolling up. In fact, you could specify a page to navigate to if something goes wrong with the JavaScript or if the user does not have JavaScript enabled.

```
<a href='fallbackpage.html' onclick="MyFunction(1,2,3);return false;">Click me</a>
```

In that case, if JavaScript is disabled, the user will be redirected to the "fallbackpage.html".

You can also not systematically use the "return false" and simply use directly the return of your function.

```
<a href='nextpage.aspx' onclick="return MyFunction(1,2,3);">Click me</a>
```

In that case, this will call the MyFunction function and if the result is false will do nothing with the navigation and if true will move the user to "nextpage.aspx." This can be interesting in a scenario where you need to confirm something with the user or if you need to validate data before moving to the next step.

How to create a fallback to html5 placeholder for Internet Explorer with Modernizr library

Release Date: 19-Dec-12
Url: http://patrickdesjardins.com/blog/?post_type=post&p=1753

Modernizr (http://modernizr.com/) is a small JavaScript library that works in parallel with your main library (like **JQuery**) and makes more advanced features work, like some **CSS3** features or **Html5** features on browsers that don't support it natively.

One feature that even Internet Explorer 10 does not handle is the attribute **placeholder**. Modernizr lets you check if the current browser supports it and, if not, create your own custom fallback.

Once you add the Modernizr library to your webpage, you can now create a new JavaScript file with a function that will test the placeholder feature. If the feature is not supported by the browser, it will execute your custom code.

```
<script src="/Scripts/Libs/jquery-1.8.2.js" type="text/javascript"></script>
<script src="/Scripts/Libs/modernizr-1.7.min.js" type="text/javascript"> </script>
```

```
2012-12-01
```

```
This is a placeholder message
```

Here is the custom code that will put in a placeholder when a browser does not have the placeholder attribute.

```
jQuery(function()
{
    // check placeholder browser support
    if (!Modernizr.input.placeholder)
    {
        // set placeholder values
        jQuery(this).find('[placeholder]').each(function ()
        {
            if (jQuery(this).val() == '') // if field is empty
            {
                jQuery(this).val(jQuery(this).attr('placeholder'));
                jQuery(this).addClass('placeholder');
            }
        });
    }
}
);
// focus and blur of placeholders
jQuery('[placeholder]').focus(function ()
{
    if (jQuery(this).val() == jQuery(this).attr('placeholder'))
    {
        jQuery(this).val('');
        jQuery(this).removeClass('placeholder');
```

```
    }
}).blur(function ()
{
    if (jQuery(this).val() == ''
        || jQuery(this).val() == jQuery(this).attr('placeholder'))
    {
        jQuery(this).val(jQuery(this).attr('placeholder'));
        jQuery(this).addClass('placeholder');
    }
});
    // remove placeholders on submit
jQuery('[placeholder]').closest('form').submit(function() {
    jQuery(this).find('[placeholder]').each(function ()
    {
        if (jQuery(this).val() == jQuery(this).attr('placeholder')) {
            jQuery(this).val('');
        }
    });
});
```

You can also set a class to style the text when it is in a placeholder mode.

```
/*Modernizr fall back style for placeholder*/
.placeholder {
    color: lightgray;
    font-style: italic;
}
```

Here is how to use it:

```
<input type="text" placeholder="This is a placeholder text" />
```

You now have the placeholder feature available for all browsers. You only need to use it as you would if the user had used a more recent browser.

Patrick Desjardins

5 SQL

This chapter groups every post written during 2011 and 2012 about SQL. Most of them are still coherent and effective two years later, at the time I published this book. If some information is outdated, I still believe it has some positive insights by providing the evolution of SQL.

Installing the AdventureWorks Database

Release Date: 05-Sep-11
Url: http://patrickdesjardins.com/blog/?post_type=post&p=83

AdventureWorks is a free database. You can find it at CodePlex.com (http://msftdbprodsamples.codeplex.com). The installation is well documented on the MSDN website but in a few steps can cause you some problems that I will try to smooth out for you. First of all, before anything, be sure that you have the latest version of SQL Server. At this moment the lastest version is SQL Server 2008 R2. This can be found at Microsoft. If you do not do this, you may receive this message:

The database cannot be opened because it is version 661. This server supports version 612 and earlier. A downgrade path is not supported.

Once the latest version of Microsoft SQL Server is installed (this can be the Express Edition), you can install the AdventureWorks Setup executable file. This will install files located at : C:\Program Files\Microsoft SQLServer\MSSQL10_50.MSSQLSERVER\MSSQL\DATA.

From there, the next step is to attach the database to your SQL Server. This is where the server may not be able to open the database because of the version. If you still continue to have this error, another solution may be to download an older version of AdventureWorks.

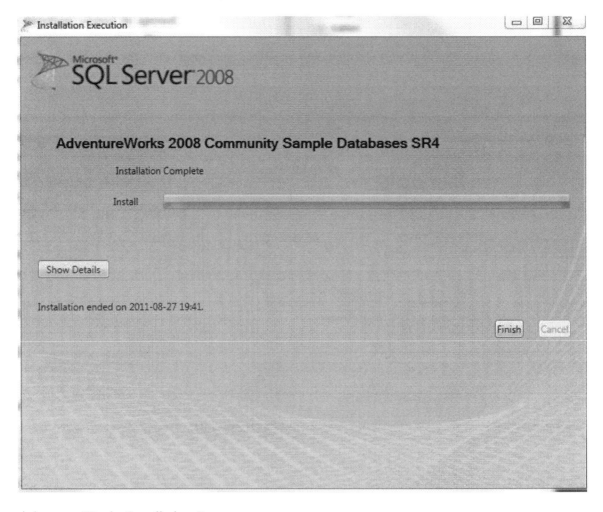

AdventureWorks Installation Process

From there, the steps at MSDN (http://bit.ly/1nnBjuu) are what you need to follow. When attaching the database you may receive this error message:

Unable to open the physical file "C:\sql\adventureworks\AdventureWorks_Data.mdf". Operating system error 5: "5(error not found)". (.Net SqlClient Data Provider)

This error occurs when the sp_attach_db is executed or when the attach is done via the Microsoft SQL Management Studio.

```
SQLCMD -S (local)\sqlexpress -E
exec sp_attach_db @dbname=N'AdventureWorks'
, @filename1=N'C:\sql\adventureworks\AdventureWorks_Data.mdf'
```

```
, @filename2=N'C:\sql\adventureworks\AdventureWorks_log.ldf'
GO
```

To solve this issue, you need to add to the directory the *Network Service* user with Read and Write access. Also, do not forget to start the command prompt of the Microsoft SQL Management Studio as Administrator.

How to back up table data with SQL Server 2008

Release Date: 15-Dec-11
Url: http://patrickdesjardins.com/blog/?post_type=post&p=640

Sometimes it can be useful to dump all data of a table in the format of an SQL insert statement.

This can be done easily with *Microsoft SQL Management Studio*. The first step is to right click on the database and select the option **Task>Generate Script**. This will pop up a wizard window.

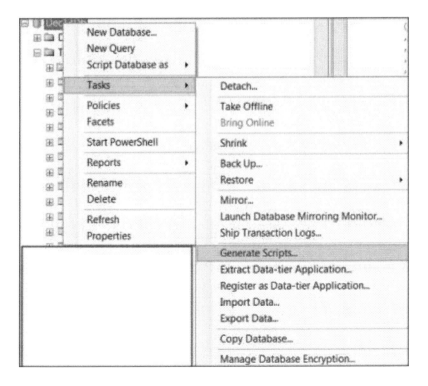

The next and last step is to select that we desire only the data.

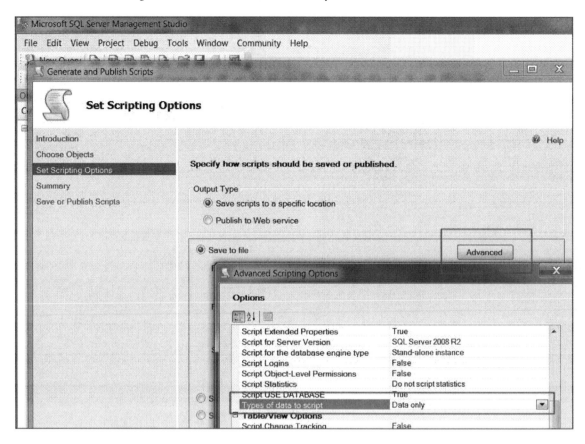

This will produce all SQL insert statements with your data.

Altering existing schema components is not allowed.

Release Date: 25-Jan-12
Url: http://patrickdesjardins.com/blog/?post_type=post&p=698

Sometimes XML can be stored in a column of a table. I personally try to avoid this, especially when it has XSD (XML Schema Definition) that will be validated on the database side instead of the code side, and even more when I'll need to get specific data into it later on in a query. Still, sometimes you have no choice because the system has been built this way.

I had a problem in an ASP.NET project which doesn't allow XML to save. After a while, I realized that the database contained an XML Schema Collections. This is found when you open the Microsoft SQL Server Management Studio under the database, into the Programmability folder, under Types and XML Schema Collection.

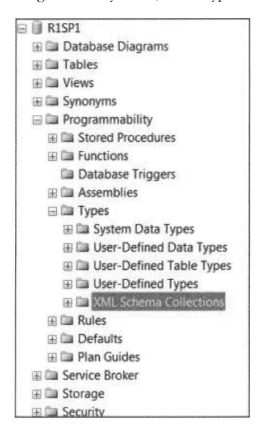

The problem is when trying to alter this schema you will get an error message.

Altering existing schema components is not allowed. There was an attempt to modify an existing XML Schema component, component namespace

To fix this, you will need to change the column type to remove the XSD validation. Afterward, you will need to drop the validation and create a new one to finally apply the new validation.

```
ALTER TABLE my_table ALTER COLUMN xml_column XMLDROP
        XML SCHEMA COLLECTION xml_collectionCREATE
        XML SCHEMA COLLECTION xml_collection AS 'YOU XSD HERE'
ALTER TABLE my_table ALTER COLUMN xml_column XML(xml_collection)
```

The user instance login flag is not supported on this version of SQL Server

Release Date: 24-Feb-12
Url: http://patrickdesjardins.com/blog/?post_type=post&p=731

When importing an existing project that you have not set up you may get when executing an SQLConnection this kind of error: flag is not supported.

Error Message: The user instance login flag is not supported on this version of SQL Server.

This can occur when the previous developer had in the connection string a reference to **"User Instance."** This needs to be removed.

A **user instance** is like a normal database instance but it is created on demand. Normally, instances are created during the creation of the database.

To remove this error, you just need to remove this configuration of the SQL connection string.

How to drop an SQL Server database and close all existing connections

Release Date: 07-Mar-12
Url: http://patrickdesjardins.com/blog/?post_type=post&p=775

Simply executing DROP [YourDatabaseName] won't work if previous connections are already made. You need to alter the database to set it to a single user and roll back every other connection. Once dropped, you can recreate your database. When creating the database, the default value is to set to multi_user so you do not have to worry about setting the value to single_user with the alteration.

```
IF  EXISTS (SELECT name
            FROM sys.databases
            WHERE name = N'YOURDATABASENAME')
alter database YOURDATABASENAME
set single_user
with rollback immediateDROP
DATABASE YOURDATABASENAME
GO
```

If you do not do the alter statement, you may get the error: **"The database could not be exclusively locked to perform the operation."**

How to modify an FK constraint with Microsoft Server Management Studio 2008 R2

Release Date: 19-Nov-12
Url: http://patrickdesjardins.com/blog/?post_type=post&p=1665

This task should be easy, shouldn't it?

Well, if you go to the Microsoft Server Management Studio (2008 R2) designer to do it and the constraint is located in a schema other than DBO, this might be more complex than you think.

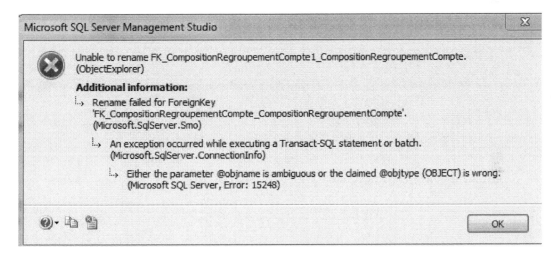

Rename failed for ForeignKey 'FK__ABC'. Either the parameter @objname is ambiguous or the claimed @objtype (OBJECT) is wrong. (Microsoft SQL Server, Error: 15248)

What's happening it that the tool is trying to use SP_RENAME with DBO as the schema. This can be verified with the SQL Profiler. It is also a <u>known bug that Microsoft</u> should have fixed in their latest release of SQL Server.

To be able to change the foreign key constraint name, you need to do it manually with the SP_RENAME function.

The syntax is 'YourSchema.YourFKNameToChange' followed by only the FK you want. Here is an example:

```
sp_rename 'YourSchema.YourFKNameToChange', 'YourNewFKName', 'OBJECT'
```

That's it!

How to execute a huge SQL file with Microsoft SQL Server

Release Date: 17-Dec-12
Author: Patrick Desjardins

Here is a small article that could be more a note than anything else. If you have a lot of SQL statements to execute, let's say a few gigs of statement, this won't load into SQL Server Manager. What you can do is to use the sqlcmd command. Open a DOS console and go where you have installed SQL Server Mananger. Mine is:

```
c:\Program Files (x86)\Microsoft SQL Server\90\Tools\Binn
```

In the console, you need to specify the server and instance you want to execute the file to. Optionally, you can write the output to a file.

```
sqlcmd -S myServer\instanceName -i C:\myScript.sql -o C:\log.txt
```

That's it. Nothing more complicated.

5 VISUAL STUDIO

This chapter groups every post written during 2011 and 2012 about Visual Studio. Visual Studio 2010 and 2012 are covered in this volume. This chapter contains information about tools that can be used with Visual studio.

ILSpy is an open-source .NET assembly browser and decompiler that is free

Release Date: 26-Aug-11
Url: http://patrickdesjardins.com/blog/?post_type=post&p=30

A few years ago, Lutz Roeder developed an assembly decompiler that was very popular, so popular that Red Gate Software bought the software and since then it is not free.

Good news, though - a free open source alternative exists. This alternative is **ILSpy** (http://wiki.sharpdevelop.net/ilspy.ashx).

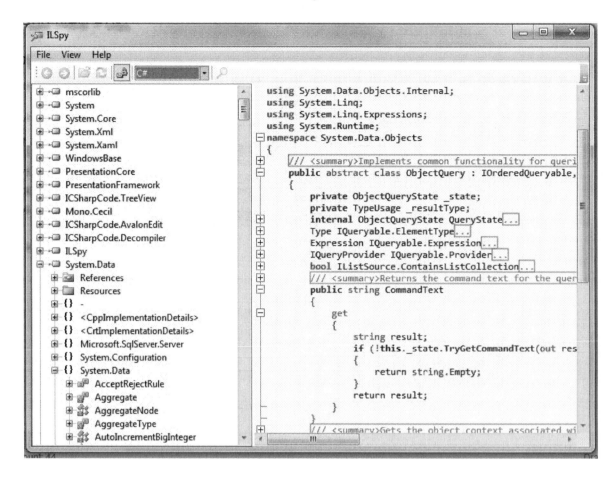

This tool lets you select an assembly and it will decompile it. It works with Microsoft Framework assembly but also yours. To select a .Net Framework, you need to load the desired DLL for: C:\Windows\Microsoft.NET\Framework\v4.0.30319 for .Net 4 framework DLL.

For Framework 2.0, the location is: C:\Windows\Microsoft.NET\Framework\v2.0.50727. It's also possible to get a 64 bit version of the code. A 64 bit .Net DLL is located in the directory C:\Windows\Microsoft.NET\Framework64\.

Also, this tool can produce IL code. **IL Disassembly** means Intermediary Language. It's also known as MSIL for Microsoft Intermediary Language. Seeing the IL is interesting to see how the C# compiler has produced code that will be read by the Virtual Machine later. This is a good way to optimize a query by comparing the produced code.

For your personal information, Microsoft .Net Framework comes with a tool called : <u>Ildasm.exe</u>. This tool can be used as a command line or with its graphical interface.

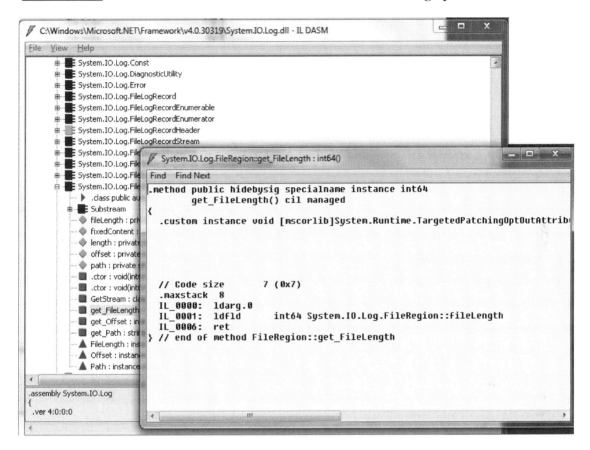

Review of NDepend

Release Date: 22-Aug-12
Url: http://patrickdesjardins.com/blog/?post_type=post&p=1284

NDepend (http://www.ndepend.com/) is an analysis tool for Microsoft .Net code. The primary goal of this tool is to let you know the quality of your code with some metrics.

You can use NDepend as software or as a Visual Studio Add-in. I tried both and preferred the stand-alone application. I found it easier to use and also did not find any real advantage to have it integrated into Visual Studio. Nevertheless, it can become handy to have it inside Visual Studio if your daily task is to optimize .Net code.

I did a run with the open source project called Nerd Dinner (http://nerddinner.codeplex.com) which is an MVC3 application. The version of Nerd Dinner is 77871 and the version of NDepend is 4.0.2 Professional edition.

The way it works is that you have to create a new project inside NDepend. This will allow you to not have to configure every time where the assemblies are to analyze, and also gives you the opportunity to compare in time the progression of your changes.

Once the project is done, you will be sent to the main user interface of the application with the project's properties windows open. This will let you choose either assembly or the solution file to analyze.

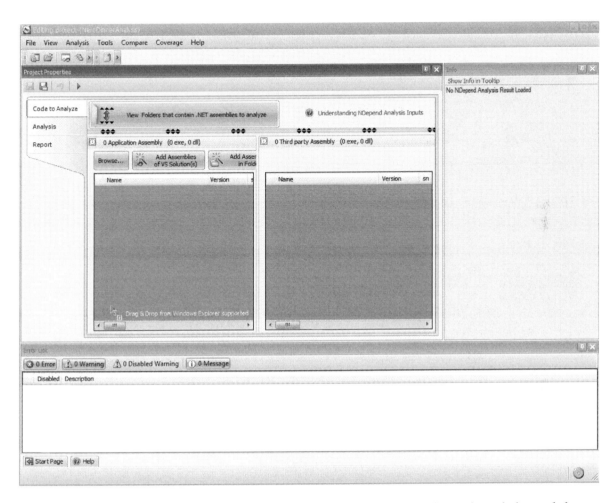

For my test, I chose the solution file which contains two projects - the main website and the testing project. Once selected you just need to press the Play button and the selected files will be analyzed. Nerd Dinner is a very small project and it took 4 seconds to analyze. When the analyze is done, your browser will pop up a webpage with a report.

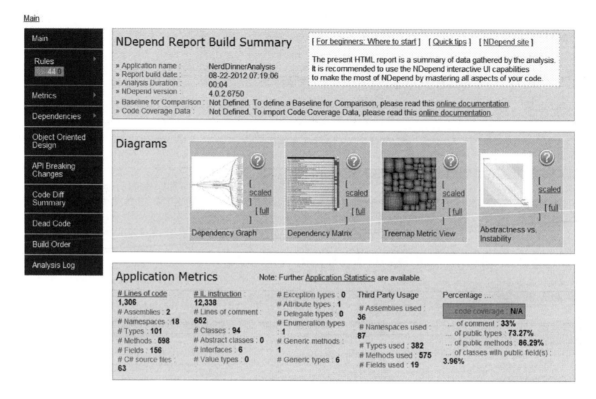

The advantage of the web report is that it lets you send the report without having to use the tool NDepend installed on the remote computer. Nevertheless, the real power of the application remains inside NDepend so it is more like a summary report than a tool to use.

The next step is to continue inside the NDepend Analysis tool and to use the **NDpend Interactive UI Graph**.

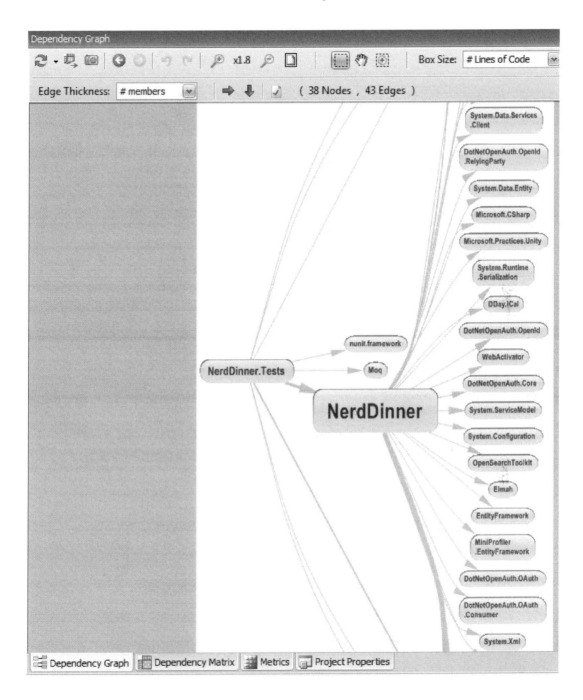

This gives you a snapshot of all dependencies your application has. This is a good tool to evaluate the coupling of your projects. Nerd Dinner project is a single DLL and another for testing. The test isn't as useful as if you had a real solution with a hundred projects inside it. You can go from there to some matrix views that will give the number of dependencies and some more information to go deeper and deeper with all relationships between assemblies. I think it can be very useful for a project of a decent size to keep control of the access. Lowering coupling and increasing cohesion is always a mission and this tool helps you to achieve it.

Next, we have the **Queries and Rules Explorer**. This tool has predefined queries that are in the form of a Linq statement. They are queries executed against your code. Not only predefined queries are available, but you can modify them and add new one as you like.

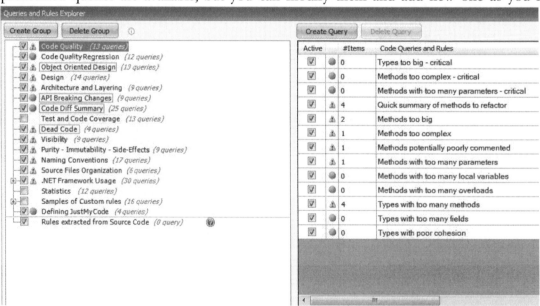

For me, this is THE killer functionality of NDepend. Let's start with an example. If we choose the category "Code Quality" and select the metric "Methods too big" we see in a panel the query itself and the result under it.

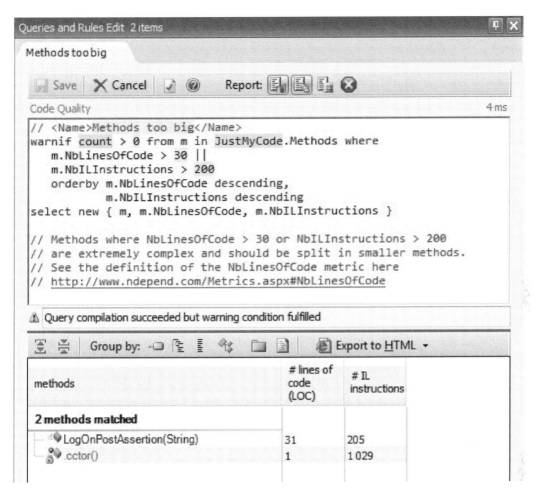

As you can see, I know that LogOnPostAssert(string) contains 31 lines of code which generate 205 IL instructions. The query was searching for a method with over 30 lines of code or 200 IL instructions. Not only that, but NDepend helps in being embedded with the query panel, which lets you expand the information with a link to their website. No need to search to know why the query has been made this way, everything is clearly stated. From this screen, it is possible to double click the method to see the code that is problematic and make necessary changes.

NDepend is a great tool to have if you care about code quality and iterative improvement of your application. You can use the tool within a few minutes of installation but it will require more hours to truly go deeper in its functionalities.

You can download NDepend and give it a try for 14 days free. After this period, the cost is

$368 for one license and goes down if you want a bundle of licenses. I think every team should have at least one version per team and periodically do a run to see if the quality goes up or down.

Visual Studio Express Database Explorer difference

Release Date: 19-Sep-11
Url: http://patrickdesjardins.com/blog/?post_type=post&p=217

When you download Visual Studio 2010 Express Edition you have to choose which version you want. Of those choices you have the C# version and the web version. Both of them seem to be similar but have some different templates. For example, you cannot create an ASP.NET website with the C# version and cannot create a Console Application with the web version.

It also has another big difference and it is the **Database Explorer**. The C# version does not connect to **SQL Server**, only to the SQL Compact or SQL file.

Here are two screenshots of the two Data Explorers. The first image is Microsoft Visual C# Express and the second image is Microsoft Visual Studio Web Developer Express.

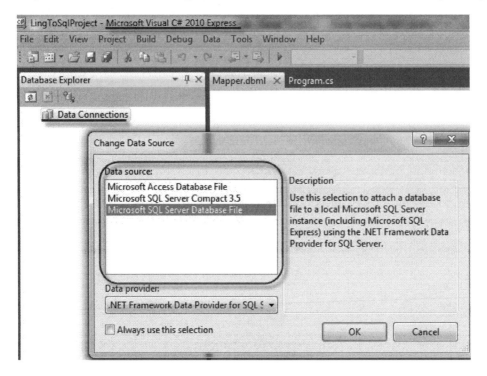

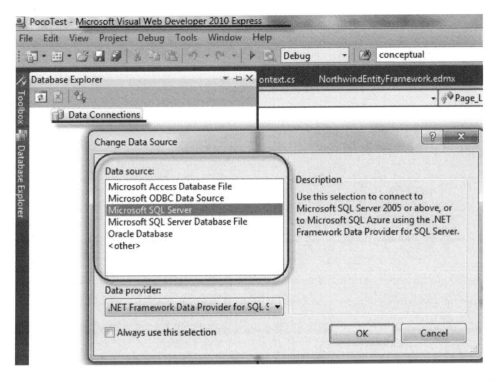

This is interesting because if you want to use SQL Profile you need to use the SQL server and not a file or a compact edition. The reason behind this is that Microsoft may have thought that the application usually does not need to have a direct access to the SQL server and, because they tried to cut functionality in each of the Express editions, the C# edition got this cut. However, it is possible to create a website with an SQL Server because usually web servers use SQL Server and not an SQL database file.

The breakpoint will not currently be hit. No symbols have been loaded for this document

Release Date: 02-Dec-11
Url: http://patrickdesjardins.com/blog/?post_type=post&p=606

Sometimes Visual Studio is not a pleasure to work with. You may sometimes arrive at a point where you compile and your new code doesn't seem to load so you decide to add a breakpoint for debugging. But, unfortunately, you have a red dot in Visual Studio that is not completely filled up. When you put your mouse cursor over it you can read the following message:

The breakpoint will not currently be hit. No symbols have been loaded for this document

From there, you can confirm that the debug file, the **PDB**, is not loaded. You can tell that in the Symbol Status column of the Module window. The Module window is **available only when debugging** under Debug>Window>Module.

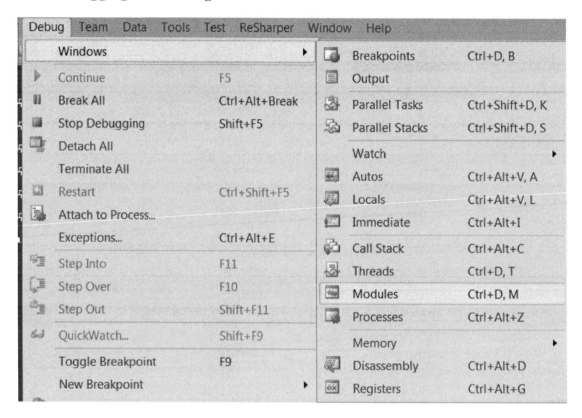

If you right click you will be allowed to load a symbol from a file. If you can go in the Debug folder and select the file, do it. If you receive a message saying that the file cannot be loaded then more steps are required.

The next step is:

1- Close Visual Studio

2- <u>Kill all processes of webdev</u>

3- Delete the Bin and Obj folders of your library that don't load

4- Open Visual Studio and compile

You may want to close IIS (net stop w3svc) before doing all those commands if you are using Asp.Net. To restart IIS simply use net start w3svc. You can also do it with the UI with IIS manager tool.

From there, you should be able to hook the PDB file (if it is not done automatically) and debug.

Edit

You may also try to :

1- Reboot

2- Delete C:\Windows\Microsoft.NET\Framework\v4.0.30319\Temporary ASP.NET Files\

3- Delete C:\yourPathTo\bin

4- Delete C:\yourPathTo\obj

5- Change AnyCPU to X86

6- Build

7- Start Debugging

How to set up Visual Studio to validate Html5 tags

Release Date: 29-Feb-12
Url: http://patrickdesjardins.com/blog/?post_type=post&p=743

If you are developing Asp.Net or Asp.Mvc and would like to have a warning or error if you are not using Html5 correctly, it is possible.

In Visual Studio 2010 you have to go into **Tools>Options>Text Editor>HTML>Validation**. From there you will be able to set up some configurations about how to display messages to you.

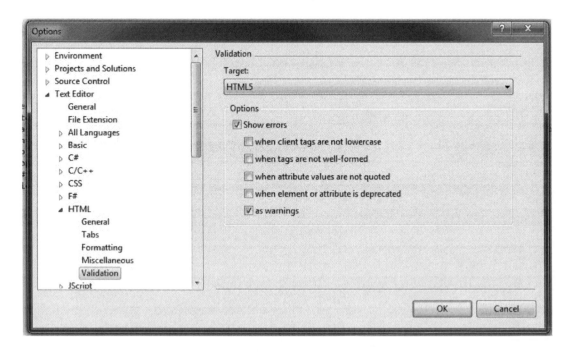

How to remove document.all from your projects

Release Date: 07-Nov-11
Url: http://patrickdesjardins.com/blog/?post_type=post&p=524

Recently, I had to work on pages which contained a lot of code that was using the famous Internet Explorer 4 document.allJavaScript method. It is not supported by all browsers and should not be used. You should use a unique identifier but I couldn't because time was limited for the change.

We already used **JQuery** so I knew that I could search by attribute.

The plan was to replace all *document.all["XYZ"]* to *$('input[name="XYZ"]')*. As you see, the XYZ changed between each file. The solution with Visual Studio (or other software that does replace with Regex) is to use the Replace tool with a Regex expression.

```
//this
document.all\[\"{(.+)}\"\]
//to
$(\'input\[name="\1"\]\')
```

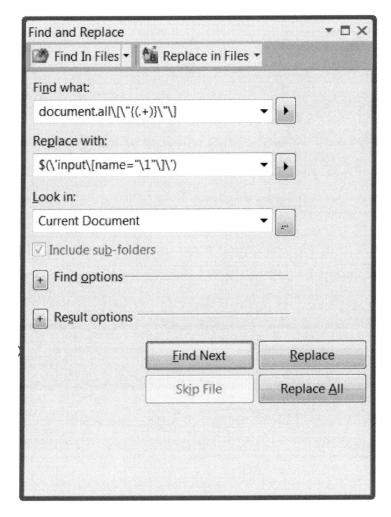

What it does is search for the string document.all["???"] and replace it with input[name="???"] and the ??? is replaced with what is found in the search and used in the replacement. This way, the name changes every time it finds a new string with document.all.

This can be good for some situations but not for code like this -

document.all["???"].value - because in JQuery the value is get by val() and set by val('new value');

To be able to do this correctly, two Replaces are required.

The first one is for the setter of the value:

```
document.all\[\"{(.+)}\"\].value(:b)@={(.+)}; //Search"
$(\'input\[name="\1"\]\').val(\2); //Replace
```

The second one is for the getter of the value

```
[^\.]document.all\[\"{(.+)}\"\].value //search
$(\'input\[name="\1"\]\').val() //Replace
```

This isn't perfect for all situations. Multiple concatenations of *document.all* may not be replaced correctly. But, I think it does the job for most situations.

How to convert JavaScript parentheses to access an array with square brackets

Release Date: 10-Nov-11
Url: http://patrickdesjardins.com/blog/?post_type=post&p=571

It can happen in an old project that array objects are accessed with parentheses instead of square brackets.

For example, MyArray[0] is in fact the first element of an array in JavaScript. But, IE lets you use MyArray(0). This is not a good practice and other browsers do not accept this syntax.

To convert easily, you can use a Regex expression. In my case, the array name was InTran.

```
InTran\({(.+)}\) //FindInTran\[\1\] //Replace
```

The curly bracket is required by Visual Studio to have a back reference but is not required by all Regex tools.

6. ENTERPRISE PATTERNS

This chapter groups a series of articles concerning enterprise patterns for web applications. They contain information about a way to create enterprise web applications. Building a web application can be done in several ways, but this one is simple and efficient. Keep in mind that these articles were written two years ago and new technologies have arisen.

Building an Asp.Net MVC website, the enterprise way

Release Date: 08-Oct-12
Url: http://patrickdesjardins.com/blog/?post_type=post&p=1468

This is the first post of a series that aims to create a Web application the enterprise way. What does it mean? It means that I won't display snippets of code, I won't code everything in the controller and I will not use a Model-View-Controller but integrate the notion of **ViewModel**. It will limit the use of **ViewBag** to transfer information to the view and let us transform the information to a display perspective without having to alter the model or to have code in the view.

Building an application for enterprise means that we will use mapper to associate information from the model to the view model. Instead of doing things manually, we will use **Dependency Injection** for most of our classes (login, persistence…) and we will abstract most of the code to be able to grow the application.

Before starting, let's check the overall architecture at the highest level.

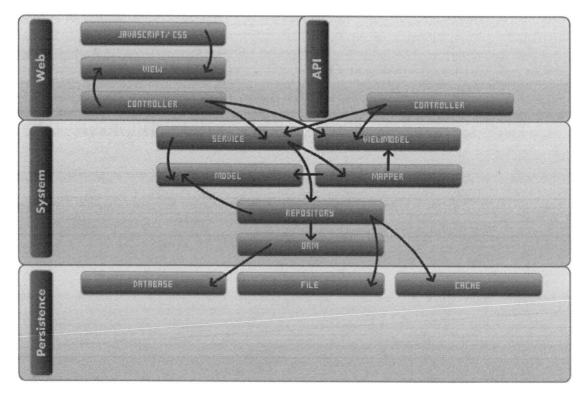

This is a big overview of an Asp.net Architecture using View Model with Asp.Net MVC.

As you can see, the JavaScript is separated from the view and this is because we will use an Unobtrusive JavaScript approach. This means that we will separate the action on the client side from the static view on the client side. The code will be cleaner and the separation of concern (from a client-side perspective) is respected. Instead of adding an action from the view we will attach the action from the controller to the view. This is quite logical!

We will also have **CSS inside style sheet** instead of using inline style or in file style. This is also interesting from a maintainability perspective because you can reuse the CSS. It is also good for performance because it reduces the HTML file to be loaded by the client and lets the browser cache the CSS file.

Concerning the view, we will use **Razor** that will be pushed by the controller in many ways. We will use View, PartialView, and JSON results that will contain partial view and Section.

As you can see, the controller does not call the repository, or call the model to transform them into a view model. A service layer is between them. The reason is that we want the controller to handle the HttpRequest and HttpResponse, and that's all. All the logic concerning the business logic, the mapping of data and the persistence of this data is handled by the service. The service layer is responsible for tasks on the Web side, the API side or any other technology it could use. It's not glued to the web with this approach and many concepts will be reused.

Finally, we will use a repository layer instead of calling directly the ORM inside the controller. Not only will it let you have a cohesive class but it lets you have a central point in your application to debug persistence more easily, and it is also a better way to change ORM later on if required. Finally, it is a good idea because you may want to have a caching system between controllers and a database (or any other mechanism). Adding this layer will simplify the whole development process from the elaboration phase to the maintenance phase.

Stay tuned in the next weeks to see the development of a project following this architecture. **Asp.Net MVC4**, **Entity Framework 5**, **AutoMapper**, **JQuery**, **Microsoft Enterprise library 5.0** for Logging &**Unity**, Microsoft Membership, **LinqKit** and many more will be there.

Enterprise Asp.Net MVC Part 1: The Planification

Release Date: 24-Oct-12
Url: http://patrickdesjardins.com/blog/?post_type=post&p=1497

As discussed before, a multipart post will be published during the next weeks concerning how to develop an enterprise web application with Microsoft Asp.Net MVC framework.

This first part will contain the project itself, the class diagram and the setup of the solution. The project will be iterative and incremental. We will establish the domain in this post, but we will enhance it in other posts. The reason we will do this is because in real life the models change. We will start slowly and add things during the next week to finally have something done.

First of all, let's define the project that we will create. I have worked out at the gym for a long time. I thought that we could build a gym workout planner. When people go to the gym, they have a plan of exercise for every group of muscles. Usually, trainers split every body part in multiple sessions during the week. So, in one week, you can go to the gym four times and train with four different workouts. This is what we call a workout with four different sessions of exercise. Each session contains different exercises. Every exercise has a name and a number of sets and repetitions. It can also contain information about what time the exercise movement is done. While a repetition is the number of times you are doing the exercise, the set is how many times you repeat a particular number of repetitions. For example, an exercise called "Leg Press" might be done in five sets of 10 repetitions each.

The Model in UML Class Diagram

If we try to translate this application into a static UML diagram, like the UML Class diagram, we have something like below.

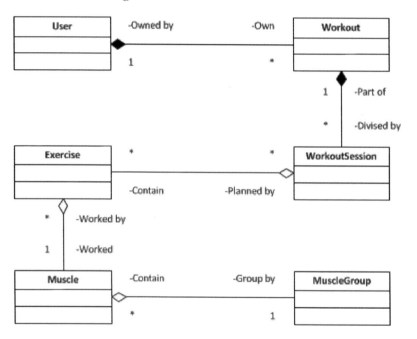

As we can see, we will have users that will be identified by the system who may have zero or many workouts. Every workout will have at least one session (in case a user wants to do the same workout every training session) or could have multiple sessions (in case the user splits his training in multiple sessions; for example, four different sessions per week). Workout sessions contain multiple exercises which are all associated with a particular muscle or muscle group. Every muscle is part of a group. For example, the biceps muscle and triceps muscle could be in the upper arm group. For the moment, let's stay simple and not elaborate further. Later, we will be able to give advice to users depending on the objectives or the muscles desired to train.

Creating a new Asp.Net MVC 4 project with Visual Studio 2012

A new project is created with the **MVC 4 project** type. The next step is to select the MVC4 template to be applied with **Razor View Engine**.

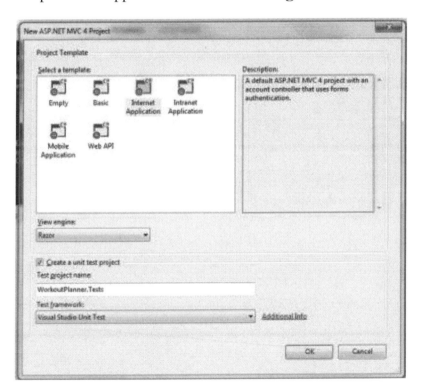

I have selected the Unit Test project to be created because as with any serious enterprise project, we will unit test most of what we will develop. Not only will it make us more secure but it will ensure that we develop good habits.

From there, we are set up to start. We have multiple possibilities. We could start by implementing Microsoft Membership straight from the beginning or we can start with the system for a single user. If we look at the model diagram, five classes of six are concerning everything but the user account. I suggest that we start with the application for a single user. By that I mean that we will remove the *User* class and develop everything for a single user a few times. The advantage will be that we will not have to configure the Microsoft Membership with Entity Framework from the start and will remove some overhead. Also, if we do not have time to implement this part of the software, we will rapidly have something functional for at least one user.

Enterprise Asp.Net MVC Part 2: Building The Model

Release Date: 26-Oct-12
Url: http://patrickdesjardins.com/blog/?post_type=post&p=1497

This is part of the enterprise Asp.Net MVC web application creation. We have before discussed the project that we will develop and now we will work on the model. We will create all classes first.

If we remember the UML class diagram, we will have to create five classes - one for the Workout, one the for the WorkoutSession, one for the Exercise, one for the Muscle and one for the MuscleGroup.

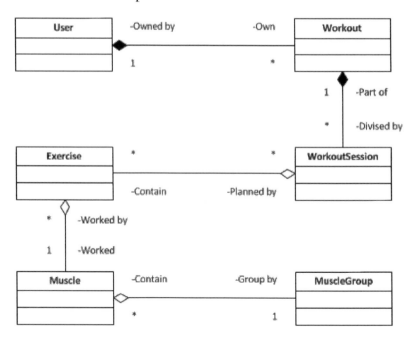

All these classes will be used to contain the business logic but also to contain the Entity from Entity Framework 5. Since we are building in **Code First** mode with Entity Framework, we have to develop all business logic (model) classes first and then the database will be generated by Entity Framework ORM.

So far, if I translate the Model diagram into classes I have :

```csharp
public class BaseModel
{
    public int Id { get; set; }
}

public class Workout : BaseModel
{
    public DateTime StartTime { get; set; }
    public DateTime EndTime { get; set; }
    public string Name { get; set; }
    public string Goal { get; set; }
    public ICollection<WorkoutSession> Sessions { get; set; }
}

public class WorkoutSession : BaseModel
{
    public string Name { get; set; }
    public ICollection<Exercise> Exercises { get; set; }
}

public class Exercise : BaseModel
{
    public string Name { get; set; }
    public string Repetitions { get; set; }
    public string Weights { get; set; }
    public string Tempo { get; set; }
    public TimeSpan RestBetweenSet { get; set; }
    public virtual Muscle Muscle { get; set; }
    public ICollection<WorkoutSession> WorkoutSessions { get; set; }
}

public class Muscle : BaseModel
{
    public string Name { get; set; }
    public virtual MuscleGroup Group { get; set; }
    public ICollection<Exercise> Exercises { get; set; }
}

public class MuscleGroup : BaseModel
{
    public string Name { get; set; }
    public ICollection<Muscle> Muscles { get; set; }
```

}

Indeed, I separate all these classes into individual files. A few modeling problems came to my mind while I was writing those classes. First, every exercise needs to be sorted for the user because every exercise is always done in a specific order. We need to add an Order property but we cannot add it to the Exercise class because the order will change depending on the workout session. For example, I may have the "Biceps Curl" exercise done first on Monday and last on Friday. Also, we will create a directory of Exercises later so we need to have the "metadata" of exercises somewhere different from the exercise or the workout session. In fact, if we put on our database glasses, this information would be in a junction table. If we put back our developer glasses, we will simply have a WorkoutSessionExercise that will have a 1:1 relationship to an Exercise. So, let's modify the model diagram and the class.

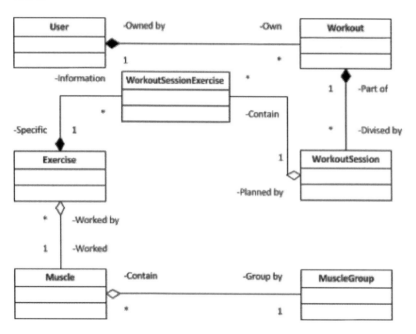

Modified Class Diagram for the Workout Planner Web Application

The modification needs to be reflected in the classes.

```
public class WorkoutSession : BaseModel
{
    public string Name { get; set; }
```

```
    public ICollection<WorkoutSessionExercise> WorkoutSessionExercises { get; set;
}
    public virtual Workout Workout { get; set; }
}

public class WorkoutSessionExercise : BaseModel
{
    public int Order { get; set; }
    public string Repetitions { get; set; }
    public string Weights { get; set; }
    public string Tempo { get; set; }
    public TimeSpan RestBetweenSet { get; set; }
    public virtual Exercise Exercise { get; set; }
    public virtual WorkoutSession WorkoutSession { get; set; }
}

public class Exercise : BaseModel
{
    public string Name { get; set; }
    public virtual Muscle Muscle { get; set; }
    public ICollection<WorkoutSessionExercise> WorkoutSessionExercices { get; set;
}
}
```

As you can see, I have also moved the repetitions, weight, tempo and all specific user/workout session information into something that will let the user add user-specific information while Exercise class has the static information, like the name of the exercise and the muscle concerned.

The BaseModel class has similar information like the primary key, which is an Integer. Later, other information will be added.

Validating the model

The next step is to add validation to the model. We could leave it up to the setter of every property where we want to have some validation, but we can also use the **IValidateObject** interface to let the ModelBinding system of Asp.Net MVC handle validation of every model object. If you want more information concerning the IValidationObject, I suggest you read this blog post about IValidationObject interface. In short, the **ModelBinding** will verify every Validate method of the model when bound back to the controller and it will also Validate the object before saving it into Entity Framework. So, we have double validation automatically executed by .Net Framework. This is a big advantage because this way we cannot forget to validate the model since the framework does it for us. To make it mandatory we will inherit the interface from the **BaseModel** class and create an abstract method that will be defined on every model. This way, we are sure that we will have models with validation defined.

```
public abstract class BaseModel : IValidatableObject
{
    public int Id { get; set; }

    #region IValidatableObject Members

    public IEnumerable<ValidationResult> Validate(ValidationContext
validationContext)
    {
        return ValidateModel(validationContext);
    }

    #endregion

    protected abstract IEnumerable<ValidationResult>
ValidateModel(ValidationContext validationContext);
}
```

All our model classes are modified to have the abstract method defined. Here is an example of a model class with validation and one that doesn't have (yet) any validation logic.

```
public class Workout : BaseModel
{
    public DateTime StartTime { get; set; }
    public DateTime? EndTime { get; set; }
    public string Name { get; set; }
    public string Goal { get; set; }
    public ICollection<WorkoutSession> Sessions { get; set; }

    protected override IEnumerable<ValidationResult>
ValidateModel(ValidationContext validationContext)
    {
        if (string.IsNullOrEmpty(Name))
        {
            yield return new ValidationResult("Name is mandatory", new[]
{"Name"});
        }
        if (EndTime.HasValue)
        {
            if (StartTime > EndTime.Value)
            {
                yield return new ValidationResult("EndTime must be after the
StartTime", new[] {"StartTime", "EndTime"});
            }
```

```
        }
    }
}

public class WorkoutSessionExercise : BaseModel
{
    public int Order { get; set; }
    public string Repetitions { get; set; }
    public string Weights { get; set; }
    public string Tempo { get; set; }
    public TimeSpan RestBetweenSet { get; set; }
    public virtual Exercise Exercise { get; set; }
    public virtual WorkoutSession WorkoutSession { get; set; }

    protected override IEnumerable<ValidationResult>
ValidateModel(ValidationContext validationContext)
    {
        return new Collection<ValidationResult>();
    }
}
```

The first example shows you some validation of the Name that needs to be defined. It also validates the StartTime that must be before the EndTime. As you can see, an error will be displayed on both properties if an error occurs.

I also defined the EndTime as **Nullable**. This will let the user not enter an ending date for the workout and, for us, give us a scenario to test with a nullable type.

The second example shows you where we do not have any validation defined. It returns a simple empty collection (that must be inherited from IEnumerable).

Localized string

The last thing that bothers me with this model is that, for the moment, we take for granted that everything is in English all the time. In fact, the workout goal could be in the user's language, but the exercise name must be translated into the language of the user. In a previous blog post, we have discussed a technique that can be used with Entity Framework to have multiple languages handled automatically. It also doesn't break any object-oriented theory. So, let's apply now the modification to the model by changing some string into LocalizedString class.

To do so, we will add this class :

```
[ComplexType]
public class LocalizedString
{
    public string French { get; set; }
    public string English { get; set; }

    [NotMapped]
    public string Current
    {
        get { return (string) LanguageProperty().GetValue(this); }
        set { LanguageProperty().SetValue(this, value); }
    }

    public override string ToString()
    {
        return Current;
    }

    private PropertyInfo LanguageProperty()
    {
        string currentLanguage =
Thread.CurrentThread.CurrentUICulture.DisplayName;
        return GetType().GetProperty(currentLanguage);
    }
}
```

This class lets you have French and English for every *LocalizedString* defined. It will add a column in the database for French and one for English.

As you can see, the *LocalizedString* does have a ComplexType attribute which will tell Entity Framework to merge the property into the owner and not to create a relationship to a table called *LocalizedString*. For example, we will use *LocalizedString* with the name of Exercise. So the Exercise will have in its table *Name_French* and *Name_English*.

```
public class Exercise : BaseModel
{
    public LocalizedString Name { get; set; }
    public virtual Muscle Muscle { get; set; }
    public ICollection<WorkoutSessionExercise> WorkoutSessionExercices { get; set;
}

    protected override IEnumerable<ValidationResult>
ValidateModel(ValidationContext validationContext)
    {
        if (Name == null)
        {
```

```
        yield return new ValidationResult("Name is mandatory", new[]
{"Name"});
        }
    }
}
```

As you can see, the Name property is now of type *LocalizedString* and we have modified the validation that now checks if the name is defined.

Enterprise Asp.Net MVC Part 3: Controller

Release Date: 31-Oct-12
Url: http://patrickdesjardins.com/blog/?post_type=post&p=1604

In this third part, we will discuss the controller. We aren't done yet with the model (we still need to add more validation) but let's talk about the controller. In Asp.Net MVC, the controller acts as the gate for the Http Request and answers back to any request with an Http Response. That is all. Its role should be limited to this task to respect the Single Responsibility Principle pattern.

But, we need to do a lot of things when a client sends information to the server. We need to convert the data in input to object, we need to convert this information to the model domain, we need to get into the database to load information and maybe to save information, we need to manipulate the data and we need to send back an answer. How can the controller be clean and at the same time be able to do all those things? Well, we will need to use the principle of separation of concern and split every task into multiple classes.

We will start with the model binding, which is the first step of any request.

Auto-mapping

In Asp.Net Mvc, the transformation of HTTP Get parameter or HTTP Post parameters into C# code is called **Model Binding**. The Model binding by default tries to convert any data to primitive type or tries to instantiate your model object if the request contains a JSON object that fits the schema of your classes. That means that you can simply use Asp.Net MVC to send all property values of your model back to the server and Asp.Net MVC is bright enough to build a new object for you.

```
[HttpPost]
```

```
public ActionResult Create(WorkoutModel model)
{
    //1)Validate model
    //2)Do manipulation
    //3)Save into the database
    return View("Create"); //4)Return a response to the client
}
```

The problem with this approach is, it works fine if you use the Model object to send information to the view, but we are using ViewModel (this was an architecture decision we made in the first part of this series). ViewModel give us the leverage to add additional information like a list of exercises that could be used in the workout, etc. So, before the first task of validating the model, we need to convert the view model back into a model object. This is where **AutoMapper** comes to the rescue.

An automapper is a library that maps a property from an object to another one. In our example, we will use AutoMapper. It is a free, open source, and widely used automapper. It is configurable or by default maps the property name automatically. I will not show you how to use AutoMapper in this article but you can find good examples in this blog or anywhere on the web.

So, once we have received the view model back from the view to the controller, we need to automap the view model to the model. That means that every time we use a controller action we need to do this task. This can be repetitive and error prone. That's why a better approach is to implement a "Model" object. This is a little bit like Microsoft did with Asp.Net MVC with the View. We will create a Model property that will hold the converted view model. To do so, we will need to modify the BaseController.

Automapper and BaseController

We will modify the BaseController and override the method **OnActionExecuting**. This will give us the opportunity to modify the code before entering the code of the action defined inside the controller.

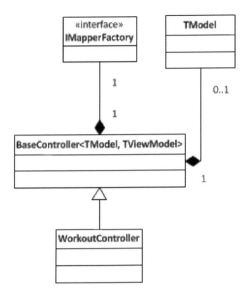

This is an overview of what we are going to do. First, we will have a concrete controller for every entity, in our case, the *WorkoutController*. Each controller inherits from the *BaseController* which is generic with two types. The first one is the model type, and the second is the view model type. The *BaseController* contains a reference to an *IMapperFactory*, which is a layer of abstraction to the AutoMapper implementation. We will come back later to the *IMapperFactory*. Finally, the *BaseController* contains a property of TModel type. That means that for the *WorkoutController* we will be able to use "this.Model" to get the model from the view model. For another entity, the Model will be of the entity type because it will use the TModel type defined by the *BaseController*. Here is the code that reflects the illustration above.

```
public class WorkoutController : BaseController<Workout, WorkoutViewModel>
{
    public WorkoutController(IMapperFactory mapperFactory) : base(mapperFactory)
    {
    }

    public ActionResult Index()
    {
    }

    [HttpGet]
    public ActionResult Details(int id)
    {
    }

    [HttpGet]
```

```csharp
    public ActionResult Create()
    {
    }

    [HttpPost]
    public ActionResult Create(WorkoutViewModel viewModel)
    {
    }

    [HttpGet]
    public ActionResult Edit(int id)
    {
    }

    [HttpPost]
    public ActionResult Edit(WorkoutViewModel viewModel)
    {
    }
}

public abstract class BaseController<TModel, TViewModel> : Controller
{
    private readonly IMapperFactory _mapperFactory;
    protected TModel Model { get; private set; }

    protected BaseController(IMapperFactory mapperFactory)
    {
        _mapperFactory = mapperFactory;
    }

    protected override void OnActionExecuting(ActionExecutingContext
filterContext)
    {
        base.OnActionExecuting(filterContext);
        if (filterContext.ActionParameters.Any())
        {
            var possibleViewModel =
filterContext.ActionParameters.FirstOrDefault(x => x.Value.GetType() == typeof
(TViewModel));
            if (possibleViewModel.Value != null)
            {
                var viewModel = (TViewModel) possibleViewModel.Value;
                var model = (TModel) Activator.CreateInstance(typeof (TModel));
                Model = _mapperFactory.Map(viewModel, model);
            }
        }
    }
}
```

Any time, inside the Update or Create, instead of using the viewModel parameter which is of *WorkoutViewModel* type, you can use the base.Model. This way to code gives us a few advantages. First, the controller is clean. No mapping is done on any concrete controller. Second, we still have access to the view model if required. Third, we do not repeat work on all controllers.

Service layer

Now that we have the data from the view, we need to do some manipulation. We will skip the validation process because it will be in another part of this series. Let's jump to the service layers. The service layer is a layer above the controller and could be used not only by the web controller but by the web api controller or any other application. It is the layer between the user interaction and the repository. It is the one that can contact the repository, the cache, or manipulate many entities to return a unique one. The service layer will be used by the controller to access the repository and to build the view model. For example, it will load a specific workout if the user calls the Edit action of the Workout controller. Not only will it load the workout, but it will give us the view model filled correctly with extra properties that could contain additional choices to be selected (like a list of exercises) and additional localized text, for example.

So, we need to modify the *WorkoutController* to have a service reference.

```
public class WorkoutController : BaseController<Workout, WorkoutViewModel>
{
    public WorkoutController(IMapperFactory mapperFactory) : base(mapperFactory)
    {
    }
    //...
}
```

will become:

```
public class WorkoutController : BaseController<Workout, WorkoutViewModel>
{
    private readonly IWorkoutService _service;

    public WorkoutController(IWorkoutService service, IMapperFactory
mapperFactory) : base(mapperFactory)
    {
        _service = service;
    }

    //...
```

```
}
```

As you can see, the *IWorkoutService* has been added. This will give us the possibility to inject the service into the controller. Every controller will have its own service.

Because most of the service will look the same we can create a base service class that I'll call IService. The IService will contain the primitive calls that are concerning getting the model, saving the model and deleting the model.

```
public interface IService<TModel, TViewModel>
{
    IEnumerable<TViewModel> GetAll();
    TViewModel Get(TModel model);
    int Create(TModel model);
    int Update(TModel model);
    int Delete(TModel model);
}

public interface IWorkoutService : IService<Workout, WorkoutViewModel>
{
}
```

We could add in *IWorkoutService* a more specific method. For example, one could require a special Get that will return an extended view model with more data. Or, someone might want to have to model from the Get instead of the view model. This type of architecture is flexible.

If we check the concrete implementation of *IWorkoutService* we will see all repository access and the automapper to convert the model to view model.

```
public class WorkoutService : BaseService, IWorkoutService
{
    public WorkoutService(IRepositoryFactory repositoryFactory, IMapperFactory
mapperFactory)
                            : base(repositoryFactory, mapperFactory)
    {
    }

    #region Implementation of IService<Workout>

    public IEnumerable<WorkoutViewModel> GetAll()
    {
        var listModel = Repository.Workout.GetAll().ToList();
        return Mapper.Map<List<Workout>, List<WorkoutViewModel>>(listModel);
    }
```

```
public WorkoutViewModel Get(Workout model)
{
    var modelToBound = Repository.Workout.Get(model.Id);
    return Mapper.Map<Workout, WorkoutViewModel>(modelToBound);
}

public int Create(Workout model)
{
    return Repository.Workout.Insert(model);
}

public int Update(Workout model)
{
    return Repository.Workout.Update(model);
}

public int Delete(Workout model)
{
    return Repository.Workout.Delete(model);
}

    #endregion
}
```

As you can see, we are using the *IMapperFactory* to map data and not directly the automapper. This abstraction gives us the possibility to mock up the mapping easily later. Also, you can see that we are doing the same with the repository. We are using *IRepositoryFactory* which is not tightly bound to any repository, or bound to the workout. That means that a workout could load exercises without a problem. The details about the repository will be defined in another article.

Conclusion

We have seen that we can have a clean controller and the use of service to help us separate the request from the repository. We also have seen that interface is preferred over concrete classes because it gives us the possibility for a mockup later on, and gives us a layer of abstraction between concrete implementation of the controller and from the repository, mapper and so on. In the next article of this series we will discuss the repository and Entity Framework in an enterprise Asp.Net MVC web application. We will come back to the controller in the article concerning validation of the model. Indeed, the controller will have its role with validation and we will see how to implement a solution that will still respect the single responsibility principle.

Enterprise Asp.Net MVC Part 4: Repository

Release Date: 02-Nov-12
Url: http://patrickdesjardins.com/blog/?post_type=post&p=1617

This is the fourth part of the series concerning enterprise **Asp.Net MVC web site**. In this article, we will discuss how to design the repository. As you can imagine, we won't use Entity Framework (or any other ORM) directly into controllers. Also, this article will focus on Entity Framework 5.0 but the concept behind it is the same—the repository must be abstracted from the controller. The main reason is that we want to be able to respect the single responsibility principle. The controller responsibility is not about how to load or save an entity but knowing how to dispatch. This is why we will follow the separation of concern idea by having classes that will handle the repository. By separating the repository we will use many classes to have a set of cohesive classes. The result will be an application well separated in concern.

Before starting, let me just make one thing clear. I won't abstract **Entity Framework** here. I do not believe that abstracting the ORM is a good idea. First, a lot of overhead is added. Second, the ORM already abstracts the database implementation, and third, the maintenance is compromised because if we want something specific to Entity Framework, we will need to do a lot of code.

Abstracting the repository: the plan

The first thing that we need to keep in mind is that every entity will need to use the ORM. Entity Framework uses what we call a *DbContext*. We need to be able to share this *DbContext* between repositories because we may want to save an entity that will use several other repositories. The same is true for loading entity. You may want to load an entity and load a second one in a different repository. Sharing the same *DbContext* lets you have the same transaction when saving and when loading instead of two queries (or more). It also opens a single connection to the database instead of several.

The second thing to keep in mind is that every entity belongs to a user. If *UserA* creates an entity, this entity should belong to him. *UserB* should access his own information. This is not true in every case, but most of the time. Even a Facebook Message is owned by you (but shared with others). So, we need a mechanism to bind data to a user account. Also, we will need to have a way to impersonate in some cases this mechanism. This will give us the leverage to save an entity to a specific user. A simple example would be in order to load the database with test data for development purposes. We may want to create entities for several users without being logged in as these users.

The third thing to keep in mind is that we want to be able to test without having to care about the database. It also means that I do not want to have overhead when testing by mocking up every method of Entity Framework. What we want is to simply mock test the repository.

Factory Method Pattern

The factory method pattern constructs objects from a single point of entry. The factory returns all repositories for every entity. It's a central point. The reason to use this pattern is that it will give us a lazy loading for all repository creations but also will give us the possibility to share the DbContext among those repositories in the creation of them. It also gives us the possibility to mock test the whole factory. The factory will be the classes shared between all controllers.

Repository Factory

The repository factory inherits from an interface. This interface will contain all entities in a repository. That means that if you want to add a new entity you need to add a new entry into this interface.

```
public interface IRepositoryFactory
{
    IWorkoutRepository Workout { get; }
    IUserProfileRepository UserProfile { get; }
    //...Other entities...
}
```

For example, in the code above, we have two entities. One is our domain, the *Workout* class, and the second is the *UserProfile* that is for the user (from the membership classes). If we wanted to add the *Exercises* entity, we would need to add a new property in the interface.

You will also notice that *IRepositoryFactory* contains an interface to the repository. So, a new entity means a new interface for its repository and for the concrete implementation of this repository.

Before going deeper with the repository class, let's check a concrete implementation of *IRepositoryFactory* for Entity Framework 5.0 Code First approach.

```csharp
public class RepositoryFactory : IRepositoryFactory
{
    private readonly IDatabaseContext _databaseContext;
    private IWorkoutRepository _workoutRepository;
    private IUserProfileRepository _userProfileRepository;

    public RepositoryFactory(IDatabaseContext databaseContext)
    {
        _databaseContext = databaseContext;
    }

    #region Implementation of IRespositoryFactory

    public IWorkoutRepository Workout
    {
        get { return _workoutRepository ?? (_workoutRepository = new
WorkoutRepository(_databaseContext)); }
    }

    public IUserProfileRepository UserProfile
    {
        get { return _userProfileRepository ?? (_userProfileRepository = new
UserProfileRepository(_databaseContext)); }
    }

    #endregion
}
```

This class takes in its constructor an *IDatabaseContext*. This will give us an interface to share between repositories Otherwise, the factory is very simple. It checks if the property has been already initialized and, if not, it initializes it with the *IDatabaseContext*; otherwise, it simply reuses the repository. This class contains for every repository a property.

Repository Classes

Every repository inherits from **IRepository**.

```csharp
public interface IRepository<T>
{
    IQueryable<T> GetAll();
    T Get(int id);
    int Insert(T entity);
    int Update(T entity);
    int Delete(T entity);
}
```

This interface defines 80% of the methods that we need for each entity. Other more specific methods like searching with a filter will be added directly into the concrete implementation of the class.

Also, every repository inherits from a base repository that holds the *DataContext* reference. This is required because every call to the repository is done by the *DbContext*. When the Repository factory passes the *IDatabaseContext* to the repository, all repositories will simply pass the object to the base in their constructor.

```
public class BaseRepository
{
    protected IDatabaseContext DatabaseContext { get; private set; }

    protected BaseRepository(IDatabaseContext databaseContext)
    {
        DatabaseContext = databaseContext;
    }
}
```

Here is the example with the *Workout* entity.

```
public class WorkoutRepository : BaseRepository, IWorkoutRepository
{
    public WorkoutRepository(IDatabaseContext databaseContext) :
base(databaseContext)
    {
    }

    #region Implementation of IRepository<Workout>

    public IQueryable<Workout> GetAll()
    {
        return DatabaseContext.SetOwnable<Workout>().Include(x => x.Sessions);
    }

    public Workout Get(int id)
    {
        return DatabaseContext.SetOwnable<Workout>().Include(x =>
x.Sessions).Single(c => c.Id == id);
    }

    public int Insert(Workout entity)
    {
        //To-do : Other stuff with complex type here
        DatabaseContext.SetOwnable<Workout>().Add(entity);
        return DatabaseContext.SaveChanges();
    }
```

```
public int Update(Workout entity)
{
    Workout fromDatabase = Get(entity.Id);
    DatabaseContext.Entry(fromDatabase).CurrentValues.SetValues(entity);
    DatabaseContext.Entry(fromDatabase).State = EntityState.Modified;
    //To-do : Other stuff with complex type here
    return DatabaseContext.SaveChanges();
}

public int Delete(Workout entity)
{
    DatabaseContext.SetOwnable<Workout>().Remove(entity);
    return DatabaseContext.SaveChanges();
}

#endregion
}
```

You do not see any details of the database connection. The only thing we see is the task concerning the saving and loading entity. We have direct access to Entry and we can use the *Set<>* and *SetOwnable<>*. As you can see, we do not need to have any access to the current user, or to the specific user to whom the *Workout* belongs because *Workout* inherits from *IUserOwnable*. You will see the detail about how it works in the next article concerning the *DbContext* (see part 5).

Conclusion

So far, so good. Now we have the controller that talks with the database. We are using the repository factory method to access the desired repository and every repository shares the same instance of *DbContext*. The result is being able to have multiple entities manipulated within the same context (same transaction). Every class has its own role. The controller handles an http request, the service handles how the database is accessed, the repository factory manages all repositories, the repository handles how their entities are stored and finally, the database context takes care of the database connection. The next article of the series, part 5, will discuss in more detail the database context (DbContext) and its role with Entity Framework 5.0.

Enterprise Asp.Net MVC Part 5: Database Context and Impersonate data

Release Date: 05-Nov-12
Url: http://patrickdesjardins.com/blog/?post_type=post&p=1623

The database context is abstracting the connection between entity and Entity Framework. We won't abstract all methods of the Entity Framework and Linq to Entity like "Where," "Select," "Find," "First," etc but we will abstract the entry point: *DbSet*. In fact, the reason is to be able to add the ability to impersonate later and to be able to configure your entity so that you need to have this DatabaseContext. The role of the factory is not to configure Entity Framework or to impersonate it. It is the database context's role to do those tasks.

```
public interface IDatabaseContext
{
    int SaveChanges();
    IDbSet<TEntity> SetOwnable<TEntity>() where TEntity : class, IUserOwnable;
    DbSet<TEntity> Set<TEntity>() where TEntity : class;
    DbEntityEntry<TEntity> Entry<TEntity>(TEntity entity) where TEntity : class;
    void InitializeDatabase();
    UserProfileImpersonate Impersonate(ICurrentUser userProfile);
}
```

For the moment, the interface of IDatabaseContext looks like the code above. We have a *SaveChanges* because we might want to do the operation over several repositories and want to manually commit changes in a specific time. This will be the role of the *SaveChanges* method. The *SetOwnable<>* method will act like the default Set method but will automatically assign the user to the entity. This will be good for loading and for saving. When in the loading, we will not have to specify every time that we want the workout for userA, etc. It will be done automatically. This saves us time, the possibility of error, and also improves the security because by default everything will be bound to the current user. The *InitializeDatabase* method will be a method to configure extra database material. For example, in this project, I am using this method to set up the WebSecurity (membership layout for WebMatrix). The last method is the method that will give us impersonation for the time of a query depending on another user profile.

```
public class DatabaseContext : DbContext, IDatabaseContext
{
    public const string DEFAULTCONNECTION = "DefaultConnection";

    public DatabaseContext(IUserProvider userProvider)
```

```
    {
        UserProvider = userProvider;
        base.Database.Connection.ConnectionString =
ConfigurationManager.ConnectionStrings[DEFAULTCONNECTION].ConnectionString;
        Configuration.ProxyCreationEnabled = false;
    }

    public IUserProvider UserProvider { get; set; }

    public ICurrentUser CurrentUser
    {
        get { return UserProvider.Account; }
    }

    public new DbSet<TEntity> Set<TEntity>() where TEntity : class
    {
        if (typeof (IUserOwnable) is TEntity)
        {
            throw new SecurityException("You cannot by pass the ownable
security");
        }
        return base.Set<TEntity>();
    }

    public IDbSet<TEntity> SetOwnable<TEntity>() where TEntity : class,
IUserOwnable
    {
        return new FilteredDbSet<TEntity>(this, entity => entity.UserId ==
CurrentUser.UserId, entity => entity.UserId = CurrentUser.UserId);
    }

    public void InitializeDatabase()
    {
        WebSecurity.InitializeDatabaseConnection(DEFAULTCONNECTION, "UserProfile",
"UserId", "UserName", autoCreateTables: true);
    }

    protected override void OnModelCreating(DbModelBuilder modelBuilder)
    {
        base.OnModelCreating(modelBuilder); //Call here some other classes to
build the configuration of Entity Framework
    }

    public UserProfileImpersonate Impersonate(ICurrentUser userProfile)
    {
        return new UserProfileImpersonate(this, userProfile);
    }
}
```

This is a small example that speaks for itself. The two interesting parts are the *SetOwnable* that uses a *FilteredDbSet* which has trimmed code from a version that you can find on the web and that we will discuss later. The other part is the Impersonate method that we will talk about now.

Let's start with the end result. For now, if you want to insert into the database a new *Workout* entity you need in the *WorkoutRepository* to do:

```
DatabaseContext.SetOwnable<Workout>().Add(entity);
```

This will automatically insert a new workout to the current logged user. If you want to change the user, you could use the Set but, because we override the Set method and check if it inherits from the**IUserOwnable** interface, this is the required interface to use the *SetOwnable* method. This way, we can get the user ID. But, to protect the developer when bypassing this mechanism, an exception is thrown if we use the *Set* method with entities that are ownable. That doesn't mean that you cannot save to another user, but it will require more work with **impersonating**. Why add some overhead and not let the developer directly use the Set when desired to save an entity to someone else's authority? Simply because all entities will inherit from *IUserOwnable* and it will be a lot easier to work with without having to always specify the user inside the repository. Also, repository doesn't have access directly to the user ID. Not providing access directly to the Set avoids the mistake of using the Set method for an entity that should not. An exception will be thrown and the developer will automatically remember to user the *SetOwnable* method instead. In the special case that the Set method must be used on an ownable class, then the impersonate method will be appropriate.

For a general entity, for example a list of statuses that are shared across all entities or shared across all users, the entity should not inherit from **IUserOwnable** because it is not a user-ownable entity. So in theory it works.

```
using (var db = DatabaseContext.Impersonate(new UserProfile {UserId = 1}))
{
    db.SetOwnable<Workout>().Add(entity);
}
```

This would be in the repository instead of the last piece of code. As you can see, we impersonate with a *UserProfile* with the ID 1. The code is inside curly brackets and gives us the scope of when the impersonation starts and ends.

The *DatabaseContext* class implementation of Impersonate simply calls a new *DbContext*.

```
public UserProfileImpersonate Impersonate(ICurrentUser userProfile)
{
    return new UserProfileImpersonate(this, userProfile);
}
```

A new class is used because we want to have a scope that is created by inheriting from *IDisposable* interface. We will create a new instance of Impersonate and dispose it to come back with the real Current User and not the impersonated one. The class is mostly the same as the *DbContext* but has a reference to the user profile before the impersonate because we want to restore it once it's done.

```
public class UserProfileImpersonate : IDatabaseContext, IDisposable
{
    private readonly DatabaseContext _databaseContext;
    private readonly IUserProvider _oldUserProvider;

    #region Implementation of IDisposable

    public UserProfileImpersonate(DatabaseContext dbContext, ICurrentUser
userProfile)
    {
        _databaseContext = dbContext;
        _oldUserProvider = dbContext.UserProvider;
        _databaseContext.UserProvider = new ImpersonateUserProvider(userProfile);
    }

    public void Dispose()
    {
        _databaseContext.UserProvider = _oldUserProvider;
    }

    #endregion

    #region Implementation of IDatabaseContext

    public int SaveChanges()
    {
        return _databaseContext.SaveChanges();
    }

    public IDbSet<TEntity> SetOwnable<TEntity>() where TEntity : class,
IUserOwnable
    {
        return _databaseContext.SetOwnable<TEntity>();
    }
```

```
    public DbSet<TEntity> Set<TEntity>() where TEntity : class
    {
        return _databaseContext.Set<TEntity>();
    }

    public DbEntityEntry<TEntity> Entry<TEntity>(TEntity entity) where TEntity :
class
    {
        return _databaseContext.Entry(entity);
    }

    public void InitializeDatabase()
    {
        _databaseContext.InitializeDatabase();
    }

    public UserProfileImpersonate Impersonate(ICurrentUser userProfile)
    {
        return _databaseContext.Impersonate(userProfile);
    }

    #endregion
}
```

We simply call the same database context method but change the current logged user profile, a single task which respects the single responsibility principle.

Enterprise Asp.Net MVC Part 6: The three layers of validation

Release Date: 07-Nov-12
Url: http://patrickdesjardins.com/blog/?post_type=post&p=1631

Validations are definitely a serious subject. If no validation is made, then the system is compromised. Whatever the architecture, whatever the hardware setup, and whatever the idea of the product, you need to implement validations to protect your system. This is why it must be taken seriously.

By default, Asp.Net MVC handles validation and also Entity Framework uses the same interface to handle validation (page 206, Model validation and Entity Framework) entities. So, why not use what is already in place and not try to reinvent the wheel? In fact, we follow the KISS[2] principle.

Here is an overview of the article in a single image.

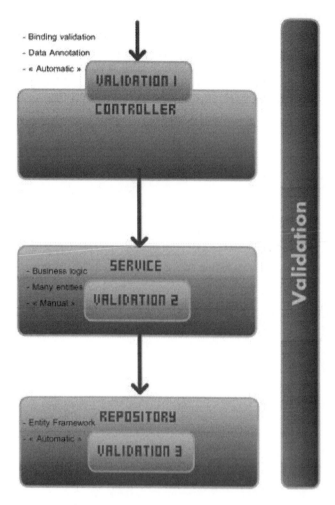

We have three layers of validation. The first layer and third layer are built-in with .Net with the IValidatableObject interface. I have already discussed (page 24, how to validate model object) this interface for validating an entity but I'll show you how to use it in a more

---

[2] KISS (From Wikipedia): KISS is an acronym for "Keep it simple, stupid" as a design principle noted by the U.S. Navy in 1960. The KISS principle states that most systems work best if they are kept simple rather than made complicated; therefore simplicity should be a key goal in design and unnecessary complexity should be avoided.

"enterprise way."

Using IValidatableObject

This interface has a single method called *Validate* that returns an error message linked to a property method. If you want a general error, you can also specify an empty string for the property name. The framework knows this interface and it automatically uses the validation when the model is bound from an Http request to your view model by the Model Binder. The .Net framework automatically calls this method when Entity Framework tries to save entities to the database. This means that you have nothing to do but to add your business logic validation.

From here, it is interesting to force every model to have this interface and this is why a good place to inherit from *IValidatableObject* is in the *BaseModel*.

```
public abstract class BaseModel : IValidatableObject
{
    public const int NOT_INITIALIZED = -1;
    public int Id { get; set; }

    #region Implementation of IValidatableObject

    public abstract IEnumerable<ValidationResult> Validate(ValidationContext
validationContext);

    #endregion
}
```

Every model has to define the *Validate* method. If no validation is required, the method is simply empty. Let's go back to the *Workout* entity and add some validations.

```
public class Workout : BaseModel, IUserOwnable
{
    public DateTime StartTime { get; set; }
    public DateTime? EndTime { get; set; }
    public string Name { get; set; }
    public string Goal { get; set; }
    public ICollection<WorkoutSession> Sessions { get; set; }

    public override IEnumerable<ValidationResult> Validate(ValidationContext
validationContext)
    {
        if (string.IsNullOrEmpty(Name))
        {
```

```
            yield return new ValidationResult("Name is mandatory", new[]
{"Name"});
        }
        if (EndTime.HasValue)
        {
            if (StartTime > EndTime.Value)
            {
                yield return new ValidationResult("EndTime must be after the
StartTime", new[] {"StartTime", "EndTime"});
            }
        }
    }
}

    #region Implementation of IUserOwnable

    public int UserId { get; set; }

    #endregion
}
```

Every time we have an error we return a **ValidationResult**. We specify a message and an array of properties that are related to the error. In this example, the name is validated and the EndTime property too, but only when this is specified.

The first layer of validation: Model Binding inside the controller

We have implemented the **IValidatableObject** and when an Http request is done to the server the controller binds the data to the model. Since we are using the **ViewModel** approach, this validation is not triggered! But, since we have a *BaseController* and already have defined the new approach of having the model automapped automatically, it hooks the validation and applies it when the ViewModel is mapped to the Model. (You have to go read the previous post of "Business" category to understand why it's automatically mapped.)

The first modification occurs in the override method *OnActionExecuting* that should be already overridden with the modification of the mapper. We simply need to check if the model bound is really an *IValidatableObject* and triggers the validation mechanism.

```
protected override void OnActionExecuting(ActionExecutingContext filterContext)
{
    base.OnActionExecuting(filterContext);
    if (filterContext.ActionParameters.Any())
    {
        var possibleViewModel = filterContext.ActionParameters.FirstOrDefault(x =>
x.Value.GetType() == typeof (TViewModel));
```

```
        if (possibleViewModel.Value != null)
        {
            var viewModel = (TViewModel) possibleViewModel.Value;
            var model = (TModel) Activator.CreateInstance(typeof (TModel));
            Model = _mapperFactory.Map(viewModel, model);
            ApplyOwnership();
            ApplyErrorsToModelState();
        }
    }
}

private void ApplyErrorsToModelState()
{
    if (Model is IValidatableObject)
    {
        var errors = (Model as IValidatableObject).Validate(new
ValidationContext(this));
        foreach (var validationResult in errors)
        {
            foreach (var memberName in validationResult.MemberNames)
            {
                ModelState.AddModelError(memberName,
validationResult.ErrorMessage);
            }
        }
    }
}
```

What we are doing is a general method that works for any entity. We verify if the Model bound from the ViewModel is really inherited from an **IValidatableObject**. From here, we do what the framework would do if we weren't using view model: calling the Validate method of the interface. We then loop all errors and assign everything to the ModelState. This will give us the possibility to act as if no view model has been used.

The code above about the method "ApplyErrorsToModelState" could be replaced with the code below to be able to validate the **data annotation** AND also the **IValidatableObject** interface.

```
private void ApplyErrorsToModelState()
{
    ModelMetadata metadata = ModelMetadataProviders
                          .Current.GetMetadataForType(() => Model,
Model.GetType());
    foreach (ModelValidationResult validationResult in ModelValidator
                          .GetModelValidator(metadata,
this.ControllerContext).Validate(null))
```

```
    {
        var propertyName = validationResult.MemberName;
        ModelState.AddModelError(propertyName, validationResult.Message);
    }
}
```

The code above validates the data annotation and the **IValidatableObject**. This can be used in a scenario where you need to have a deeper validation process. For example, here is the same code as above with enhanced validation in the mapping. This required splitting both validations.

```
private void ApplyErrorsToModelState(TModel model, TViewModel viewModel)
{
    //Data Annotation validation
    ICollection<ValidationResult> result;
    ValidateDataAnnotation(model, out result);
    foreach (ValidationResult validationResult in result)
    {
        foreach (string memberName in validationResult.MemberNames)
        {
            ModelState.AddModelError(memberName, validationResult.ErrorMessage);
        }
    }
    //IValidatableObject validation
    if (Model is IValidatableObject)
    {
        IEnumerable<ValidationResult> errors = (Model as
IValidatableObject).Validate(new ValidationContext(this));
        foreach (ValidationResult validationResult in errors)
        {
            if (validationResult is EnhancedMappedValidationResult<TModel>)
            {
                var enhanced = (EnhancedMappedValidationResult<TModel>)
validationResult;
                var viewModelPropertyName = _mapperFactory.GetMapper(model,
viewModel).GetErrorPropertyMappedFor(enhanced.Property);
                ModelState.AddModelError(viewModelPropertyName,
validationResult.ErrorMessage);
            }
            else
            {
                if (validationResult.MemberNames.Any())
                {
                    foreach (string memberName in validationResult.MemberNames)
                    {
                        ModelState.AddModelError(memberName,
validationResult.ErrorMessage);
                    }
```

```
            }
            else
            {
                ModelState.AddModelError(string.Empty,
validationResult.ErrorMessage);
            }
        }
    }
}
    /*
    //This validate underlying entity which can be not fully loaded in the case of
reference
    * ModelMetadata metadata =
ModelMetadataProviders.Current.GetMetadataForType(() => Model, Model.GetType());
    * foreach (ModelValidationResult validationResult in
ModelValidator.GetModelValidator(metadata, this.ControllerContext).Validate(null))
    * {         var propertyName = validationResult.MemberName;
    * ModelState.AddModelViewModelToErrorsMap(propertyName,
validationResult.Message);
    * }*/
}

private bool ValidateDataAnnotation(object entity, out
ICollection<ValidationResult> results)
{
    var context = new ValidationContext(entity);
    results = new List<ValidationResult>();
    return Validator.TryValidateObject(entity, context, results, true);
}

[HttpPost]
public ActionResult Create(WorkoutViewModel viewModel)
{
    if (ModelState.IsValid) //This is the default Asp.Net MVC way to validate
entity
    {
        //Save the entity
    }
}
```

This is great because it is the default way to validate an object that has been bound in MVC. The *IsValid* not only validates our business logic but also validates all data annotations that could have been set. It's even greater because people who are used to using the ModelState for validation will not have to learn a new way to act with controllers because it is the same.

The second layer of validation: Service layer

So far, the validation works fine but it doesn't handle the situation when you need to validate across many entities. You could have a case where you need to validate an entity depending onthe value of others' entities. It can also be a validation from some values that are inside the database. Since Model does not have access to the repository, at this moment we could not validate. To solve this problem, the second layer of validation is required and the perfect place for it is in the Service layer. The reason is that this layer does have access to all entities and also has access to all repositories. Contrary to the first layer of validation, this one will require a manual explicit call for validation. The concrete implementation of this second layer of validation will be done with the *Workout* entity. What we want to implement is a validation that the active user cannot create more than three workouts per month without a premium account. That means we need to go check in the database the number of workouts for a specific user for a specific month. This could not be validated in the *Workout* class because it does not have access to the database.

```
{
public int Create(Workout model)
{
    int amountWorkout = Repository.Workout.GetAmountWorkoutForCurrentMonth();
    if (amountWorkout > 3) //More than 3 workouts done without premium account
    {
        throw new ValidationErrors(
            new GeneralError("You have reach the limit of 3 workouts "
                + "per month, you need premium or wait the next month"));
    }
    return Repository.Workout.Insert(model);
}
```

This gets the number of workouts for the month and if it is over a certain threshold will raise the error.

The error is handled by the controller that verifies that the action executed has been completed without error. Here is the *Create* action of the *Workout* controller with the first layer validation and with the catch for the second layer.

```
[HttpPost]
public ActionResult Create(WorkoutViewModel viewModel)
{
    if (ModelState.IsValid)
    {
        try
        {
            _service.Create(Model);
        }
        catch (ValidationErrors propertyErrors)
```

```
        {
            ModelState.AddValidationErrors(propertyErrors);
        }
    }
    return View("Create");
}
```

The exception type is *ValidationErrors* which is our custom error handler. The reason is that we do not want to use a specific exception from other layers. This is why cross-layered classes will be used to transport exceptions through all layers. This will be discussed after the third layer of validation.

The third layer of validation: Persistence layer

The persistence layer is where the call to the database is made. This is an automatic validation with Entity Framework that calls the **IValidatableObject** interface of the entity before saving it to the database.

But, since we do not want to raise a **DbEntityValidationResult** up to the controller because it is a class that belongs to Entity Framework (System.Data.Entity.Validation), we will use our own exception classes.

We will create an interface that will hold the property name in error and also the error message.

```
public interface IBaseError
{
    string PropertyName { get; }
    string PropertyExceptionMessage { get; }
}
```

Two classes will inherit from this interface—one for a property error and one for a general error.

```
public class PropertyError : IBaseError
{
    public string PropertyName { get; set; }
    public string PropertyExceptionMessage { get; set; }

    public PropertyError(string propertyName, string errorMessage)
    {
        this.PropertyName = propertyName;
        this.PropertyExceptionMessage = errorMessage;
    }
}
```

```
}

public class GeneralError : IBaseError
{
    #region Implementation of IBaseError

    public string PropertyName
    {
        get { return string.Empty; }
    }

    public string PropertyExceptionMessage { get; set; }

    public GeneralError(string errorMessage)
    {
        this.PropertyExceptionMessage = errorMessage;
    }

    #endregion}
}
```

Then, we add the interface *IValidationErrors* which holds all *IBaseError* to be sent back through all layers.

```
public interface IValidationErrors
{
    List<IBaseError> Errors { get; set; }
}
```

The first implementation can be used anywhere, like in the service layers.

```
public class ValidationErrors : Exception, IValidationErrors
{
    public List<IBaseError> Errors { get; set; }

    public ValidationErrors()
    {
        Errors = new List<IBaseError>();
    }

    public ValidationErrors(IBaseError error) : this()
    {
        Errors.Add(error);
    }
}
```

The second is more specific to the database.

```
public class DatabaseValidationErrors : ValidationErrors
{
    public DatabaseValidationErrors(IEnumerable<DbEntityValidationResult> errors)
: base()
    {
        foreach (var err in errors.SelectMany(dbEntityValidationResult =>
dbEntityValidationResult.ValidationErrors))
        {
            Errors.Add(new PropertyError(err.PropertyName, err.ErrorMessage));
        }
    }
}
```

The last one is used by the repository. In fact, when we **SaveChanges()** to the database, we need to validate before Entity Framework executes the SaveChanges. Of course, we could let Entity Framework execute but we would have to catch the exception. Since there is a way without having to catch an exception, I prefer to use it.

If you remember correctly, our DatabaseContext inherits from **IDatabaseContext** which has a SaveChanges() method. We simply need to override this instead of relying on the one from DbContext, and call the DbContext one if everything is fine.

```
public override int SaveChanges()
{
    var errors = this.GetValidationErrors();
    if (!errors.Any())
    {
        return base.SaveChanges();
    }
    else
    {
        throw new DatabaseValidationErrors(errors);
    }
}
```

The exception thrown will loop all errors and be triggered to a higher level. In fact, this exception is raised to the service layer, which doesn't handle the exception. So, the exception will be raised to the controller layer. This is the same patch of exceptions as having an exception thrown from the service in the layer two because of business logic validation! We are reusing the same mechanism and this is possible because of the exceptions classes we have created which are abstracted with interface.

Model State and custom exceptions classes

If you remember, the controller does have a catch for ValidationErrors.

```
//...
catch (ValidationErrors propertyErrors)
{
    ModelState.AddValidationErrors(propertyErrors);
}
```

By default, the model state doesn't have this method that accepts our interface IValidationErrors. This is an extension method.

```
public static class ControllersExtensions
{
    public static void AddValidationErrors(this ModelStateDictionary modelState
                                , IValidationErrors propertyErrors)
    {
        foreach (var databaseValidationError in propertyErrors.Errors)
        {
            modelState.AddModelError(databaseValidationError.PropertyName
                    , databaseValidationError.PropertyExceptionMessage);
        }
    }
}
```

Using **IValidationErrors** lets us handle errors from the service layer or the database error. In fact, at this point, it does not really matter because we want to loop through all exceptions and use the model state to attach, when there's no exception, to the correct property (or if a general exception to the string.empty which will be a global error message).

Conclusion

Validation of the model could be more complex. It could have used external classes for each validation. We could have created our own system for validation messages and not use the **IValidatableObject** interface. We could have completely not used the ModelState and created our own HTML helper with a custom mechanism for validating across all layers. We could have added a layer of abstraction between Entity Framework and the service and handle validations there. But at the end, having a solution that is short and efficient seems to be better from my point of view. The current solution gives a lot of flexibility concerning the validation and keeps the code easy to maintain. In fact, adding a validation is two steps. First, where should the validation be coded? Second, add the validation. I have seen patterns for validation that go so beyond MVC and respect even more the single responsibility principle that adding a single validation takes over 30 minutes. For me, this is not acceptable. Abstraction levels never should make the development of the code harder. In theory, adding levels of abstraction does not cost a thing, but in real enterprise code, where people have to maintain the code base, this can lead to problems.

The solution proposed here uses layers previously defined without adding overhead to handle validation.

Enterprise Asp.Net MVC Part 7: Securing action with role authorization

Release Date: 10-Dec-12
Url: http://patrickdesjardins.com/blog/?post_type=post&p=1730

In a previous article of the enterprise Asp.Net MVC series we chose to allow anonymous not by default and to secure to a logged user most of the actions possible. This is great but not enough if we want to have some actions available only for a specific role. In this article, I will show you how to authorize a specific role to be mapped to action and also keep the security for anonymous. Also, we will see how to have a custom error page for unauthorized action instead of the login screen that Asp.Net MVC redirects to when the authorization is unsuccessful.

First of all, we will need to create a new Authorize attribute. This is not because Asp.Net MVC 4 does not provide the attribute but because Asp.Net MVC 4 acts the same way for **authorized access (401)** and a **forbidden access (403)**. We want when it is an authorized access (not logged) to redirect to the login screen and when it is a forbidden access (not being in the role) to be redirected to a view saying something else, and not the login form.

```
[AttributeUsage(AttributeTargets.Class | AttributeTargets.Method, Inherited =
true, AllowMultiple = true)]
public sealed class AuthorizeAttribute : System.Web.Mvc.AuthorizeAttribute
{
    public AuthorizeAttribute()
    {
        ErrorArea = string.Empty;
        ErrorController = "Error";
        ErrorAction = "Index";
```

```
}

    public string ErrorArea { get; set; }
    public string ErrorController { get; set; }
    public string ErrorAction { get; set; }

    public override void OnAuthorization(AuthorizationContext filterContext)
    {
        base.OnAuthorization(filterContext);
        if (AuthorizeCore(filterContext.HttpContext))
        {
            return;
        }
        if (filterContext.HttpContext.Request.IsAuthenticated)
        {
            if (ErrorController != null)
            {
                filterContext.Result = new RedirectToRouteResult(
                                   new RouteValueDictionary(
                                            new {action = ErrorAction
                                                , controller = ErrorController
                                                , area = ErrorArea}));
            }
            else
            {
                filterContext.Result = new HttpStatusCodeResult((int)
HttpStatusCode.Forbidden);
            }
        }
        else
        {
            filterContext.Result = null;
        }
    }
}
```

This is the attribute class. This class checks if the user is authenticated and, if not, will redirect to the normal process and return a 401 http status with the login form. If the user is authenticated, the status code is changed to 403 if no controller is specified; otherwise, it will redirect to a specific controller/action. By default, I have set a controller and action; this way it is more user friendly to have a real page inside the page layout than the default 403 IIS page. Of course, it is up to you to choose what you prefer. However, I believe that not only is it more user friendly but it gives you the possibility of logging forbidden access and having a custom message.

To use this new **AuthorizeAttribute**, we need to change the default filter set to every action.

In Asp.Net MVC 4, you need to search for FilterConfig.cs

```
public class FilterConfig
{
    public static void RegisterGlobalFilters(GlobalFilterCollection filters)
    {
        filters.Add(new HandleErrorAttribute());
        filters.Add(new Views.AuthorizeAttribute());
    }
}
```

Line 6 has been replaced by AuthorizeAttribute. This will not make such a big change since the access by default is not set. But, when an action is protected by a specific role, this is where the custom authorize class shines.

```
[HttpGet]
[Views.Authorize(Roles = Models.Roles.ADMINISTRATOR)]
public ActionResult Create()
{
    var x = ServiceFactory.Exercise.New(Model);
    return View("Create", x);
}
```

As you can see in the code above, if the user is not an administrator then this will be redirected to the default error page.

At any time, you also can specify a specific controller and action if for a special case you need to do something else for a forbidden access.

```
[Views.Authorize(Roles = Models.Roles.ADMINISTRATOR
                , ErrorController = "CustomerController"
                , ErrorAction = "LogAndRedirect")]
public ActionResult Create()
{
    var x = ServiceFactory.Exercise.New(Model);
    return View("Create", x);
}
```

To conclude, it is possible to have distinct pages for authorized access and forbidden access. I strongly believe it is important to do something different since it is counterintuitive to display the login form when someone is already logged in, but without the right role. It is fundamental that the user know what is going on and this is why a redirection to a custom error's controller seems the natural solution to this problem.

ABOUT THE AUTHOR

Patrick Desjardins is a Microsoft Most Valuable Professional (MVP) in Asp.Net since 2013. He has studied software engineering and he is known for his analysis, resourcefulness, and abilities to find effective solutions quickly. Since his early professional career, his focus has always been to keep up to date in order to provide quality services to meet customers' needs. Patrick is a professional who has a well-developed work ethic and who has the desire to perform both in quality and timeliness. His area of interest is Web development, which he embraced since the early 2000s. For many years Patrick has continued to train daily in new technologies and apply all theories learned to various projects. Patrick is a huge fan of Microsoft technologies' .Net which he used to develop professionally since 2004. By contrast, since 2002 he developed in PHP many projects that make him someone with multiple perspectives on how the web can be developed. His main focus is to help people to embrace Microsoft technology in an enterprise environment. He is a strong believer in Asp.Net MVC and Entity Framework to help create quality websites for professionals that follow good standards with Html5, CSS3 and design patterns.

.Net Knowledge book

This book is a melting pot of several articles about Asp.Net MVC, Entity Framework, JavaScript, CSS, C# and SQL. They are scenarios that happen in the everyday work of developers who use these technologies. They are divided into short articles that are easy to understand. This book is ideal for anyone with intermediate to advanced knowledge of Microsoft web stack and who wants to learn more about how to deal with practical cases. Subjects vary, from how to use the Model Binding to how to update complex objects with Entity Framework. This book includes articles written during 2011 and 2012. It is volume 1 of a series of books that will be out in the future. I strongly believe that the content of this book is a must to anyone who works with Microsoft Asp.Net in enterprise.

Here are some subjects discussed in the book:

Asp.Net MVC ModelBinding, Sections, Templates with Editor and Display, C# Sealed Method, .Net Transaction, how to handle circular references with Entity Framework, managing connection pool with EF, creating HTML Extensions, the difference between CSS displays, the difference between join, inner join, left join; what to use between view data, view bag and temp data, using dynamic keyword, caching, proxy creation with Entity Framework, the object context life cycle, working with 404 errors, using resource file, session and http handler, dynamic JavaScript and CSS with Asp.Net controller, master page, compare linq collection, html 5 and Internet Explorer, NDepend, localizing property, logging with Entity Framework, Expression, CGI extension with IIS, contants, cookies, foreign key and MSMS, Ajax call for partial view, anonymous object, ILSpy, performance counter, POCO object, debugging Asp.Net MVC, ModelState, MemoryStream, method parameters, MvcHtmlString, Asp.Net action name, best practices for developing enterprise Asp.Net MVC website.

About the author:

Patrick Desjardins is a Microsoft Most Valuable Professional (MVP) in Asp.Net since 2013. He has studied software engineering and he is known for his analysis, resourcefulness and abilities to find effective solutions quickly. Since his early professional career, his focus has always been to keep up to date in order to provide quality services to meet customers' needs. Patrick is a professional who has a well-developed work ethic and who has the desire to perform both in quality and timeliness. His area of interest is Web development, which he has embraced since the early 2000s. For many years Patrick has continued to train daily in new technologies and put all theories learned into practice in various projects

Printed in Great Britain
by Amazon